two lots of love from Allison

SPARKS FLY UPWARD x

ALLISON PETERSON

Pink Press

First published in Great Britain by Pen Press

All paper used in the printing of this book has been made from wood grown in managed, sustainable forests.

ISBN 978-1-78003-408-9

Printed and bound in the UK
Pink Press is an imprint of
Indepenpress Publishing Limited
25 Eastern Place
Brighton
BN2 1GJ

A catalogue record of this book is available from the British Library

"Yet (wo)man is born unto trouble, as the sparks fly upward" Job 5:7

For Gill, my family and friends

ONE

Autumn, 2002. The flight from Gatwick to Edinburgh is full this Friday evening. Yawning businessmen down their first beers of the weekend and contemplate the domestic or other prospects awaiting them. I, on the other hand, am flushed with fear, awaiting the touchdown, which always seems to occur while we are still travelling at excessive speed. The purser warns us not to fiddle with our safety belts until the aircraft has come to 'a complete stop'.

Flying is still a trial, although I no longer approach it with the assistance of Scotland's chief export: my family and friends were until recently accustomed to find me in an altered state of consciousness when I emerged, somehow, from Arrivals. Indeed, in the good old days when I was nursing, before drug checking became obsessive and before awareness of the real benefits of barbiturates took them off the menu, I could get through especially long-haul flights on 400 milligrams of sodium amytal and a few doubles of scotch.

I no longer have the stamina to drive from the south coast to St Andrews, a distance of nearly 600 miles by road, and rail travel has become an expensive extreme sport. So flying is the least unsatisfactory mode of travel now that I am visiting the land of my birth so often. Especially since Mother died and poor Father is less than able to cope alone.

Marion and Cheryl meet me at what my Canadian great nephew, Gavin, calls the 'hairport', and we swish off in Marion's smart car to an even smarter restaurant for dinner. My Canadian *nephew*, Scott, says there are three standards of excellence in dining: three star, five star and 'Marion approved'. And he is right. Mercifully, nouvelle cuisine seems to have declined in popularity over the past few years; we are no longer served with a couple of miniature mint leaves over which has been drizzled a fine but unidentifiable syrup. Scottish cuisine has become heartier again, and we dine well.

Marion is more slender than I have ever seen her. She seems tense and somehow translucent. With her carapace of competence and authority, she outlines our schedule for the weekend. I will stay overnight at her elegant home near the foot of Arthur's Seat, and she, Cheryl and I will together drive to St Andrews to see Dad tomorrow morning – just in time for coffee.

The route is beautiful, across the Forth Road Bridge which I drove over on the day of its opening, nearly 40 years ago, with my first lover. We drive through the villages and small towns of Fife, the familiar farmland now pale and grey. My throat is thick and aching, my eyes threatening to leak. We agree to stop off in South Street for flowers for Mum's grave, but on the whole our conversation carefully confines itself to current practicalities.

Cheryl fell in love just before Mum died, and her new love seems to have sustained her through the unspeakable grief we have experienced since. Cheryl is 18 years younger than I, and the youngest of us four sisters. She has developed a philosophy of life which is relentlessly positive and optimistic. Her eulogy at Mum's funeral ended with the assertion that 'we will survive', although she could not really have known whether we would. But she may have been right. We may indeed 'survive', but in altered form. The chief difficulty for the four daughters is that Mum was the lodestar in a proverbially dysfunctional family, the 'dysfunction' stemming from the fact that our father had Asperger's syndrome, something which we could not have known during the decades of our youth.

I weep like a baby in the flower shop, ashamed that my younger sisters have to do the choosing and paying. I thought I had perfected a technique for crying inwardly, but it is clearly not 'watertight'.

We make our way to Dad's house. He greets us at the front door, his arms raised in a stilted and curious form of blessing, his eyes staring at a point somewhere beyond us. We are only slightly late for coffee, which consists of a cupful of tarry liquid merrily boiling away in an old aluminium pot on the electric cooker. For reasons unknown, he prepares coffee in a conventional coffee maker, with its own hotplate for keeping it warm, and then transfers it into the other pot on the cooker. We find ways of stretching the liquorice-like liquid four ways and make our way to the sitting room.

Father's cat, prescribed for him immediately after Mum's funeral, rolls over in ecstatic greeting, purring like a grampus. Dad has always loved cats (and hens and owls), and relates well to them, although he throws books at poor Mustafa when Mustafa does what cats do, such as scratching the backs of chairs or triumphantly bringing in struggling, half-dead mice and birds.

Father is ordinarily unable to look at us or to rehearse the conventional enquiries customarily made of relatives who have not been with him for some time. In his own way, he is probably pleased to see us, but he is not able to say so in the normal way. He instead fastens upon some preoccupying frustration, such as an odd peep coming from the smoke alarm, a lost chequebook or MOT certificate, or the

3

accelerating difficulty of parking anywhere near the house. Or the scandalous proposed consecration of an openly gay bishop in the American Episcopal church. He knows that I am gay...

Marion empties the laundry basket which, after two weeks, contains little actual laundry. She strips his bed and pops the little bundle into the washing machine. Father has never operated a washing machine in his life, nor a cooker or any other domestic appliance. He has been pretty hot on car mechanics and a gifted organist in his time; now, at 85, he continues to play the organ for country parish churches every Sunday, although he occasionally plays a verse that exceeds the number in the hymn book, or muffs a chord. But what we call the 'routine activities of daily living' are largely beyond him – and always have been. He has a home help who cleans the floors and toilets for an hour a week.

His bungalow has seen better days. The window frames are slowly disintegrating, the exterior paintwork gently peeling. Marion pays for the maintenance of the rather fine garden in which we all sat a year ago making a videotape recording at the behest of Cheryl, whose prescient observation that 'we might not all be together again' resulted in a poignant interplay of the family's current concerns and pursuits. There is a lovely moment in that recording, shot in the magnificent grounds of Rufflets Hotel, when I am asking my frail mother, who is taking tiny but determined steps toward a steep flight of stone stairs, 'You're surely not going down those steps, are you, Mother?' to which she immediately replies, 'What's the matter, dear? Too much for you, are they?'

I once managed to watch the tape after her death, but only after a few beers. Today, I am no nearer to watching it – or opening the lid of a box in which I keep some photographs of her, a splendid collection of her school medals, her passport and various other relics of her saintly life. I frequently wonder whether my sisters are making such a poor fist of their grief as I. Frances, 20 months younger than I, lives in Canada, and is so securely medicated on long-term antidepressants that she suspects they protect her from the full feeling of losing Mum. Shortly after her death, we found, on Mother's desk, an airmail letter beginning 'Dearest Frances...' She had got no further.

Marion, the third sister, is approaching 50. I have always seen her as in some ways closest to Mum. Marion has certainly been the family's saviour over and over again, especially when poverty and ignominy threatened to engulf them some time after Frances and I had left home. At the age of 18, I resolved to get as far away from my father as I could and, to this day, have never lived in the same country. Frances entered nursing training and subsequently married. Mum, Marion and Cheryl were left to bear the increasingly dire consequences of Father's bizarre personality and behaviour.

Father has shrunk further every time I see him. For 50 years, I experienced him as tall, fat and strong, with a voice like a foghorn and a terrifyingly huge hand, which stunned as it hit you across the side of your head for some misdemeanour. Other factors conspired to bring about in me an enduring school phobia, but being walloped by Father must have assisted its development, at a time when administering the 'tawse' or 'strap' was in vogue in Scottish schools. And I experienced the sharp sting of the strap on several occasions, for long-forgotten misdemeanours; I do remember the scarlet welts which followed.

As I look at him now, I do not know how I feel about him. Pity, perhaps. He has always dressed formally, even when on holiday, and still wears a collar and tie every day, if not his clerical collar. He may not change his clothes as often as Mum tactfully prompted, and the familiar grey

5

socks are good for a fortnight between washes now, but he still appears reasonably kempt. Far from mellowing with age, Father remains pedantic, dogmatic, irrational and 'grumpy', as Mum used to observe. His perceptual universe is dislocated from ours, and always was. The effects of this huge, loud and insidious source of truth or reality on his children can only be inferred. All four of us have had problems with food; all of us have been on antidepressants – three long-term; all of us have severe problems with self-esteem and at least two of us have contemplated self-destruction.

Now we are his lifeline. He has never had a true friend in his entire life and, since Mum died, of his two acquaintances, both clerical, one has died and the other subsists from one blood transfusion to the next. His weekly round consists of almost daily excursions to Boots, fretting about one or more of his galaxy of prescriptions or a new symptom which, ten to one, is the side effect of one of the myriad medicines. He may totter, listing markedly to starboard, to the mini-market at the end of his street, for the staples of his larder: bread, cheese, corned beef and malt whisky. Other highlights include frequent trips to the health centre about his dry mouth or the recalcitrant gastrointestinal tract, which refuses to yield the daily, perfectly formed movement to which he is entitled. Or he may visit one of his three chiropodists. These, together with playing the organ on Sunday, constitute his weekly schedule.

The house is filled with books, despite numerous attempts – on the part of others – at culling over the years. Church of Scotland Year Books from the year dot, biographies of the great classical composers, works on witchcraft, collections of horror stories reside alongside the Daily Telegraph's Financial Guide for 1957. For reasons unclear to us, Father is steadfastly resistant to disposing of

6

any of them, and we dread the moment when he has to be parted from his library. Poor Mother's modest collection of French and German books is evidently of no interest to anyone, and they will no doubt find their way to a charity shop or, if we are pressed for time, a clearance firm's dump. Her poetry books will rest in our own collections. But most of the enormous library, which has taken 70 years to build, will disintegrate and die in a matter of days.

The few items of furniture which have not been bought by Marion have been inherited from long-dead relatives: there is little of market value and less of discernible style. Mother had an eye for elegance and colour, but chronic poverty thwarted any wish she might have had to create a handsome home. It is ironic to think that her married life began in the university chapel a few yards away, and that her final glimpse of the world, just along the street, was also within yards of it.

Although Mother was born in Peterhead, most of her childhood was spent in Dundee and St Andrews, and it was there that her father, James Carnegie Ramsay, became Head Postmaster at the General Post Office in South Street. Grandfather began his working life as a messenger for the General Post Office, and was subsequently in the telegraph section where he was first in the UK to receive the news of the start of the Russian Revolution in 1917. He and Grandmother latterly lived in a semi-detached house in Nelson Street, St Andrews, where Frances and I stayed for family holidays when we were very young. Grandmother died when I was four, and I remember sitting on the kitchen table at our manse in Whalsay – one of the Shetland Islands – when Mother got the news. I weep when I think how she must have felt: learning at the tender age of 30 that her mother was gone, being too far away and too poor to attend the funeral, and having begun to realise that she had contracted the strangest of marriages.

TWO

The Shetland Islands are the farthest north of the United Kingdom, and Unst, the island on which I was born, is the most northerly of these. I was born in the manse of Uyeasound, and this was my father's very first charge, to which he was inducted in 1942, the year of his marriage. When I subsequently enquired of him why he had chosen such a remote parish, he explained that there were at that time few vacancies in the Church of Scotland from which to choose. How times change! I do not know whether he may also have been influenced by the fact that his paternal grandfather had ministered in Whalsay before him, or that his father was born there. But I do know that poor Mother was thoroughly unhappy in Shetland, where she and Father spent eight years in two parishes: four in Unst and four in Whalsay.

There were virtually no trees on either island, and Mother experienced the whining winds as ceaseless: she attributed her lifelong rheumatological problems to the Shetland weather. I myself recall the environment as unremittently bleak, damp and cold. My memories of Shetland, which we left when I was six, are of deep gloom and fear. Looking back, I am certain that my poor mother was suffering from multiple bereavement prior to and following the time of my birth. She had been an exceptionally outgoing, adventurous and happy young woman in a loving family, close to her parents and three older sisters. The dux of her school, Madras College, she went on to excel at St Andrews University, where the advent of World War Two prevented her from achieving the requirements of an honours degree in modern languages: she was unable to spend the necessary periods living and working in France and Germany. She was captain of the university tennis, swimming and hockey teams, and had many close friends.

The year before I was born, Mother gave birth to a full-term, dead baby, who was male. My father told me, many years later, that he had buried his son in a cave on the coast of the island. Nowadays, full-term babies born dead are, I understand, given the full Christian burial rites. Perhaps that was not the case in 1943 – or his isolated circumstances, being the only clergyman on the island, rendered the customary ceremony impractical.

Not long before her death, Mother told me that, quite soon after their marriage and move to Shetland, Father began his lifelong series of intense attachments to other women. Twenty years later, it was one of these which led to his ultimate expulsion from his church in Canada. That, and the culmination of a permanent and gross financial ineptitude, led to the family's effective bankruptcy and return to Scotland.

It would not, therefore, be surprising if Mother had been depressed. On moving to Shetland, she had lost the companionship of her many friends, her sisters and parents. Within a few years, she lost her first child and then her mother. And, with the first signs of Father's psychological infidelity, she had lost the exclusive devotion of her new husband. Throughout her life, Mother seemed to me to be tired, sad and anxious. Of course she knew times of happiness, but I believe that her marriage was deeply unhappy. She had no way of accounting for her husband's extraordinary attitudes and behaviour. There was little or no evident warmth in him, little sense that he respected or even recognised any of us as autonomous beings of intrinsic value.

Frances, who was to undergo six years of four-days-a-week psychoanalysis, agrees that we felt *as if we hardly existed* in Father's life: unless, that is, we somehow irritated him, in which case he would regularly bellow with rage. Or smack us hard on the side of the head.

I began school at the age of four. The school was at Broch, on the island of Whalsay, and the teacher was Miss Margaret Stewart. There were several age groups of pupils in the same classroom, so it was a pretty small school. My recollection of Miss Stewart was that she was kind and smiling. The same could not be said for some of the older pupils.

I have no doubt that one or the other of my parents must have walked with me to the school when I first began, but thereafter I went to and from school on my own, a journey of two miles in each direction. On several occasions, on the way home, I was waylaid by a group of much older children and diverted from my homeward route. There is an indelible memory of being made to lie down while one or more big boys inserted wedges of raw potato up my anus. How they laughed! I did not actually remember this until I was in my thirties, and I have no idea whether I told my parents anything about it at the time. I do, however, very clearly remember Miss Stewart regularly exhorting us not to 'loiter on the way home'. Whether she had any inkling of the extracurricular activities, I shall never know.

Another ineradicable recollection is of the day when, on my way home from school, several of the older children asked me whether I'd like a sail in the black canvas dinghy

10

which was tethered against the shore of a small loch. They helped me into the dinghy, and pretended that they were joining me. Suddenly, they jumped back onto the shore and kicked the dinghy out into the middle of the loch. And off they went, laughing. I have no idea how much later it was when I saw my father walking toward me over the hill, nor of how I was brought back to the edge of the loch. But I do remember the first sight of him at the top of the slope, wearing a haversack and walking with a long, knobbly cane.

Other recollections are mere fragments. Before I went to school, I developed a fascination for cigarettes, although my father only smoked a pipe, and Mother smoked one solitary Balkan Sobranie on very special occasions. But the headmaster's wife, Mrs McWhirter, who occasionally looked after me, was a true devotee of nicotine, and I followed her about, marvelling at her habit of leaving a lit cigarette in each room of the house. I think I identified cigarette smoking with a particular sort of insouciance: somehow, if you smoked you could protect yourself from all evil...

At any rate, one of my first criminal activities occurred when I was visiting a family – the Wisharts – who lived in a very small cottage by the sea, not far from the manse. I appropriated a packet of cigarettes, and made my way home. I was in the garden when, not long afterwards, the irate woman of the house stormed up to the front door of the manse, demanding to see Mother. As I realised what was happening, I hid behind a bank in the garden. Toward the end of her life, Mother told Cheryl, our family archivist, how furious the woman had been, although I was four or younger when the incident occurred. I think Mother was pretty humiliated by the episode, and one component of my continuing grief consists in the endless humiliations, disappointments and anxieties to which I subjected her throughout my life. If only I could have managed some sort

11

of tangible reconciliation with her; if only we could have talked about these things. Somehow, we never could.

Another little fragment of recollection consists of the scene at Whalsay harbour, where women gutted the freshly caught fish with impressive speed. We travelled from that harbour to Lerwick several times, the first leg of any journey south to the mainland. Then, from Lerwick, we would go by 'steamer' to Aberdeen. We sailed in the *Earl of Zetland*, and the passage was invariably choppy; the thoughtfully provided little red cages containing cardboard bags regularly received Frances's and my pre-passage refreshments. And I can still smell the unique, sooty aroma of the smoky steam billowing from the funnels. I believe the regular captain used to tease the wan and trembling passengers by saying, 'You'll be glad to get back to terra cotta, then?'

I returned to Shetland just before my sixtieth birthday, partly to check the territory against my memory, partly to revisit possible or actual locations of traumatic events, and partly to close a chapter of fear, sadness and incomprehension.

THREE

We left Shetland in 1950, when I was six and Father had completed eight years of ministry in the Church of Scotland. I expect Mother was hugely relieved to leave behind her those austere, bleak islands, with the moaning wind, driving rain and clinging mist. New pastures tend to evoke in us the futile hope that things are bound to get better, and perhaps poor Mother hoped that she would feel less isolated and utterly alone in dealing with a strangely unfeeling, unpredictable husband.

Father was inducted to the parish of Mossvale in Paisley. Our manse lay immediately beneath the flight path of what was then Abbotsinch 'aerodrome', now Glasgow Airport. The parish was in a fairly poor area of Paisley, and our house stood on a busy main street. As was typical of Scottish manses at the time, the house was cold, dark and damp. It did, however, have a generously sized garden, complete with a massive and highly productive pear tree, some raspberry bushes and enough room for Dad to establish a henhouse and run. There was also a steading or series of outhouses, in part of which was kept the coal for the drawing room fire, and anthracite for the Rayburn in the kitchen. When I got my pocket money on Saturday – sixpence, I think – I would buy a packet of five Woodbine cigarettes and disappear into the steading, where, with the very first puff, I felt grown up and invulnerable.

After my experiences of school – or, rather, post-school events – in Whalsay, I hoped and prayed that my parents would forget about sending me to another school. That hope was nourished by the fact that it probably took several weeks to get me enrolled in the local school. Since a week is a year in a six-year-old's life, there was some reason for my optimism. Hope was, however, extinguished when I was eventually taken to Mossvale School, and thus began a period of reinforcement of my fear of intrusion and assault. Mossvale was essentially a slum school, and the mores and rituals there were tough and aggressive. A particularly terrifying custom, when someone had a birthday, was to seize the unfortunate individual in the playground for 'nips and dumps'. The victim would be nipped by the gang of aggressors for the number of years the poor child had attained: imagine being nipped 12 times, anywhere on the body, by a crowd of excited juveniles. But the 'nips' were less frightening than the 'dumps', which entailed being thrown into the air and then let go, so that the birthday boy or girl crashed to the ground. Bruised and bleeding, the unfortunate child was then taken to the little van from which buns were sold at playtime, and commanded to buy some for their assailants. I made a point of never revealing my birth date to anyone, especially when we were asked to state it in the classroom; the teachers must have thought me singularly dull.

On one occasion, when I had something of a panic attack just before I ought to have left for school, I lay on the kitchen floor, screaming and crying, altogether in a state of terror. I will never forget Father's response, which was to kick me sharply in my side and bellow at me to be on my way.

Again, I can recall only facets of life at Mossvale. Somewhere along the line, I had acquired a morbid dread of war, in particular war with the then Soviet Union. Indeed, I used to interrogate any available adult as to how highly they rated the risk of conflict with the USSR: it is possible that at least one babysitter declined to repeat the experience because of my dark preoccupation. While at Mossvale School, I learned that Stalin had died, and this gave rise to a sense of relief on my part. Little did I – or anyone else, for that matter – then know the nature and extent of Stalin's war on his own people. Or whether his successors would attempt to thaw relations with the Western world.

Our form teacher at Mossvale was called Miss Burns. She was tall, strongly built, and somewhat intimidating. It was a common practice for children to pass round rude notes or drawings when lessons were in progress, and it so happened that Miss Burns noticed that I had just received one such grubby little piece of paper, upon which was drawn a diagram whose significance was entirely lost on me during the brief glimpse I had had of it before being summoned to the front of the class and instructed to explain it to everyone. I did not understand what it was about, but felt utterly humiliated and baffled by my exposure in this way. Miss Burns thereafter seemed to take a close interest in me, and there were occasions when I actually thought she was following or lying in wait for me. The only thing I remember learning at Mossvale School was taught by Miss Burns: in the course of one particular lesson, she produced a piece of white paper upon which there was a large blot of black ink. We were invited to state what it might represent, and various answers were offered. When our perceptions had finally run out, she told us that it was simply an ink stain, and that the most important thing to remember about it was that it could never be erased. Thus bad behaviour might never be eradicated. Or forgiven?

Father must have disapproved of Mossvale as an institution of learning, so I was transferred to Paisley Grammar School. This school was some distance from Mossvale, so I had to get the bus across town. My little sister Frances was similarly transferred. PGS was a very different place of learning: everyone wore uniform, and even our hat brims had to be turned down in a particular way. Here I encountered the phenomenon of 'homework', but, for reasons which still elude me, I could never get to grips with it. I was sent to see an educational psychologist called Dr McLaren, who gave me endless tests to do. Once, while I was waiting to see Dr McLaren, her secretary said to me, 'You had better pull your socks up, Allison,' an injunction with which I immediately complied, thereby inducing great hilarity all round. The joke was entirely lost on me, as was the purpose of my visits to Dr McLaren.

Whether Dr McLaren had anything to do with it I shall never know, but I was suddenly removed from the form I was in to one in a higher year, where I knew no one and where the 'homework' expectations were even greater. Things cannot have been going well, for I remember that my mother had to meet my form teacher, who said to her, 'If Allison worked half as much as she *worried*, she'd be top of the class.' Mother reminded me of this from time to time over subsequent years, but I came to recognise that this really was a case of the pot calling the kettle black: no one worried as intensely as Mother.

While we were in Paisley, Marion was born – in a private nursing home – in 1954. Now that Mother has gone, we have no idea who paid for the confinement, but Frances and I had to stay with another minister's family until Mother and Marion came home. I remember feeling very strange being away from Mum for what seemed an age, and we both remember that we were not allowed to visit her; we were instructed to stand outside on the lawn, while Mum waved to us from her window. I do not know whether Frances felt the same, or whether we were able to give each other comfort or support. Perhaps we were too young, at ten and eight, to have the sense to look after each other. In fact, I am inexpressibly ashamed to say that, according to family reports, I wasn't much of a sister to little Frances, and I believe that I bullied her. Frances was petite, pretty and well behaved, whereas I was already becoming something of a black sheep in the family. My impression of myself was that I was ugly, stupid and bad.

Marion was born with a raised strawberry mark right on the top of her head, which pulsated while she was being fed. And she had red hair. This surprised us all, as there were no near relatives with red hair. But there was no mistaking her paternity; she had a miniature version of Father's nose.

While we were at Mossvale, the minister and organist of Paisley Abbey had a spectacular falling out, as ministers and organists often do. The official reason for the dispute was something to do with divergent views on appropriate musical praise, but I now suspect that it had rather more to do with the organist's deep appreciation of 'beautiful' male choristers. My father, a gifted organist himself, offered the Abbey organist both a home and a job. Thus Karl Pearce Hosken came to live in our house, and became organist at Mossvale Church. KPH was one of nature's true eccentrics. He described himself as Cornish rather than English, and evidently came from a distinguished family, although we never met any of his relatives. Indeed, I recall no mention of, or contact with, any member of his family. He almost invariably wore a kilt and a ring with a large stone, and carried a handsome walking cane. Following the schism at the Abbey, a contingent of KPH's supporters came over to Mossvale with him, and I am sure that the quality of the praise there improved no end. Whether KPH supplanted an existing organist at Mossvale, I shall never know. KPH

17

subsequently became organist at St Machar's Cathedral in Aberdeen, where a replication of the Abbey debacle eventually occurred...

We were desperately poor, so much so that we came to be sent parcels from a Miss Fiddes of the Distressed Gentlefolks' Aid. It had not yet become apparent to Frances and me that Father was pathologically incapable of managing money. Mother was blessed with both common sense and frugality, but was never allowed to manage the family budget. In those days, there were no charity shops, and the wearing of second-hand clothes was a mark of shame rather than economic virtue.

New pastures beckoned, and we exchanged the grey city landscape for the rural beauty of Perthshire in 1956.

FOUR

Nine miles from Perth, Bankfoot lies in the parish of
Auchtergaven, on the way to Dunkeld and the Highlands.
The manse stood at the edge of the village, largely bordered
by fields. There were extensive lawns, a stable block and a
walled garden.

Mother was a keen gardener, and Father mowed the
lawns with a noisy, smelly motor mower. A burn rippled
past along the boundary of our grounds, and Frances and I
often played down there, constructing a little hideaway
house under the bordering trees and a crossing over the
burn. Marion subsequently called the hideaway her 'fairy
house'. A tree stump beside the burn became a favourite
pedestal for Marion, and we still have photographs of her
standing upon it.

Frances and I were enrolled in the local school, just
down our front drive and over the bridge. The teachers
seemed pleasant and gentle, and it was here that we sat the
11 Plus examination. At that time, children who got the top
marks in the 11 Plus were sent to Perth Academy to study
'two languages', Latin and French. Those who did less well
also went to the academy, but to study only one language,
namely French. Everyone else went to Perth High School,
the secondary modern school. The result of my 11 Plus was

that I would be studying only one language. I recall being perfectly content to do so, since I was too anxious about school or scholarship to settle down to study, and the less homework there was, the better. Father, however, was furious, and actually contacted the Director of Education for the whole county, insisting that I be reclassified to study both Latin and French. I even recall the director's name – Lachlan B Young.

Lachlan B Young acceded to Father's demands, and I consequently embarked upon the 'two languages' course at Perth Academy. I have often wondered what Mother must have made of all Father's manoeuvring of my schooling: she was, after all, a trained teacher and, judging by her school and university performance, even brighter than Dad. In any event, I clearly had some problems with my first year at Perth Academy and, once again, found myself attending a psychologist. His name was Mr Birkett, and he chain smoked, bit his nails, called me by the wrong name, and overran our sessions occasionally, causing me to miss my last, fare-paid, bus home to Bankfoot. Needless to say, I can recall no benefit – or consequence – of my attendance at Mr Birkett's office.

As if my school phobia were not enough to satisfy my neurotic needs, I had become increasingly aware of my developing lesbianism. Ever since I was a toddler, I recall having dreams of a tall, strong, lovely, long-haired woman looking after me and protecting me. During the Paisley years, aged six to ten or so, I experienced strong affection for certain adult women, although never consciously in a sexual sense. I can never remember feeling close to Mother in either a physical or an emotional sense, although I have always idealised her – and still do, yet I recognise that this is also a common component of intense grief. The stereotypical dynamic psychologist will of course say that my lesbianism is a direct consequence of failing to bond

20

properly with my mother and having a pathological relationship with my father. Although this may indeed be a part of it, I have long been convinced that my extreme-end-of-the-spectrum orientation is attributable more to genetic than to environmental influences.

I developed a great passion for a girl in my class at Perth Academy, when I was about 13. We became very close friends, in an entirely platonic sense, until my father was called to a charge in Newfoundland, Canada, in 1960, and we became separated by the Atlantic. Deirdre was an exceptionally gifted singer, and her parents were also musical; Jimmy Shand, the Scottish Country Dance Band leader, often came to dinner at their house. He was a modest, shy man, who had the intriguing habit of removing his false teeth prior to eating.

I doubt very much whether Deirdre ever suspected how much I adored her throughout our three years of friendship. She was intensely preoccupied by a male nurse she'd met at a Highland Mod, and who lived in Inverness. They exchanged frequent, passionate and lengthy love letters, which she would read out to me. My feelings were never overtly erotic: I just longed to be physically and emotionally close to the loved one. I had never encountered a lesbian in life or literature, and truly believed I must be alone in bearing this terrible affliction. There was no question of mentioning it to either of my parents – or to anyone else, for that matter.

My father and I sometimes went walking, although neither of us was, or ever would be, keen on much physical exercise. But these were no ordinary father-daughter bonding sessions. Father would deliver lengthy monologues about himself, his haemorrhoids, his financial worries, his pastoral work with troubled parishioners and his views about the universe. He spoke to me as if I were another chap sharing a good malt, and this didn't strike me at the time as

21

strange. A most potent memory is of his telling me that he had contemplated suicide because of his financial problems. I subsequently hated him for unburdening himself to his own child in this way, because it merely intensified my feelings of fear and foreboding. Much later still, I resented his shameless hypocrisy in declaring that 'No Christian has any right to be depressed' when my sister Frances's severe and protracted depression reached his attention. His judgement struck me at the time as not merely hypocritical, but theologically unsound...

Our part of Perthshire was an intensely agricultural area, and our friendship with especially two of the local farming parishioner families engendered in me the desire to become a farmer. The chief attractions, it seemed at the time, were that you got to drive glamorously powerful machines like Massey Ferguson tractors and massively majestic combine harvesters. You were also allowed to wear dungarees and stout boots. One glossed over the less romantic activities of potato harvesting, the mucking out of byres, and dawn milking in the bleak mid-winter.

And so I graduated from the Dandy and Beano to the Young Farmer's Weekly, and took to answering advertisements for agricultural products, particularly if free samples were involved. One day, when I returned from school, Mother somewhat agitatedly told me that an agricultural representative had unexpectedly arrived at the back door, and had offered to demonstrate a state-of-the-art manure spreader. No doubt Mother explained that the interested party was 12 years old and attending school at the time of his visit.

An advertisement for the British Mushroom Industry caught my attention, and I saved up my pocket money to buy a bag of mushroom compost, which I laid out in the former stable. As I write, the unique aroma of the compost, as I forked it over, returns as if it were yesterday, and I can remember the deep sense of satisfaction I experienced as the promised button-cap fungi emerged some weeks later.

Encouraged by my success with growing food, I turned to the breeding of livestock. Accumulated pocket money was invested in a pair of guinea pigs, who were duly installed in the stable block and cared for in accordance with the instruction manual. To my huge joy, mother guinea pig became visibly pregnant, and my delight was unbounded when she gave birth to five guinea piglets. And then tragedy befell. For reasons which I could never fathom, especially considering my devotion and diligence in their care, one or both of the piglet progenitors consumed their offspring. I broke my heart and either sold or gave away the cannibals.

While we were in Bankfoot, Father bought an old Alvis. I think it was a 1922 Firefly, and its registration was definitely YJ 672. Having been taught all the main registration areas by Father, I recognised that YJ represented Dundee. The Alvis was black, and had red leather seats. The front doors opened forwards, and there were broad running boards. Because its exhaust was extraordinarily loud and smoky, the villagers christened it the Bomb. I cannot easily convey the extent of my embarrassment at the sight and sound of Father's car. I would do anything to dissociate myself from it. Occasionally, Father would insist on driving Frances and me to Perth Academy, presumably because he had some business in town. Despite my protestations that we were more than happy to use the bus, he would simply insist. I tried every means to secure our disembarkation some distance from the school, praying that none of our contemporaries would see us emerging from this dreadful vehicle.

Whereas I think we were always aware that people readily and warmly took to Mother, I don't think I had any conception of how people – parishioners or otherwise – regarded Father. It did occur to me that, especially in church, he spoke in rather a strange way: oddly formal, rather antiquated, 'posh'. He pronounced some words in a peculiarly idiosyncratic way: 'yellow' became 'yillow', for example. Father was particularly prone to including Latin or Greek phrases in his ordinary discourse, and would do so in colloquial exchanges with people who could not possibly have known what he meant. Many years later, I was surprised to hear him say that he had 'preached churches empty', which may have indicated some level of awareness that his preaching was not always reaching the flock. It would perhaps have been heartless of me to ask him to return to that remark and elaborate.

Father's Aunt Mary came to live with us while we were at Bankfoot, although I have no idea quite how or why this came about. When her mother died in 1923 and Father was six, Aunt Mary left her Catholic convent, before taking final vows, to look after her widowed father and his young grandson at their home in Aberdeen. Father's parents were at this point effectively touring the United Kingdom, while his father moved from job to job – or posting to posting in the Royal Flying Corps, precursor to the Royal Air Force. From all accounts, Aunt Mary was a devoted and loving carer of her father and nephew. One particularly poignant story my father discovered was that, unbeknownst to *her* father, Aunt Mary would make 'tablet' (crisp English 'fudge') and sell it to people in the local cinema queue in order to supplement the domestic economy. That, and her decision to become a Catholic in a strongly Protestant family, gave me cause to admire her greatly.

In her old age, Aunt Mary was given a room at the front of our house, and brought with her a budgerigar called

Peter, to whom she frequently spoke and was devoted. I now wonder whether young men of her day were attracted to her in droves, as she was a strikingly beautiful young woman. Her devotion to Catholicism was, however, developed early and remained of central importance to her until her death in the convent where she spent her final years. On Sundays, Father would drive Aunt Mary to a Catholic church in Dunkeld, about five miles from Bankfoot, and then come back to prepare for his own morning service at Auchtergaven Parish Church. I still have an image of her, sitting low in the Bomb's front passenger seat, only her hat visible, on the way to Mass. Whatever his faults, Father was an ecumenist long before it became fashionable.

I committed one of my worst sins of all time against Aunt Mary. Having no private income, she lived solely on her modest state pension. At least partly because of my father's profligacy with money, we were in a constant state of financial embarrassment, and subsisted on potato or tomato soup followed by ice cream on most weekdays. We were consequently in no position to enrich Aunt Mary's material life. And yet, she would from time to time enquire about my stamp collection, which countries were underrepresented therein, and give me some of her precious pension to buy stamps. In spite of this, I remember stealing a ten-shilling note from her purse, and using it, I think, to buy even more stamps. That money must have been a very significant proportion of her income at the time, in the late 1950s. To confess this now and in this way evokes inexpressible shame, pain and remorse. Since I was myself received into the Catholic Church some 30 years later, I often pictured Aunt Mary in heaven, enjoying a chat with my mother; truly a pair of saints.

One incident, involving both Aunt Mary and the district nurse, lives on in the family's archive of memories. While

25

Aunt Mary was still able to get about, albeit with a pronounced limp and a hat too well drawn down over her forehead to afford an adequate field of vision, she was one day returning from a trip to the village post office. She failed to notice the approach of Nurse Morrison's grey Austin A45 as it barrelled down the road from the village main street to the manse, and started to cross over. Nurse managed to bring her car to a shrieking halt, and, shaking, she found that Aunt Mary was both unhurt and unruffled. While Nurse gave Aunt Mary a lift home to the manse, Aunt Mary extracted a promise from her not to tell 'Charles' about the encounter, lest she (Aunt Mary) have her freedom curtailed. Nurse gratefully kept the promise.

A few years ago, Auchtergaven Parish Church was entirely gutted by fire: the roof and whole interior were destroyed. So far, no cause has been identified. And this event brought to a close yet another chapter in the history of our family.

As we approached our fourth year at Auchtergaven parish, Father cast about for a new charge. Two possibilities crystallised in his thinking: one in Canada, the other in Tasmania. In 1960, we began a new life in Newfoundland, Canada, all of us doubtless hoping for a higher quality of existence, whatever that might mean to each of us individually. For my egocentric self, I hoped we would have a large American car and that I could finally buy a guitar...

FIVE

On February 7, in 1960, a BOAC Super Constellation flew us into the New World. We departed from Prestwick, bound for Gander in Newfoundland, but fog drove us on to Moncton, New Brunswick. Landing in the middle of the night, we found the airport deserted but for the presence of a bleary-eyed customs officer who, somewhat to our surprise, seized upon little Marion's hand luggage, which consisted of a doll in a small canvas bag. Father's dog collar may have inhibited further scrutiny, and we were conveyed to the airport hotel for the night.

Our first Canadian breakfast was a feast to remember. I ordered buckwheat pancakes with sausages, and, when the dish arrived, I assumed that the contents were to be shared among the five of us: there were six pancakes, about a foot in diameter, swimming in maple syrup and accompanied by at least as many sausages. This first taste of Canada was auspicious – we were truly met with warmth and generosity. Then we were airborne again, to Gander International Airport in Newfoundland. Here we embarked on the final leg of our journey to St John's, the capital of Newfoundland, which was deeply clothed in snow, as we were taxied to the Newfoundland Hotel, where we stayed for a few weeks until our new home was ready.

27

Father was duly installed as minister of St Andrew's Presbyterian Church, and we moved into the new blue-shingled manse in Chestnut Place. For the very first time, we had the luxury not only of central heating – a great joy after years of cold, damp Scottish manses – but of a refrigerator. Not long afterwards, our joy was unbound when a second-hand black-and-white television was added to our home comforts. Frances and I were enrolled at Prince of Wales College, and Marion at a kindergarten next to PWC. We discovered that, in most subjects, our Scottish schools had been slightly ahead, so managed to integrate ourselves reasonably well into the new system. Teachers and students seemed far warmer, less challenging and critical, than their Scottish counterparts. And corporal punishment was unknown.

In retrospect, I see how delightful the Newfoundlanders were, how welcoming, hospitable and sincere. Many of the congregation of St Andrew's Presbyterian Church were university people from the Old World, and we made many good friends. Mother, in particular, with her gift for friendship (inherited by our Cheryl), maintained strong bonds with a wide range of 'Newfies' until her death, even though the family returned to Scotland in 1974.

My recollection of Newfoundland is of huge lakes and vast plantations of firs – and deep snow for half of the year. When we first arrived, in 1960, there was no paved road from St John's to Corner Brook, on the other side of the island, and the Trans Canada Highway, from east to west, was a pot-holed dirt-track. It had the merit, however, that you could perceive the distant approach of another vehicle from the cloud of sandy grit pluming out behind. Similarly, journeys 'round the bay' of the Avalon Peninsula were pioneering treks along dusty, single-track roads to little 'settlements' of brightly painted wooden shacks by the sea. There were all sorts of myths and legends about the denizens of these clustered homesteads, few of them flattering. Their dialect was hard to decipher, and there were encapsulated residues of old Cornish – 'thee's and 'thou's, for example – and Irish in their speech. The 'bay boys' were cruelly characterised as the intellectually challenged products of consanguinity.

Formerly British, Newfoundland confederated with Canada in 1949, becoming Canada's youngest province. Many Newfoundlanders laid proud claim to British ancestry, and people from 'the old country' were highly regarded. St Andrews Presbyterian Church, of course, had strongly Scottish elements in the congregation. St Andrew's Day and Burns Night were celebrated with gusto.

Frances and I joined the junior choir and the church-linked Canadian Girls in Training (CGIT), an oddly titled organisation if ever there was one. The leader was an English physiotherapist called Margaret, for whom I developed a fancy. At the time, I assumed that she was straight and that I was the only deviant on the planet. She also ran the junior choir, although she herself was never much of a singer. She had an enormous talent for burlesque, however, and many were the church socials at which she shone. She was also a great amateur tennis player, and, as far as I know, continues to play in seniors' matches to this day. She had a huge zest for life, and was a thoroughly decent soul. It was not until I was in my fifties that I was told that her sister, who was married and also lived in Newfoundland, had been killed in a fire that had evidently been started by her own cigarette. It is also probable that she had been drinking, as she and her husband were devotees of the warming cup. As far as I know, Margaret never formed a partnership with anyone, and, what with the loss of her sister in these terrible circumstances, I wonder whether her life has been as bright as she invariably portrayed.

Between Grades 9 and 10, when I was 16 and looking for a summer job, I became a nurse's aide at the Hospital for Mental and Nervous Diseases on the Topsail Road just on the edge of St John's. Frazier Walsh, the physician superintendent, was a member of our congregation, and effected my very first appointment in the real world of work. Frazier was a short, round manic-depressive Irishman for whom I developed a high regard. He told me that, when he sensed that he was about to enter a depressive phase, he booked leave and went fishing in the centre of the province, all by himself, until his black dog slunk away. In later years, I learned that he had ever more severe attacks of depression, and, convinced that he was bankrupt and rotting from the inside, had periods of hospitalisation.

When, in the mid-1960s, my family ultimately reached crisis point as the combined result of Father's catastrophic mismanagement of money and obsession with one of the sopranos in the church choir, Mother managed to secure a job as ward clerk at St Clare's Mercy Hospital, the RC hospital in which Frances had done her general nursing training. This was one of the few jobs my mother actually enjoyed, and it was here that she encountered poor Frazier when he was severely ill toward the end of his life. But it was Frazier who first introduced me to the world of psychiatry, and instilled in me an interest which has persisted to this day.

At 16, to be regarded as an adult with a proper job was magical. I wore a white uniform, white stockings and shoes, and felt immensely proud. On one extremely hot day, one of our charges 'escaped', and I was detailed to pursue her, despite my puppy fat which was rapidly becoming fully grown dog fat. The sun was raising bubbles of tarmac on the Topsail highway, and, as I puffed and panted after our escapee, my white shoes and stockings became splattered with hot tar. I do not recall whether I ever caught up with the patient...

The superintendent of nursing at Topsail Road was a slim, elegant and supremely efficient matron in the old style. Every day, she would visit each ward and examine all aspects of the domestic and therapeutic environment. One day, when she had made her stately way into the large ward bathroom in which I was cleaning, she remarked that she had never seen the toilets so beautifully clean. I do not believe I have ever had a prouder moment in my entire life. I ascended into heaven and stayed there for some time.

At the tender age of 16, and enjoying my first encounter with 'mental patients', I made what I considered the revolutionary discovery that 'the mentally ill' were not radically different from ordinary people. I thought I had made a kind of philosophical breakthrough. Psychiatric phenomena fascinated me, a fascination which has never diminished. There were moments of real distress, however. The consultant psychiatrist in charge of the Topsail Road patients had a preference for 'straight' ECT, that is, electroconvulsive therapy *without* general anaesthesia. This meant that not only did it take several of us to hold the convulsing patient on to the bed, but the poor patient emerged from the experience feeling physically and mentally terrible. Several patients told me that they felt they had been 'in hell'. I reported this to my superiors, but the practice continued until the consultant left the hospital: it was explained to me that the patients couldn't *possibly* experience anything while they were in the throes of a grand mal seizure; they were, after all, unconscious.

Aversive though this experience was, I did witness a 'miracle' wrought by the dreaded – and to this day still controversial – ECT. When I first went to Topsail Road, I met Mrs Shepherd, who was suffering from very severe depression. She could hardly walk without the support of two nurses. Her hair hung greasily down her back, her eyes were almost closed, her skin sallow and her breath foetid. She was unable to speak. This was her umpteenth episode, but, following a course of ECT, she became a different person – animated, charming and thrilled to be her old self again. No doubt ECT knocks off billions of neurones, but possibly not as many as I have sacrificed through alcohol abuse...

Encouraged by this introduction to the world of psychiatry, I resolved to study medicine and, when school recommenced, I actually began to do homework and take study seriously – for the first time in my entire school career. I am certain that the atmosphere of encouragement and absence of physical and psychological punishment enabled me to make the transition. By the time I matriculated 18 months later, I had come second in the provincial examinations. Because we had not been resident in Canada for the requisite three years, I was ineligible for a provincial scholarship – there were no government educational grants – but, at the eleventh hour, General Motors of Canada offered me a substantial scholarship to run for four years. There was one proviso: I had to maintain 'straight A's' in each academic year. This daunting requirement, and falling hopelessly in love with a gorgeous but straight fellow student, finished me. As if that were not enough, I found that the pre-med course consisted entirely of pure sciences and advanced mathematics, subjects in which no member of our family was proficient, least of all me. At 17, deeply and hopelessly in love, and with a congenital tendency to panic at the lowest of hurdles, I became a 'Christmas graduate' of Memorial University of Newfoundland and began my career of nutty decisions and lost opportunities.

It would be altogether misleading to imply that there were no lighter moments in my life then. One family in our congregation became particularly important to me. They were of Scottish lineage, the McKinlays, and lived on Le Marchant Road in St John's. The father, Gavin, worked for the Canadian National Railway, and was a highly skilled welder: two brass candlesticks he made for my parents reside proudly on our mantelpiece today. Gavin was a deeply thoughtful, gentle, handsome man, and I wished he could have been *my* father. Mabel, his wife, was an ebullient, funny, adorable soul whom I truly loved. I remember her coming round to our house to give Mother a 'perm', and Mother's face lighting up as she listened to Mabel's jokes and anecdotes. I think Gavin was the nearest thing to a friend Father ever had, as I was recently reminded by his eldest daughter, Jean, how Father had persuaded Gavin to help him with some church organ repair or modification he was attempting to undertake at St Andrew's: the two would stand solemnly and silently together, smoking their pipes, pondering the next stage in their endeavours.

Schools at that time in Newfoundland were denominational. Whereas Frances and I had gone to the United Church of Canada Prince of Wales College, Jean had gone to the Anglican Bishop's College. But we met in the St Andrew's Church junior choir, and in the hideously titled Canadian Girls in Training. The fact that Jean was almost completely tone deaf did not deter her from contributing lustily to Sheep May Safely Graze. We had a private deal whereby we would always stand together at choir practice or in church and, when she went particularly wildly off-key, I would give her a bit of a kick. Jean had a lot of her mother about her and, despite the routine fallings-in and -out of adolescence, we were great friends. Indeed, we try to meet when I am in Ottawa visiting Frances. Jean knew I was 'mad', but seemed to accept me anyway. And that is the mark of a true friend.

Newfoundland had so many advantages over Scotland, although I was incapable of recognising that at the time. The people were nicer, the cars more glamorous, the restaurants more exciting and society less rigidly hierarchical. I have often wondered whether, had I not run away at 18, I would have been better off staying in Canada. I wish I could re-experience the inside of my head then; I wish I could see and feel the things that drove me to get as far away as I possibly could from my 'situation'. It was not as if I'd felt desperately homesick for Scotland, although I do recall mournful trips to Signal Hill to look out across the Atlantic and picture the next piece of land, the English coast. Life in Scotland had been far from easy. We had been permanently poor, and home life was fraught. Father and Mother didn't exactly have out-and-out rows, but Father frequently shouted us down, while Mother did her best to keep the peace. My lifelong struggle to achieve a spiritual perspective was probably 'bedevilled' by an enduring vision of the tall, stout Man of God, dressed in long, black robes, booming repeatedly about us 'weak and miserable sinners' with 'no health in us' – and at home regarding us all as fools. He had an appalling temper, and it was rarely possible to predict when he would next explode. His likes and dislikes were idiosyncratic, to say the least. A few of his favourite things were Leyland buses, the Conservative Party, vintage motor cars, Charlie Chaplin and Harold Lloyd, owls, hens and the Adored Woman of the time: he was wild about Gladys Ripley for a while, for example, the classical pianist whom he had never met, but from whom he managed to obtain an autographed photograph which he displayed in his study for years. By contrast, among his chief hates were Volkswagen Beetles, guitars in church, electronic organs, the Labour Party, dirty fingernails and most forms of meat.

Although I often longed to belong to a 'normal' family, and to escape from the eternal anxiety about having too little to live on, it was not evident what was 'wrong' with Father until the later stages of his life. He was simply the all-powerful controller of the family destiny: he was in charge. We all knew, at some level, that he was constitutionally illogical in matters great and small, and yet we allowed him to bellow his way to victory every time. Mother was too gentle with him; too eager to avoid a noisy, blustering row. 'Blessed are the peacemakers.' Whereas Mother and Frances tended to settle for peace by means of diplomatic circumnavigation, I was more inclined, by the time I reached adolescence, to argue the toss with Father. I can still recall the way my leg muscles ached with the tension experienced in the course of futile debate with God/Father. As Trollope would say, Father 'Knew He Was Right'.

My escape back to the Old World was partly an attempt to put a real distance between Father and me. But it was also an attempt to escape from intolerable aspects of myself, had I but realised it. In the first place, I had encountered the double-edged misery of unrequited lesbian love. In the second, the brief experience of studying advanced mathematics and pure science had persuaded me that I was, indeed, a fool. And so, despite the many attractions of Newfoundland, I returned to Scotland in 1962 to undergo psychiatric nurse training. As Father so helpfully observed: 'Nursing is a profession in which brainless young ladies attempt to redeem themselves.'

When I left Newfoundland in September, 1962, I had only lately become aware that Mother was expecting Cheryl, although I had observed that she seemed to have put on a little weight – a Very Good Thing, since she had always tended to eat rather too little. I have always suspected that, given our chronic shortage of cash, she under-ate in order to allow the rest of us more generous helpings. Evidently, she thought that she had embarked on the menopause, and was as surprised as anyone to be pregnant at the age of 45. By the time of Cheryl's birth, on October 22, 1962, I was 2000 miles away, learning how to become a psychiatric nurse. I did not have the pleasure of meeting her until she was three years old and I had finished my training. When, a month after I had started my training, Father's telegram arrived announcing Cheryl's birth, uncharitable colleagues put it about that the child was actually mine, and that I had fled to Scotland to escape disgrace.

In Newfoundland, despite the enticing glimpses of the independence that might be conferred by the world of work, and that enthralling first encounter with psychiatry, I was a thoroughly confused mess. It did not occur to me to talk to anyone about my troubles. Being gay was both a sin and a social disaster, being in love and unable to 'confess' it an all-consuming torture which infused life by day and nightmares at night. Being fat was also a matter of deep shame and humiliation. I had not yet discovered the special effects of inhaling tobacco, and my sole tranquilliser became food. There was a shopping mall quite near our manse, with a delicatessen called Monty's, where I would buy tubs of ice cream and enormous bags of cheese snacks to wolf in my room. When there was no one at home, I would draw all the curtains in the living room and fry panfuls of onions. I did not want to see – or be seen by – anyone.

SIX

Leaving home was a strangely liberating experience. Although I knew that I would especially miss my gentle mother, it would be good to exercise my own will and do things my way, whatever that might turn out to be. I had gone to Canada with my mother and father and little sisters only two years before, and here was I at 18, striking out on my own. Needless to say, every 18-year-old imagines that she is fully mature, and I was no exception.

In fact, I was a couple of stones overweight, absolutely naïve and totally lacking in any practical skills. I could not make a pot of tea, had never cooked anything except fried onions in my life and had only the vaguest idea how to wash and iron clothes. I lacked the most basic common sense and was generally a social disaster. Although I subsequently regretted having chosen nursing, I do realise that the three years of training certainly – if painfully – knocked off a few corners and disabused me of some of the more bizarre prejudices I had unwittingly picked up from Life With Father. And I did learn how to make a decent pot of tea.

Murray Royal Hospital was a fairly typical old 'asylum', complete with handsome grounds and its own farm. It stood on the far side of the river Tay from the main city of Perth, an agricultural market town to the south of the Scottish highlands. As asylums go, Murray Royal was reasonably benign if inevitably somewhat institutional. For most of the three training years, I lived in the nurses' home and received my weekly rations of tea and sugar in Largactil tins. The ancient home sister, Sister Keith, was a strict but amiable old duck who limped markedly to the left and wore comfy slippers along with her black uniform dress and white lacy cap. Sister Keith ensured that the home was properly cleaned and that propriety and decorum prevailed. Nurses had to be in by 11.00 pm and no male visitors were permitted after 9.00 pm.

Our rooms were scrupulously cleaned every week by a team of 'maids', a fact which illustrates how times have changed since last century: nowadays you would be fortunate to find any hospital *ward* cleaned properly at all, far less weekly. Needless to say, there were anomalies in the order of priorities. Murray Royal was a psychiatric hospital, but there was a tendency to value cleanliness, order and strict rules of precedence over therapeutic interactions with patients. Highly polished floors, sparkling clean toilets and baths, and immaculately made beds indicated that all was well; everything under control. Once, when I was sitting talking to a patient, the ward sister asked whether all the stockings had been darned.

I have to say that the matron, Annie FY Smart, was ahead of her time in wisdom and humanitarianism. It was Annie FY Smart who helped me to stay the course, despite the inevitable frustrations and tedium one experienced during 13-hour shifts and 48-hour weeks. When, in a moment of exasperation while I was in my third year, I asked her what psychiatric nursing was really supposed to be about, she replied simply 'Being with the patient'. I have never forgotten, and have often repeated, that wonderful answer. It is particularly refreshing to recall it when all around are preoccupied with contemporary government targets and obsessions with 'safety,' 'accountability' and myriad other empty approximations of genuine value.

After classroom learning the basics of human anatomy and physiology, hygiene, medicine and other exotica, female students were invariably posted to Ladies 3 for their first ward experience. The point of this posting was that, if you could survive it, you were considered likely to complete the training period. The senior sister on Ladies 3, Sister Reid, had been there from time immemorial, and was considered to be as mad as a rabbit. In fact, she was merely very eccentric, but struck terror into the students' hearts. Ladies 3 was a 'refractory' ward, where the most disturbed patients lived, many of them having been there for their entire adult lives. This was a locked ward, and consisted of two elements: one was a dormitory of about a dozen beds, in which patients lay curled up, some doubly incontinent, others screaming for help or shouting obscenities. The other part of the ward consisted of single rooms, one of which was kept as a place where a patient could, if necessary, be restrained while acutely disturbed.

In those days, the ward kitchen doubled as the nursing office, and Sister Reid would direct operations from the kitchen. On one occasion, I was carrying a large tray containing a dozen bowls of porridge for the dormitory patients, when I slipped and fell on the highly polished corridor floor. Most of the bowls were smashed to pieces, and the porridge globbed down the corridor walls. In mortal fear, I slunk into the kitchen to advise Sister Reid of the disaster. With her back to me, she said, 'Nurse, these bowls are unbreakable,' and dismissed me.

On another occasion, she and I were wheeling a deceased patient on a trolley from the ward round to the mortuary, a journey through part of the grounds. A quarter of the way there, Sister Reid ordered me to go back and fetch my cape. I foolishly protested, saying that I would be all right, thank you, and that I wasn't at all cold. We came to an abrupt standstill as she bellowed, '*Nurse, will you do as I say and go and get your cape at once!*' As we were in the middle of the grounds, in full view of everyone and respectfully conveying a dead person on her last journey, I was, so to speak, mortified.

Part of me realised that I was the proverbial square peg in a round hole. I was not cut out for nursing at all. I had few practical skills and even less common sense or 'nous', and I inwardly chafed against the fossilised hierarchy and pointless, archaic rituals involved. But two considerations kept my nose to the grindstone for those seemingly interminable years. For one thing, I needed to prove to my parents that I wasn't a quitter, and for another there was the occasional joy of 'getting through' to people who were seriously ill. Indeed, this has remained a source of satisfaction in my life, and I profoundly regret that I didn't at least attempt to train as a psychologist. And, had I been less hopeless at mathematics and physics, I might have persevered with the three-year pre-medical course and ultimately gone on to study psychiatry. I have to confess to a mixed envy and fury when I encounter so many psychiatrists today to whom I would not present my dog.

But when resentment and regret subside, I believe I owe a great deal to my years at Murray Royal, not least the acquisition of advanced tea-making skills. I learned how to budget, for one thing. Given my father's hopelessness in managing money, I was financially independent out of sheer necessity. After the deductions for board and lodging, I was left with £4.4/- per fortnight. Since I had become a professional smoker at 17, much of my wage went up in smoke and, toward the approach of the next pay day, frugality prevailed. Mercifully, there was no easy credit in those days: no plastic cards to dull our economic senses.

Most of the established staff at Murray Royal had worked there for their entire adult lives, and were indeed a formidable establishment. In consequence, we student nurses stuck together and became very good friends. Another of my many regrets is that I did not keep up with most of them after qualifying. Now I come to think of it, another of the great benefits of those years was that I became conscious of being 'middle class', and of having a hitherto unrecognised sense of 'differentness' from 'the working class'. I gradually came to see – and feel – the truth of human equality. Although I have no recollection of explicit indoctrination during childhood, I had somehow acquired the view that 'the working class' were less intelligent than 'the middle class'. No doubt part of this was conditioned by my parents' worship of higher education: the only 'real' letter my father ever wrote to me consisted of a five-page, single-spaced exposition of my folly in 'dropping out' of Oxford University years later.

One must ultimately encounter and deal with the phenomenon of one's sexuality. Although I was born, I believe, at the extreme end of the sexual orientation spectrum, being profoundly embarrassed about being gay – I still cannot comfortably use the term 'lesbian' – I strenuously tried to maintain the appearance of 'normality'. It creases me even now to recall my wearing 'firm support corselettes', nylons and stiletto heels. Trousers for women were, even then, for occasional wear only, skirts and frocks the norm. Scotland in the early 1960s was no place for sexual deviants and, besides, our psychiatric textbooks clearly listed homosexuality as a formal mental disorder.

I was therefore almost grateful when an unprepossessing chap from the hospital works department, delightfully named Benjamin Braithwaite, invited me out on a 'date'. This little foray into heterosexuality concluded with my being pressed against the outer wall of the Administration block and being invited to savour the delights of his manhood – and his manhood was, indeed, pressing. Like the proverbial News of the World reporter, I made my excuses and escaped, virgo intacto.

A few miles away from the hospital lay Scone Aerodrome, where pilots and flight engineers from overseas were trained. It was almost mandatory for student nurses to 'go out with' these rather glamorous chaps. Again hoping to establish my credentials as a 'real woman', I went out with an Iraqi flight engineer and had my very first experience of full sexual intercourse. This took place on a bench in a chilly little garden overlooking the river Tay in Dundee. I was not transported in ecstasy, and have an abiding memory of his tearing open a packet of Durex with his teeth. As for the sexual act itself, I found it undignified and vaguely humiliating. Moyaed Gibrail was a perfectly nice, funny and clever fellow, but I could not appreciate his physical charms in any sense at all. I occasionally wonder whether we bombed him to bits along with thousands of others in 2003...

My sexual orientation was not my only burden. When I was posted to Ladies 2, a ward for 'chronic' but unchallenging patients, I steadily gained weight largely as the result of pure boredom. During the 13-hour days, there was precious little to do except make the beds, dispense the medicines and prepare morning and afternoon tea. A fellow student and I both grew daily larger, and had to endure the embarrassing admonitions of Miss Mitchell, the sewing mistress, as she inserted extra panels in our uniforms. Too many cups of tea with too many crunchy, floury Scottish breakfast rolls exacted, so to speak, a heavy toll.

I can still see Ladies 2 in my mind's eye: the long, brilliantly polished corridor off which were the patients' rooms, with the regulation bed, bedside locker, one upright chair and a wardrobe. Private patients had their own rooms, while non-fee-paying patients were housed in small, four-bed dormitories. We were then unacquainted with the concepts of 'rehabilitation' or 'self-help', and we nurses made all the beds and generally waited on these sadly institutionalised women. In the centre of the corridor was the long day room, complete with log fire and television set. Here the ladies sat for most of the day, waiting for the next meal or cup of tea.

I can remember several of the patients very clearly. One, an admiral's widow, was diagnosed as having 'general paresis of the insane', but we were instructed that she was not under any circumstances to get wind of her diagnosis. She was a tall, strikingly handsome elderly lady whose chief joy in life was her daily trip into town to place a bet on the horses. Her case was often referred to in teaching sessions as exhibiting the sign of 'confabulation', where the patient camouflages memory loss with imaginary accounts: an occasional feature of chronic alcoholism. Another was a female psychiatrist who suffered from severe recurrent depression, and who had had more than 300 ECTs during the course of her illness. In those days, the stigma of mental illness was very real, and I very much doubt that she was allowed to practice her profession between depressive episodes.

But my favourite patient was a Dundee pharmacist's wife who, among other things, believed herself to be titled. She wished to be known as 'Lady Grace', but we were strictly forbidden to address her thus, on the ground that it is wrong to collude with delusions. It was because she looked so distressed when addressed as plain Mrs B that I acknowledged her title when senior staff were out of earshot. Lady Grace was a tiny, wizened little soul who was convinced that malign forces were pouring a poisonous substance called 'puric acid' into her teacup. She consequently refused to drink her tea when its level reached

43

about half an inch from the bottom of the cup. I was happy to replenish her cup beyond that level when no one was looking. Since she had been living in this ward for over 30 years, I felt that my small acts of rebellion were unlikely to compromise her recovery.

Lady Grace and I grew fond of each other, so much so that she accorded me a title of my very own – 'Lady Hilda'. One day, to my huge surprise, Lady Grace asked me to take her out for a walk in the hospital grounds; she had resisted the outside world for so many years that I felt pleased and honoured to comply with her request. I helped her into her coat, donned my cape and we set off for the front door. Outside, leading down from the impressive front door, was a flight of five deep steps. We paused at the top of these for a moment. To my intense dismay, and in what felt like an eternity, I saw that Lady Grace was preparing to fly down the steps rather than walk in the conventional manner. I was paralysed. Suddenly she took off, grasping me firmly by the hand, and we both flew to the foot of the steps and rolled over together in the grand front drive. Simultaneously shocked and seized by an involuntary attack of the giggles, I noted out of the corner of my eye that Lady Grace, too, was giggling.

Some of the patients were clearly not ill in any recognisable way. At least one pleasantly cooperative and almost entirely self-caring middle-aged woman had been labelled a 'moral defective', having had a child 'out of wedlock' at an early age, and had been in hospital ever since. Each ward also had a quota of 'mental defectives' and, on Ladies 2, three perfectly unremarkable, stable souls were in permanent residence. Others had had an episode of illness – depression, for example – and recovered satisfactorily but had in the process become somewhat institutionalised. Two of these women worked shifts on the hospital switchboard for decades.

44

Away from the main hospital building, and partially secluded by a ring of trees, was Gilgal, then described as the 'psychoneurosis unit', to which I was posted, presumably because I spoke nicely. The sister in charge of Gilgal was especially fond of horse-racing, and followed the form assiduously: she was not to be disturbed under any circumstances during a race. She was somewhat taciturn and forbidding, so one felt ill at ease in her presence. On Tuesday mornings, patients who were prescribed electroconvulsive therapy (ECT) were given a preliminary injection of atropine, a drug used to dry up body secretions and hence reduce the risk of choking during the treatment. In those days, atropine was dispensed in tablet form to the ward, and on one occasion it was my duty to dissolve each tablet in boiling water from the kettle on the ward kitchen stove. One obtained a teaspoonful of the boiling water and popped an atropine tablet into it, then drew the solution up into a syringe. On one awful Tuesday morning, Sister was sitting in her customary position immediately beside the stove as I prepared to tip one atropine tablet from a phial of 24 into the teaspoon. Sister's proximity unnerved me, and my hand shook slightly, thus tipping the entire contents of the phial into the kettle. I do not recall her reaction.

During my third year of training, I fell resoundingly in love with a post-registration student who had come to Murray Royal to take her Registered Mental Nurse training. Bobbie was a slightly plump girl from a Perthshire farming family, and enviably competent, especially in the professional and domestic spheres. I think that an unconscious part of the attraction was her motherliness: she had the confidence and easy cuddliness which my poor mother seemed to lack. She also had a great sense of fun, and we played practical jokes on one another from time to time, greatly to the irritation of our rather sober superiors. Together, we discovered the joys of yoghurt when it first appeared in the early 1960s. We also discovered the delights of camping, and had several heavenly holidays – along with a third student friend – around Scotland. My lifelong predilection for alcohol may have stemmed from our tendency to imbibe copious quantities of brandy on these holidays, but is much likelier to have become established a few years later, when an ostensibly lesbian partner turned out to be transsexual. To this day, however, I cannot abide the smell of brandy.

On one of these camping holidays, as the three of us lay side by side on our invariably deflating airbeds, Bobbie and I wordlessly found ourselves in each other's arms. Blissfully unaware that our companion camper was wide awake and observing our embrace, we were too absorbed in each other to notice. Our horrified friend stole silently out of the tent, found her way to the nearest telephone box, and 'phoned the physician superintendent at Murray Royal. We were never made aware of his response to our friend's shocking report, but we were not called to account on our return to work.

When I finished my training in 1965, I flew 'home' to Newfoundland to see my family – and to meet my new little sister, Cheryl, for the first time. Two hundred milligrams of sodium amytal and a few stiff scotches saw me safely over the Atlantic to Gander International Airport. Father met me there, and explained that we would be giving a visiting American a lift back to St John's. This colossal man had been on a fishing trip in central Newfoundland. Shortly before my return, I had seen a documentary on the training of US marines. In my post-flight state of altered consciousness, I expatiated at some length on the evil techniques employed to instil a murderous rage in these soldiers, and on the iniquitous position of the supposedly Christian clergy who associated themselves with a killing machine. When I eventually drew breath, the tall fisherman sitting next to Father in the front seat turned round and said to me: 'Ma'am, you're talking to the Chaplain-in-Chief of the United States Marines.'

When we finally reached St John's, my poor mother had overcooked some bacon for tea. God knows why I remember this, but somehow this rather trivial recollection has always induced in me a sense of intense sadness – and embarrassment on her behalf. I had so often dreamed of seeing her again after these three years in Scotland, but never found a way of telling or showing her any of the love and affection I felt for her when we finally met. Mother was not one of nature's huggers, and I have always experienced difficulty in being touched at all. I could never sense what she really thought or felt about *me*, but I suspect that she always regarded me with apprehension. I regarded her as a kind of saint; a somewhat ethereal, fragile soul for whom an embrace might somehow be harmful. But I continue to feel that she regarded *me* as a volatile, rebellious and generally contrary 'problem'. Conspicuous failure at school in Scotland and a couple of referrals to educational psychologists no doubt consolidated that view. If only these 'professionals' had *told* me what concerns had led to these referrals – indeed, if only my *parents* had done so, I could perhaps have talked about my fears and insecurities.

My new little sister was a robust little blonde with a ready warmth and wit. At three, she was a bundle of beauty and energy. I like to think that we took to each other immediately, and we had some hilarious encounters during my stay. I hired a VW Beetle, a breed of car of which my passionate motorist father for some reason disapproved. One morning, when Father was out of town, I was assigned to convey Cheryl to her nursery school. It was mid-winter, and the snow lay deep and crisp and uneven as the result of overnight ploughing activity. When I got Cheryl out of the house and indicated the way to the car, she stood stock still

47

in the snow and firmly announced, on seeing the Beetle, 'I'm not going in *that*!'

On another occasion, when I was to collect her from her nursery school, I noticed that she was sitting on a stool, facing a corner of the playroom, and that standing over her was a pinkly stern Mrs Brooks, the leader, firmly telling Cheryl that 'No one tells *me* to shut up'!

I asked Cheryl whether she'd like me to take her to an A&W drive-in for a root beer and a hot dog. She seemed keen, so off we went. I ordered the promised root beers and hot dogs and noticed that, while we were eating them, Cheryl was staring all around the car park. She explained that she was looking for the poor hot dog...

The family lore has embedded within it the account of the first time I supervised Cheryl's bath time. All went well until, having drained the bathtub, I tried to get her to come out. She instead stood on her head, naked as the day she was born, asking, 'Are you nuts, or something?' – a frequent expression of Father's when he was disinclined to respond to a request.

But the pleasure of being home was soon shattered when I discovered that Father had been having a 'spiritual' affair with a soprano in the church choir. He had taken a conspicuously greater interest in his personal grooming, stooping even to the use of Grecian 2000 on his greying temples. Frances had noticed that Father was regularly driving down Soprano's street, often going out of his way by miles. He arranged a series of recitals with the Canadian Broadcasting Corporation in which he played the organ and she sang works by Bach. As he became increasingly besotted, awareness of his obsession spread like a bush fire through his congregation and beyond.

Mother was devastated. This was far from the first time that Father had developed an overwhelming preoccupation with another woman, but it was probably the most dramatic, and had catastrophic consequences. Any reference to the impropriety of his obsession drew excoriating denials and protestations that his interest in Soprano was purely musical, spiritual and altruistic. He denounced those who challenged him about this and took to wearing a black tie and lying down on Sunday afternoons, repeatedly playing tapes of his recitals with Soprano. He portrayed himself as the misunderstood, wronged victim of trivial, petty minds. He joined a gun club in St John's, and obtained the necessary police licence to possess a firearm. He threatened to blow Soprano and himself into oblivion if people refused to accept the innocence of his intentions and sentiments. On one terrible occasion, presumably frustrated and infuriated by others' appeals to reason and morality, he threw his handgun onto Marion's lap in what I took to be an act of histrionic manipulation: a demented attempt to warn his decriers of their ignorance and misunderstanding. Marion was eight years old at the time.

No words can possibly convey the misery and impotence we all felt. Mother was utterly wretched and, at one point, actively suicidal – Father had had to order Frances to entice Mother out of their en suite bathroom, where she was evidently intending to cut her wrists. I almost managed to persuade Mother to leave Father and to come with me to Scotland, where I proposed to change career tack and to undergo district nurse training in order that she and I could be housed. For the briefest of moments, I could see that Mother was contemplating my proposal. But the moment passed, and she sank back into her role as dutiful minister's wife.

By this time, however, Father's congregation took matters into their own hands. The kirk session confronted him about the looming scandal, and Father was ultimately forced to resign. There followed his very first mortgage – on a gloomily gothic house in a poor part of the city – and a series of low-paid jobs. He had an unsuccessful stint as a life insurance salesman, drove trucks for an ice cream factory, briefly lectured in English at the university and finally became a librarian at the Arts and Culture Centre. The family economy suffered more than ever, and Mother was forced to return to teaching in a 'rough' school, where she was somewhat traumatised by the students' unruly behaviour; it would seem that she had some form of psychological collapse. At any event, she left teaching and got a job as a ward clerk in the hospital in which Frances had trained. This turned out to be the only job which Mother actually enjoyed, although the pay was low.

Meanwhile, I returned to Murray Royal as a staff nurse, and then saw an advertisement for a course in 'Psychiatric Treatment Methods and Group Dynamics' to be run jointly by the Royal Edinburgh Hospital Department of Psychiatry and Dingleton Hospital, the first therapeutic community in Scotland, run by the father of 'social psychiatry', Maxwell Jones. Professor Henry Walton and Max Jones sought to train a small group of carefully selected psychiatric nurses to a level somewhere between nursing and psychiatry. I was one of the four chosen. The course comprised six months in the Department of Psychiatry at the Royal Edinburgh Hospital and six months at Dingleton Hospital, a small district psychiatric hospital in the borders. We worked in the Professorial Unit at the Royal Edinburgh, where the professor at the time was Morris Carstairs, and learned the rudiments of group psychotherapy with inpatients. We also attended the lectures for the Diploma in Psychological Medicine, but were not permitted to sit the examinations. A condition of the course was that we would undergo group analysis for the six months, and as an early result of this it emerged that three of the four of us were gay. When this was reported to Professor Walton, we were advised that he was not amused.

Toward the end of this part of the course, Bobbie got a job as a ward sister at the Royal Edinburgh, and she and I moved temporarily into a room at my cousin Donald's third floor flat in Bruntsfield. We roasted ourselves over an electric fire and fried 'cheesy dreams' – sandwiches of cheese coated in tomato ketchup – on our little Belling ring. This was my very first 'live in' relationship, and it began well. Although we had little in common, we got along together very well, and we both turned out to be cheerfully natural nest-builders. At that stage, neither of us thought that we would not be partners for life. Scotland, in the sixties, was pretty 'homophobic' – a real misnomer, since the problem is hardly an irrational fear so much as a deeply rooted prejudice. On the whole, we attempted to conceal the nature of our relationship from the world – even, absurdly perhaps, from my cousin and his wife. The only people officially in the know were my three colleagues on the diploma course.

After the six months at the Royal Edinburgh, we four 'advanced' students then moved on to Dingleton, daily travelling the 40-odd miles between Edinburgh and Melrose in Tom's elderly Mini, all four of us smoking throughout the journey, thus combining the benefits of active and passive smoking. Which all seemed perfectly natural at the time.

The therapeutic community experience was strikingly different from the rather academic months at the Royal Edinburgh. We learned how to see the institution itself as a therapeutic agent, where staff and patients were part of an egalitarian social structure in which any member of the community might help another member to recognise the effects of their behaviour on others. For legal purposes, the physician superintendent, the chief nurse and the hospital secretary maintained their roles in theory, while in practice they were to be seen primarily as members of the

51

community rather than leaders. It is a moot point as to whether this was really the case. Maxwell Jones himself was a highly charismatic figure: a tall, handsome man who wore Bernat Klein suits, drove a Jaguar and had a flirtatious demeanour toward attractive young females. Whilst I found the notion of therapeutic community deeply attractive – and do so to this day – I did not take to Max himself. Rightly or wrongly, I felt that he was, paradoxically, revelling in his own importance, and that he was a somewhat heartless philanderer. Indeed, when he eventually left Dingleton to take up a professorship in the US, he abandoned his then wife, a beautiful Scandinavian, and ran off with a student nurse.

The year had been almost exhilarating, and I felt I had benefited enormously. The future looked promising, and I looked forward to continuing a career in psychiatric nursing, hopefully at an 'enlightened' institution. When the course finished, I was offered a sister's post in the new Young People's Unit at the Royal Edinburgh. This turned out to be the only job I ever actually enjoyed. I had barely been there a year before the course of my life changed radically and, in several respects, disastrously.

SEVEN

Bobbie and I moved out of my cousin's flat in Bruntsfield Place and into our first real home – another third floor flat close to the Royal Edinburgh Hospital, where we both now worked. Few flats in those days were centrally heated, and we cheerfully hauled sacks of coal up the three flights of stairs in our tenement building. Apart from a downstairs neighbour, who repeatedly played Abide With Me loudly on her piano at odd times, we were truly content in our domestic cocoon, and Bobbie enjoyed cooking and baking – especially her 'millionaire's shortbread', a shortbread base with a layer of condensed milk topped by chocolate. The expression of my addictive personality was in those days confined to Dunhill International cigarettes.

My appointment to Tipperlinn House, or the Young People's Unit, was my first ward sister's job in the new unit, just outside the main grounds of the Royal Edinburgh. I was 24, embarking upon the next step in what I still assumed would be my career in psychiatric nursing. The staff all wore mufti and addressed one another by their Christian names – rather *avant garde* at the time. It was nevertheless clear that Dr John Evans, the psychoanalytically trained consultant psychiatrist in charge of the unit, was the boss. He was a tall, fairly well covered chap, with floppy hair and a distinctly Welsh brogue. The unit was to be run on psychoanalytic lines, with features of therapeutic community. We three 'sisters' – actually two sisters and a male charge nurse – were to run psychoanalytically-oriented groups with the parents of our adolescent patients. We each had five psychiatrically disturbed adolescents in our care, so the groups consisted of ten parents. Commitment by the parents to these groups was a condition of the treatment of their offspring.

For me, this was truly a dream job. Very few elements of conventional psychiatric nursing were involved, and every team member felt they were valued contributors to the recovery of their patients. In those days, of course, there were few 'outcome measures', but we became aware of the progress of our youngsters in the course of follow-up out-patient appointments. The physical unit itself was a large Victorian mansion, elegantly decorated and furnished according to various experts in these fields. The underlying theory was that, if our patients were looked after in a well-appointed environment, they would appreciate the fact that they were being respected, and we would experience a minimum of damage to the fabric of the house. This proved to be the case.

We held community meetings, in which patients and staff together discussed and decided domestic arrangements, resolved conflicts between or among the community 'members' and analysed crises such as epidemics of self-destructive behaviour. As far as was practical, the community would decide how the unit should be run, with the obvious exception of legal and exclusively clinical matters.

Patients had a wide variety of problems. Some were referred by the forensic services: one young man had been in prison, having been convicted of arson. Others had extreme forms of adolescent angst – violent aggression, for example, or severe identity problems. Others again had formal mental illnesses or disorders: depression, early schizophrenia, obsessive-compulsive disorder (OCD), for example. I especially recall an endearing schoolboy whose OCD had so paralysed him that he could not ascend a flight of steps without halting at every third step to pray frantically. He eventually recovered.

We charge nurses took it in turn to 'sleep in', there being no waking staff on duty during the night. On one occasion, when it was my turn, I became aware of a slight scuffling sound from one of the bedrooms, and could just about make out a boy's voice, asking who was on sleeping-in duty. When the answer was 'It's Allison', another voice said, 'We'd better get back to bed, then'... There was no further sound that night, beyond the occasional soft snore.

In those days, I was convinced that Freud was right about everything. There was plenty of evidence as to the existence of the unconscious mind, and Freud's interpretation of dreams made sense, as did the array of personality defence mechanisms. Aficionados of psychoanalytic theory and practice resembled not so much clinicians as worshippers of an arcane religion. We managed to interpret most behavioural phenomena in psychoanalytic terms, and objectors to these formulations were accused of 'denial' or 'defensive' strategies.

In retrospect, I view our 'successful outcomes' as attributable more to the respect and attention – and affection – we showed our young people than to the application of psychoanalytic theory. It was obvious to any observer that we cared quite deeply for our patients. It may have been the demonstrably positive effects of our 'treatment' of our charges that made the job so enjoyable. I would cheerfully have stayed in that kind of therapeutic setting for the remainder of my working life.

Although I failed to see it at the time, my world began to implode when I fell in love with one of the senior registrars, Wendy Acton. She seemed to represent much of what I most admired in another woman: warmth, care, humour and competence. Dr Evans also admired her to the extent that he urged her to go on to the Tavistock Clinic in London when she had completed two years at the Young People's Unit. He clearly saw, as I did, her potential as a gifted clinician.

To begin with, I had no idea – and there was no overt signal – that Wendy reciprocated my developing love for her. We got on really well as colleagues, and shared a similar sense of commitment – and humour. By this time, Bobbie and I had moved into a larger flat a few streets away from the hospital, and continued to enjoy our life together. We worked hard, but socialised little: our partnership was still largely secret, and it simply did not occur to us to explore the gay 'scene' in Edinburgh. In fact, I do not believe that we even knew whether there *was* such a thing. That is how 'closeted' we were. We went to the odd concert – I remember going to see the Alexander Brothers and Frankie Vaughan, for example – but that was about the extent of our cultural life.

One evening, when Bobbie was in Perthshire visiting her mother, the doorbell rang and I was astonished to find Wendy Acton in the doorway. I seem to remember she was 'just passing' and thought she'd just 'pop in'. I invited her in, and imagine we had a coffee; I still had not begun my love affair with alcohol, so almost certainly had no 'strong drink' in the house. Heaven knows what we talked about, but there was no disclosure of romantic sentiment on either part.

I mentioned Wendy's visit when Bobbie returned from Perthshire, and attributed it to conventional friendliness: after all, we got on really well at work. Inwardly, however, I was inevitably stirred emotionally by the encounter, and perhaps half hoped that it might signify something beyond friendship.

Some time – probably weeks – later, Wendy invited me round for 'supper'. She explained that her partner, Maggie (a senior nursing officer in the main part of the Royal Edinburgh) was away, and that she could 'use some company'. I was surprised and delighted by the invitation, and would have been even more surprised had I known at the time that Wendy was no cook. Nevertheless, she managed to provide something perfectly edible, and we settled down for a post-prandial chat. Suddenly, *a propos* nothing, she announced, 'If you're not careful, I'll make a pass at you.' I was temporarily bereft of speech, which she evidently took to be an expression of horror or shock, whereupon she began to apologise and begged me to 'forget' she had said anything. I seem to remember saying something like, 'No, no, it's fine, really...' I stayed the night...

While I was thrilled and flattered that Wendy should reciprocate my feelings, I was thrown into torment about betraying Bobbie. I decided not to confess my infidelity immediately: after all, the affair might not progress beyond the status of a brief 'fling'. But it did indeed progress, and in no time at all, Wendy was suggesting I come down to London with her while she attended an interview for a senior registrar post at the Tavistock Clinic in the Department of Children and Parents. I cannot remember how I explained the London trip to poor Bobbie, but I duly accompanied Wendy on the day of her interview. We went to the film *Funny Girl* in the evening, and stayed overnight in a hotel. I felt extreme excitement about our romantic adventure – but agonised about the as yet unsuspecting Bobbie.

Wendy was offered the Tavistock job, and submitted three months' notice to the Young People's Unit. Again, she asked me to come down to live with her in London. I had been working at the unit for only 18 months, and knew I would regret leaving a job I enjoyed so much. But my joy at the prospect of being with Wendy overcame both my disappointment about the job and acute guilt about leaving Bobbie. I chose to tell Bobbie about the end of our relationship while she was on duty, in her office. It was an act of abject cowardice, which I deeply regret to this day. Bobbie had little alternative but to hide her shock and hurt until her shift ended.

The remaining weeks in Edinburgh were amongst the most painful of Bobbie's and my life. One evening she did not come home after work finished, and later telephoned me from the Forth Road Bridge, announcing her intention to throw herself off. I managed to persuade her to come home, but heaven alone knows how, since I was unable to offer the slightest comfort in her profound distress. I had set my compass in the direction of London, and nothing was going to deter me – not even the fact that I had hardly got to know the person with whom I was effectively eloping.

Actually, Wendy and I each had an entirely mistaken perception of the other. I saw her as a confident, highly competent professional woman with a delicious sense of mischief, and she saw me as a motherly, mature woman. We were both wrong, as it turned out – and with devastating consequences. How different our life trajectories might have been had we had more time to get to know each other before embarking on such a bridge-burning enterprise. But time was one luxury we did not possess.

The parting from Bobbie was heartbreaking for both of us, albeit in different ways. Our colleagues at the Young People's Unit were visibly shocked by the nature of Wendy's and my departure, and an attempt was made to persuade me to stay. But I have never been good at compromise or 'second thoughts', and Wendy and I were both in the honeymoon stage of our relationship. We had set our course, and that was that.

We rented a tiny flat in North Finchley, and I got a sister's job at the Northgate Clinic for 'psychopathic' young men in Hendon. Presumably because of my early experiences with male youths in Shetland, I had never been comfortable working with men, and the aggressive behaviour with which we were regularly confronted rendered the job particularly stressful. Matters were not helped by the fact that the (male) nursing officer in charge of the clinic took a dislike to me from the outset. I believe he thought that the unit I'd come from in Edinburgh was too 'fancy' for his liking, and seemed to seize any opportunity to undermine me. On one scary occasion, when I was in charge of the clinic on night duty, a group of patients surrounded me, brandishing syringes and demanding that I open the drug cupboard. I was simply terrified, but managed to summon up the strength to order them firmly to back off. Which, to my astonishment, they did. My boss did not comment on the incident, merely raising his eyebrows when I reported it to him.

A few weeks into the job, I developed a chest infection and gratefully went off sick. I then suffered a spontaneous pneumothorax, which allowed me to extend my sick leave. Before I had left Edinburgh, a psychologist at the YPU had suggested that I might like the London School of Economics, an institution of which I had not heard, but to which I enthusiastically applied – anything to let me escape from the ghastly Northgate Clinic. To my huge relief, I was accepted and began a two-year, full-time course in Social Administration. The LSE was my saviour in several respects, not least because it enabled me to escape from my job, but also because it provided me with a deeply enjoyable distraction from Wendy's revelation, soon after we had arrived in London, that she believed that she was a man wrongly inhabiting a woman's body.

Words cannot convey the extent of my shock and initial disbelief. This could not possibly be true. I had fallen in love with a real woman, had cherished and adored every part of her, especially those features which distinguished her as a woman. Her slender physique, gorgeous little breasts, those lovely ankles, beautifully curved legs... the sexy court shoes, elegantly tailored skirts and frilly blouses. How could I have fallen for a woman *who wasn't there; who did not, after all, exist?* The whole thing was an illusion – or a delusion. My sanity was on the line. And there was no one in the world in whom I could confide, no one to whom I could convey my sense of dislocation from reality; my ultimate nightmare – not merely losing the object of one's love, but discovering that they never existed in the first place.

I can no longer recall how I reacted to this news, but I was naïve enough to imagine that I loved 'her' enough to assimilate it, and agreed to help her explore the options available – if indeed there were any – in 'reassignment'. But love was not enough. In a sense, this decision ruined my life. And it undermined the rather fragile sense of self-confidence that I had only just acquired in early adulthood. The wholly negative experience I had had at the Northgate Clinic diverted me from psychiatric nursing, as did the highly positive experience of studying at the LSE. My happy sojourn at the LSE simultaneously enabled me to meet some of the most eminent figures in politic philosophy and political theory of the time – people like Richard Titmuss, Brian Abel-Smith, Howard Glennerster, Tessa (now Baroness) Blackstone and other luminaries – and allowed me to hang on to the filaments of self-respect I had so recently gained. I do not believe that, without this experience, I could have endured the hellish journey in what

I came to call 'no man's land': the lonely path toward a goal which the media and the world in general knew nothing of at the time. There was no internet in those days, of course, and discovering the pathways to 'gender reassignment' was painfully slow, rather like a game of espionage.

In the early 1970s, the small world of gender reassignment was a secret one, and the only service we could discover in the UK was based at the Charing Cross Hospital in London, under the direction of Dr John Randall, a consultant psychiatrist. We managed to get an appointment with a social worker at Guy's Hospital York Clinic, Margaret Branch, with whom Dr Randall worked on reassignment cases. Almost immediately, in our first meeting with her, Mrs Branch asked Wendy what occupation 'he' might follow after reassignment, as he couldn't possibly continue in medicine. This dumbfounded us, as we had not anticipated such a radical change of career. As it turned out, she was being disingenuous; indeed, she herself had been directly involved in the case of the reassignment of a female-to-male GP – and subsequently arranged for us to meet that individual. The reference to the necessity for a career change was, it turned out, Mrs Branch's way of testing Wendy's resolve.

In those days, it was not possible to change one's birth certificate: that became possible only very recently. So Wendy would always be stuck with a female passport. It proved possible – but only by the most circuitous means – to change most other key documents such as driving licence by means of specially arranged interviews with the relevant departments. The fact that such changes had been achieved in the past was not generally known, so individual bureaucrats invariably had to refer to their managers for individual decisions. I experienced a sense of achievement as each of these documentary changes was accomplished, and this mitigated the initial apprehension I might otherwise have felt.

And, of course, these minor triumphs were supplemented by huge quantities of alcohol and Valium. Every little step of 'progress' was celebrated by gallons of cider or beer, terminated only by the torrent of vomit which became the norm for me after each 'celebration'. Wendy, on the other hand, tended to become belligerent and bellicose. Neither of us was remotely capable of comforting the other: we were isolated both from the world and from each other. I could no longer contemplate love-making: for one thing, Wendy had grown to hate her breasts and genitals, and hated to be touched as if she were a woman, and, for another, she took to insisting that I call her clitoris her 'willy'.

I thanked God for the LSE, and, when I was either there or at home studying, I could at least partially insulate myself from the grotesque collapse of my relationship with my vanished lover – the lover who never was. And I regarded my contribution to securing Wendy's transition to manhood as a miniature crusade: something that had to be done; a way of helping another human being toward self-realisation. And so the distraction of academic study, the pursuit of a 'just' campaign – and liberal quantities of alcohol and tranquilliser – enabled me to get through the days.

One of the most difficult documentary changes involved the General Medical Council, who initially affected not to know that a previous member had successfully had her registration changed from female to male. I had to exercise unprecedented patience and tact during this protracted and gruelling process. I think that we ultimately had to invoke the assistance of the Medical Defence Union. To complicate matters, the GMC insisted upon the production of two references to attest to 'Ben's' continuing medical competence. One of the Royal Edinburgh referees,

Professor Walton, declined to provide such an assurance on the ground that he did not know the person now named as Edward Benjamin ('Ben') Peterson. And the psychoanalyst who was conducting 'Wendy's' training analysis while 'she' was still working at the Tavistock Clinic stated that he could not attest to 'her' future stability given the anticipated psychological and physical challenges inevitably posed by the reassignment process. There was presumably the additional difficulty that traditional psychoanalysts tended to believe that problems of gender identity could be solved by psychoanalysis. I had to muster my utmost debating skills – and respectful demeanour – in order to persuade the GMC that the practical dilemmas posed by potential referees were insuperable and unreasonable. In the end, re-registration was accomplished, but it had taken months of metaphorical blood, sweat and tears in what had felt like a real war of attrition. When I look back to this agonising time, I can see the GMC's difficulty. In fact, 'Wendy's' heavy social drinking had escalated during the year of 'living the other way round' (and mine had begun), and accelerated throughout the period of major surgery and hormone treatment. The stress was phenomenal for us both, and would have been severe even for people more secure in their personalities than we were.

To some extent, I succeeded in separating my life as a student at the LSE from my life as the partner of an individual undergoing a 'sex change'. But the price I actually paid for enduring the three years of reassignment was high. I had of course resorted to the transient relief of alcohol, and, when the tensions were at their greatest, joined Ben in adding Valium 10mg tds to the toxic levels of tranquillisation by alcohol. At the time, we joked about needing Valium to get ourselves together enough to go to the pub...

One of my abiding memories is of sitting in lectures at the LSE while stunned and nauseated by hangovers. I wrote most of my essays under the influence of Blackthorn Black Label Cider and, to my real surprise, managed to gain a distinction at the end of the course. This helped to restore a little of my thoroughly battered self-confidence. And it was while I was at the LSE that 'Ben' embarked upon the series of surgeries which were designed to obliterate Wendy's anatomical womanhood. In those days, no self-respecting surgeon would carry out reassignment surgery, so it was a case of casting about for a surgeon prepared to operate and possibly risk his professional reputation if news of the surgery were to be broadcast. It took time to get the name of a surgeon willing to undertake a bilateral mastectomy, and he was an Australian general surgeon who had never performed a mastectomy in his entire career. The result, from a cosmetic point of view, was disastrous. Ben looked as if he had been the victim of a serious gangland stabbing: there were grotesque zigzag scars all over his chest. Thereafter, Ben took to explaining that he had been involved in a serious car crash.

As I have indicated, it is impossible to express how it felt to have one's erstwhile female partner have such significant signs of womanhood removed in a procedure which resulted in such a visible act of butchery. I realised that Ben was just relieved to be rid of those detested betrayers of his 'real' self. To me, however, they were part of what I had loved in Wendy-as-woman. Since I was an end-of-the-spectrum lesbian, I was saying 'goodbye' to someone with whom I had once been in love, but whom I had hardly got a chance to know. In truth, I was devastated and heartbroken but, at the time, could not afford to let myself feel this. I remained focused on the project in hand, to the exclusion of any other consideration.

The next major step in the transformation involved a 'total' hysterectomy, again negotiated with the customary difficulty of securing the services of a specialist surgeon sympathetic to the reassigning individual and prepared to absorb the risk of professional opprobrium should the information 'leak' out generally. Again, the fact that the operation was performed by a general surgeon rather than a gynaecological specialist meant that Ben was taking a calculated risk in having a non-specialist carry out the procedure. And, again, the resulting scar was inevitably larger and longer than those resulting from conventional hysterectomy by specialist surgeons: Ben was going to have to explain further scarring in terms of trauma rather than those of elective surgery. Once again, Ben was only too delighted at the time to be rid of the despised betrayers of his 'real' gender. But he later came round to resenting and regretting the aesthetic disasters that had been visited upon him.

As if these surgeries were not in themselves traumatic enough, Ben's heart stopped in the immediate post-operative period, with the result that he had had to be resuscitated on both occasions. Following the second lot of surgery, he was clearly suffering from anaesthetic-induced confusion. He pulled me close to him, saying in a confidential whisper, 'I know you'll think this is funny, but I can see little pixies hopping in and out' of the ventilator high up in the wall of his room. Mercifully, he forgot about the pixies when he was fully 'round' from the surgery.

Again in retrospect, I can see that the hormone treatment, which began the moment the one year living as a male had expired, was having not merely a physiological effect. Ben's musculature changed quite dramatically from a female to a male contour, and he began to grow a beard. All of this transformation was accompanied by a significant deepening of his voice. I was not prepared for the speed nor

65

the extent of the physical changes, but neither was I prepared for the nature and depth of the *personality* changes which were, if anything, even more disturbing to me than the physical. Wendy's gentleness and liberalism gradually gave way to an aggressive, reactionary illiberalism: he took, especially when drunk, to decrying my 'lesbianism' and to physically attacking me. I was shocked and devastated, but felt there was no one to whom I could turn for advice or comfort. We were still living in 'no man's land', with 'Wendy' still working at the Tavistock, complete with female wig, clothing and facial makeup – but with a closely shaved face and deepening voice. I have no way of knowing what 'her' colleagues must have thought at the time; they could hardly have failed to notice the changes in their erstwhile female colleague. Perhaps they thought that she was suffering from a glandular disorder which was really none of their business.

One of the really gruelling aspects was the extreme isolation – hence 'no man's land' – we were expected to endure while the transformation was achieved. We were effectively instructed to sever all our social allegiances for the entire reassignment period, which began with what was initially prescribed as a two-year period of living as a male without any of the hormonal or surgical procedures taking place. In the event, Dr Randall reduced this period to one year for Wendy – partly, we surmised, because there had been several suicides of people who were unable to tolerate the awful period of 'living the other way round' before starting active 'treatment', and, partly, we suspected, because Wendy was a fellow psychiatrist.

The 'living the other way round' was a veritable hell. Wendy was expected to continue working as a female, while living as a male in her off-duty life. At the time, we were living in a tiny upstairs flat in Golders Green, with our landlady living downstairs. If we planned to go to a pub in the evening, Wendy had to wear a 'maxi' length coat to conceal her male attire, and we had to leave the house as stealthily as we could, to escape our landlady's attention. By this time, Wendy had had her hair cut in a short male style and was wearing a female wig to work at the Tavistock. She therefore cut a curious figure with her long coat, men's haircut and men's shoes. These were such nerve-racking occasions that I was sometimes physically sick when we got home. We had cast off the friends we had had when Wendy was Wendy, and neither of our families was yet aware of the situation.

EIGHT

Toward the end of 'her' two years at the Tavistock Clinic, Wendy Patricia Acton became Edward Benjamin Peterson and it was 'Ben' who applied for a consultant post in 'mental subnormality' at Leavesden Hospital in Hertfordshire. He had explained his situation, and the advice he had been given was that he needed to step aside from adult psychiatry until his credentials as a male consultant had been established in a 'less demanding' setting. A sympathetic consultant at Leavesden was evidently prepared to accept the 'risk' in employing a newly reassigned applicant, and I still have a photograph of Ben arriving at Leavesden Hospital, complete with briefcase, on the first day of his first job as a male. We moved from Golders Green into a flat in a terraced house in Watford, where the Polish landlord and his wife lived on the premises. By this time, Ben had grown an impressive beard, had developed a convincing baritone voice, and actually looked every inch a conventional male.

As far as I can recall, Ben seemed to be happy enough at Leavesden, although he was hardly able to apply the kinds of knowledge and skills he had acquired during his senior registrar years in Edinburgh and London. There was a conveniently located little hostelry close to the hospital gates, and he and I would sometimes meet for a leisurely, liquid lunch there. He stuck to his current favourite, Greene King ale, while I downed generous glasses of Moussec. Heaven alone knows how or if his luncheon affected his afternoon performance, but in those days it was quite common for medical and nursing staff to have an alcoholic drink or two at lunchtime.

Having succeeded in his first employment as a male consultant, Ben applied for and got a consultant's post in child and adolescent psychiatry at Peterborough District Hospital. We bought our first house – a 'chalet bungalow' – in Peakirk, a village on the periphery of the town. I soon grew to loathe the fenland: those vast, grey-brown expanses of flat land with occasional scraggy trees, dark, threatening skies and an air of doom and death. Or was it just me? I got a job as a trainee social worker, posted in the little town of March. As Ben became ever more aggressive and critical of my orientation, my demeanour, the way I dressed and so on, I gradually invested more and more energy in buying smart, fashionable dresses, wearing makeup, plucking my eyebrows, and even went the length of joining a beauty club which sent monthly collections of mascara, lipstick, foundation creams and perfumes. I can even feel a shiver of embarrassment now when I think about it – 40 years later.

Really, the Peterborough years were a time of contortion and distortion for us both. Ben became steadily louder and increasingly paranoid – about me, about colleagues at work and sundry others. The most mundane of conversations might suddenly explode in a barrage of swearing, throwing glasses to the floor or physical assault. The Peterborough constabulary soon knew the route to our house. Our drinking accelerated, providing further fuel to our frequent brawls. Ben was losing his equilibrium, such as it had been, and I was losing my sense of who I was altogether. We made few friends, largely because we were too immersed in our drinking and fighting to take the trouble to do anything at all that did not involve alcohol.

This was undoubtedly the nadir of our lives. We were desperately unhappy and insecure, facing each day with dread, living only for the next drink. Ben saw himself as a 'social' drinker, but I knew that my relationship with alcohol was one of desperate need: I could not countenance a life without it. Whilst I might have thought of myself as a 'functioning' alcoholic, insofar as I seemed to be able to do academic work to a satisfactory level, I knew I was, by any definition, a lush. And, especially in the early seventies, alcoholic women were beyond the pale. My sense of shame was absolute.

While I found aspects of my trainee social worker job occasionally interesting or even entertaining, I soon recognised that a career in social work was not for me. Although the era of political correctness had not yet dawned, there was nevertheless more than a whiff of sanctity and preciousness about some of the more senior social work trainers and managers which I found indigestible. I became bored and restless, and knew I had to do something to change things when I found myself buying draught sherry in dodgy-looking bottles in garages in the fens. There I was, with a bottle between my knees, driving to my next appointment. I hope I was sensible enough to pull into a lay-by to take a swig, as it would have been positively dangerous to drink while driving...

Despite the terrible ending of our relationship, Bobbie and I had resumed contact, and, at an especially low point in my life with Ben, I arranged to spend a few days staying with a former girlfriend of Ben's in Leith – a retired school doctor – and to spend some time with Bobbie and her mother, who were now living just outside Edinburgh. I drove from Peterborough to Midlothian in my beloved little Renault 4, and was enjoying the break away from Ben until the mid-point in my northern sojourn when, after a particularly bibulous evening with Bobbie, I insisted on driving back to my temporary lodgings at Leith. Bobbie was no great drinker and, I subsequently gathered, had urged me not to drive. But the combination of alcohol and my customary pig-headedness led to my overriding her pleading, and I set off for Leith at an ungodly late hour. I have no recollection of what happened next, but 'came to' in a police cell somewhere in Edinburgh. My temporary landlady was summoned from her bed, and collected me from the police station, tight-lipped with embarrassment and fury.

I had evidently managed to negotiate only a few streets away from Bobbie's house before colliding with a – stationary – car which, it turned out, belonged to a Church of Scotland clergyman. Freud would have loved that. Someone called the police, who removed me to their 'place of safety'. A police surgeon determined that I was approximately four times the 'safe' limit, and I was charged in the customary way. A subsequent summons to appear in the High Court of Edinburgh materialised after my ignominious return to Peterborough.

Rather touchingly, Ben had arranged for me to see his former, Jungian, analyst, the eminent Dr Winifred Rushforth, about 'my' problems while I was staying in Edinburgh. I was not aware that analysis might prove a useful tool in the resolution of an alcohol problem, but, theoretically, of course, a full-blown analysis might expose some of the neurotic substrata of *any* problem – addiction and transsexualism included. But a more immediate answer to my problems was called for, and one session on a cracked leather couch, covered in a tartan blanket, did not promise to be that. Dr Rushforth had analysed Ben's brother, whose homosexuality was resolved over the course of five years and resolved so convincingly that Peter decided to marry

71

and have children. Sadly – predictably? – his homosexuality resurrected itself; the marriage was ended and a gay union established which, as far as I know, has persisted these 40 years.

When I received the summons to return to Edinburgh, I consulted a gay lawyer friend, who advised me that there was no defence to such a charge, drink-driving being a 'summary' offence: either you had committed it or you had not; you were not required to have *mens rea* or an intention to commit the offence. If the evidence showed that you 'did' it, you were automatically guilty, and must bear the consequences. As it happened, Ben had been charged with precisely the same offence some weeks before at a court in Biggleswade, and had been duly deprived of his licence. It looked as if we were both to be so deprived, so things had reached a pretty pass.

With the desperation of our situation in mind, I resolved to do everything I could to escape the withdrawal of my driving licence, and I arrived in Edinburgh with a mentally prepared statement in what should legally have proved a pointless defence. To my shock and dismay, I found my cousin, Helen, waiting to greet me at court. I still have no idea how she found out about my appearance, but she was at the time working as a midwife and living in Penicuik, just south of Edinburgh. My shame was immediately compounded, but I was not to be deterred from making an impassioned appeal for the retention of my licence. I have little recollection of the basis for my defence, but certainly mentioned depression and my firm intention of seeking help for my resulting alcohol addiction. To my – and everyone else's – astonishment, I was fined £10 and had my licence endorsed, but not withdrawn. Indeed, when I was back in Peterborough, I got a sweet little note from a writer to the signet – who was awaiting the next case – congratulating me for my performance, and advising me that the decision in my favour was almost certainly illegal.

Despite my speech to the court, I did not immediately 'seek help' for my addiction, but became Ben's chauffeuse until *his* licence was returned. By which time, of course, my drinking had simply resumed its normal pattern.

With Ben back on the road, I 'considered my position'. I was not quite old enough to embark on Jung's mid-life period of introspection, but I made a cursory analysis of my life thus far: a difficult, phobic, lonely childhood, turbulent adolescence and then a period of relative stability when doing my three years of psychiatric nursing training. A great job at the Young People's Unit in Edinburgh, then a very successful – and hugely enjoyable – two years at the LSE. But why was I so off-course now? I felt I had lost any sense, fragile as it undoubtedly was, of being a person of some worth. The discovery of my sexual orientation at a very early age – probably no later than six (take note, Dr Freud; no latency period for me!) – had given me a deeply rooted sense of differentness and wrongness which was, during the time with Ben, cruelly inflamed. My relationship with him had become a malignant disaster, and my academic qualifications, such as they were, did not naturally pave the way for any particular career. I had entirely lost my admittedly slender moorings.

Part of me realised that alcohol was, if not the cause, then certainly the fuel of my decline, and I decided to seek treatment for my dependence. Because Ben was a hospital consultant in the Peterborough area, it was decided that I would go to a supposed Alcohol Treatment Unit in Yorkshire – Scalebor Park in Burley-in-Wharfedale. We were led to believe that there was a designated ward or unit for alcoholic patients, but it turned out that only the males were housed in a self-contained unit, whereas the poor females were admitted to a conventional acute psychiatric

73

women's unit. I was mortified. From the moment of admission, my outdoor clothing was removed and I was confined to bed for some unfathomable reason. The regime was authoritarian; I was warned that 'just because you were a ward sister doesn't mean you'll get any special privileges here', and pains were taken to inculcate the truth of that. As if matters were not sufficiently depressing, Ben had extracted a firm promise from me not to reveal the nature of his former gender status. Which had perhaps been the key driver of my descent into addiction. I was consequently unable to share much of the cause of my misery in group therapy, which was held once weekly in the alcoholism unit – where the majority of fellow patients were, of course, men.

The unofficial criterion of alcoholism at the time was 'drinking as much as (the consultant-in-charge of the unit)'. In the evenings, we were taken in a hospital minibus to local AA meetings; those church hall rooms wherein, amidst clouds of Capstan Full Strength fumes, we heard the dreary litany of alcoholic stories. Otherwise, after the weekly hour of group therapy, one languished back on the acute ward. I became increasingly depressed and terminally bored. The nursing staff judged me to be a suicide risk, so I was sectioned under the 1959 Mental Health Act and prescribed Largactil, an anti-psychotic, at a high dose. But I was not psychotic; just profoundly frustrated by the unproductive 'therapy' and my incarceration in a ward full of acutely disturbed women. When I expressed my rage and frustration to an elderly female psychiatrist, she advised me that I had a personality disorder, and I proceeded to prove her wrong by re-arranging some of the furniture in her office. To have such a diagnosis in those days was a form of psychological death sentence, and in mainstream psychiatry today, 40 years on, it is still a label which attracts opprobrium. Looking back, I have recently begun to wonder whether she was right: that I was an alcoholic lesbian with a personality disorder.

There were then no, and are now few, units set up for the treatment of personality disorder. Indeed, when I was myself in psychiatric nursing, personality disorder was universally regarded as untreatable, a view which is still widely held today. When I was nursing, there were unofficial 'blacklists' of people with personality disorder who were not to be admitted under any circumstances. They were not 'legitimate' patients with 'genuine' illnesses. Very recently, Dialectical Behaviour Therapy – a refined form of cognitive behavioural therapy – has been promoted as an effective treatment for people with personality disorder. In the US (of course) the psychotherapist Marsha Linehan, effectively the 'inventor' of DBT, has suggested that an important element in the development of the condition is the 'non-validation' of the child by their parents and the child is consequently not affirmed as a worthwhile, individual human being. The unshakeable conviction that I was both 'bad' and 'stupid' I drew from my early life plays on as a bass line to my life today. I believe that these 'messages' are hardwired neurobiologically, and that they are consequently impossible to erase. Skilled psychotherapy may assist in their attenuation, but not their extirpation.

The treatment 'contract' at Scalebor Park was for six weeks. Ben drove up to see me about halfway through, and insisted that we lunch in a nearby pub, where he sank several pints of strong ale. He justified this by pointing out that I would have to get used to people drinking around me when I was discharged. The fact that we had both been convicted of drunk driving did not deter him from driving back to Peterborough that afternoon. Over lunch, I explained that I thought the 'treatment' was actually making matters worse, and he agreed to talk to my consultant on the following Monday. Whether he actually did so I shall never know, but he told me that he would come up on the following weekend and take me home.

And so I endured a fourth week of tedium and demoralisation, counting the hours until my release. Ben duly arrived. My cases were packed, and, as I went to the dormitory to collect them, Ben suddenly raced away down the corridor, across to the car park and, before I could comprehend the situation, started the car and drove off at speed. I had never felt so betrayed or so desolate. This was one of the final nails in the coffin of our relationship. When he collected me at the end of the six weeks, I was broken. And, within a day or two, eased my sense of desolation with the usual antidote. Finally, I recognised my need to escape from Ben and Peterborough.

During one of my tutorials at the LSE, my supervisor had suggested that I had the kind of mind which could lend itself well to the law, by which I hope he meant the *study* of the law. Surprised and flattered, I had asked him where he thought I might best do that. Since he himself was an Oxford man, and I myself had no influential connections in the legal world, he proposed that I go to Oxford. And so now, when I felt I had reached the bottom of my personal pit, I completed an UCCA application form for a few universities outside Oxbridge, but also wrote to Somerville and St Hilda's at Oxford. The UCCA applications were serious – Bristol, Reading, the LSE and a fourth I cannot recall. I was turned down by Bristol and the LSE – the latter on the rather pompous ground that I had been privileged enough to have studied there already – and accepted by Reading. The applications to the Oxford colleges were really for a bit of a lark. Somerville delivered a haughty rejection, but St Hilda's invited me for interview.

Fortified by five triple-X barley wines at lunch time, I attended an interview with two law dons at University College. The barley wines enabled me to canter through convoluted legal conundrums with ease and confidence: so much so that I was sorry when the meeting ended. I then managed to find my way to St Hilda's, to be received by the principal, Mrs Bennett. She treated me to tea and shortbread, advised me that the UC men would be pleased to accept me to study 'Jurisprudence', but Mrs Bennett herself wondered whether I wouldn't in fact prefer to study a rather 'softer' subject – English, perhaps?

Ben was vehemently opposed to my going to Oxford, although there was a perfectly practicable route by public transport between Peterborough and Oxford. I could not quite fathom why he should object, since he and I were a toxic combination. In fact, shortly before I was due to start my first term, he bought an enchanting Beagle puppy and begged me to stay at home to look after her. Indeed I did fall in love with Felicity, but I decided, as is my wont, to proceed with my master plan regardless. And so I bought a new briefcase, some sober clothing, and moved into a post-grad house in Boulter Street, within easy walking distance of St Hilda's. My room there had obviously been a box room, given its dimensions. Heating was provided by a tiny gas fire operated by a coin-operated meter. The other women in the house included a descendant of Nehru, who was engaged on a doctorate on Yeats, and a student of social administration who appeared to eat little apart from boiled cabbage.

To begin with, I enjoyed the lectures, but ran into difficulties with Roman Law. I had explained to the UC dons that I had in fact negligible Latin, and was reassured that the Roman Law tutor would be sensitive to that. In the event, however, the tutor could not help himself, and persisted in conducting the tutorials in Latin. Tutorials in those days were generally with two students, and my 'other student' had clearly emerged from a public school with a thorough grounding in the language. After pointing out my difficulty on several occasions, I lost confidence and stopped attending. A sense of intense panic percolated through me, and I became convinced that I was a fraud; I was in the wrong place, doing the wrong thing.

My life seemed to be an irremediable catastrophe. My relationship with Ben was effectively over, and I had allowed myself to become ensnared by a delusion of academic competence which was wildly beyond my reach. I was a fantasist, a failure – a complete mess. My parents, devout worshippers of academia, had been thrilled when I went to Oxford; it was perhaps my one and only *redeeming* feature; they would be Disappointed.

The more I writhed, the greater became my conviction that all was, well and truly, lost. My relationship with Ben was hopeless, I had let my family down, and I had deluded myself in thinking that I was cleverer than I really was. It is that sense of hopelessness, of having metaphorically painted oneself into a corner, that draws one toward the lure of self-annihilation. Guilt, despair, humiliation and a sense of inevitability. Having severed some truly priceless friendships during the 'no man's land' period, there was no one to whom I could turn. My family were still in Canada, and I was in any case doubtful that they would understand my situation.

Ben had introduced me to Anafranil, a tricyclic antidepressant, soon after we arrived in Peterborough and while our relationship was deteriorating dramatically; also to Valium, and I had remained on both drugs ever since. I obtained a fresh prescription of Anafranil and Valium, bought a bottle of gin, and repaired to my little room in Boulter Street. I knew enough about the business to take smallish quantities of tablets at suitable intervals, and not so much gin that there was a danger of throwing up.

I awoke in the John Radcliffe Hospital a day or so later, and have since wondered whether that hospital holds the record for resuscitating suicidal students. A nurse was taking my blood pressure, saying, 'My, you are a very lucky lady! We thought we'd lost you a couple of hours ago!' In no time, I was being interviewed by a psychiatric social worker, and exercised every technique in my armoury of dissemblance to persuade her that I had had a temporary aberration and just wanted to get on with my life; I knew that being detained in a mental hospital is the last place you want to be when you are enjoying a radical life crisis.

With my life, if not my sanity, restored, I had to endure the humiliation of facing Mrs Bennett, Principal of St Hilda's, and my 'moral tutor', Doreen Innes, upon my return to Boulter Street and, officially at any rate, to the continuation of my studies. I explained the collapse of my 'marriage' and my doubt that I had the academic capacity to carry on with the course. Mrs Bennett, I recall, was briskly British, advising me to 'get on with the Mods and postpone arguments about who is to have the teapot' until the end of the academic year. 'There is nothing in your reports so far to indicate that you won't easily pass the Mods.' Ms Innes pointed out that suicide attempts were par for the course, as it were, and that it should not act as a deterrent to getting back on track. They were probably both right, but my confidence was gone and my innate stubbornness persuaded me that all was lost and that I must change direction immediately. I resigned from the course, and received a courteous reply in which I was told that they would hold open a place for me until the beginning of the following academic year.

NINE

Having unmade my bed, I could not thereafter lie on it. I gave myself a fortnight to find a residential job somewhere and move out of Boulter Street. I think it was at about this point that I wrote to tell my parents that I was leaving Oxford. I do not recall a response on my mother's part, but my father wrote a lengthy epistle, in his usual sermon format, advising me that I was making the biggest mistake of my life and would regret my impulsivity forever. It was the first time that he had ever written a 'real' letter to me, albeit in his customary unfeeling style. In a way, he was right. I did eventually come to regret 'dropping out', and realise that, quite apart from any advantage an Oxford degree might confer in career terms, 'the Oxford experience' was unique, and would have been a priceless chapter in my life.

Quite by chance, I picked up a copy of Gay News in the little newsagent's shop on the Cowley Road and, for the first time in my life, turned to the contacts page. There I noticed a tiny ad, beginning: 'Affectionate, bisexual female graduate, 40s, seeks...' I do not remember the remainder, but made a desultory reply, and arranged to meet her in London a few days later. Margaret turned out to be 19 years my senior, a graduate of Lady Margaret Hall (Oxford), and to be married with three teenage children. At our first meeting, we went to a tiny gay women's club just off the corner of Trafalgar Square, called Matty's Bar. There, we exchanged further details about each other and had a few drinks; well, she probably nursed one while I had my usual quick succession of beers. I learned that she was a true blue-stocking intellectual with immensely varied philosophical and cultural interests.

Margaret was married to a Cambridge-educated actuary with Sun Alliance in Horsham, and she insisted that he would have 'no problem whatever' with her 'seeing' women: he was entirely comfortable with his wife's bisexuality, and would be happy to meet anyone his wife 'befriended'. Some years before the placing of her ad in Gay News, Margaret and her husband had had a *ménage à trois* with their au pair, Raymonde. Predictably, perhaps, and in a very short time, I was invited to live with the family while I got a job somewhere. With equal predictability, Margaret's husband developed a sexual interest in me. I, of course, did not reciprocate, but felt at a distinct disadvantage given that I was at the time homeless and jobless. I redoubled my efforts to get a job with accommodation.

In 1974, I applied for a job as superintendent of a children's home run by the London Borough of Southwark in Bermondsey. Rather to my surprise, I was offered the job, although I had no experience of working with children and had no idea what to do with them. A major attraction of the job was that there was a self-contained flat within the home for the superintendent. The home itself was incorporated within a housing estate, on the premise that the children would be integrated into the local community. Since a significant number of our neighbours supported the National Front, and an equally significant number of our children were black, the policy was seriously misguided.

Matters were not helped by the regular anti-social acts of our children – urinating into neighbours' milk bottles, for example. Successive attempts were made to close us down, and senior social services managers made regular efforts to appease our aggrieved fellow tenants. After my time, the neighbours eventually succeeded in having the home closed down.

This was my first management job, and, although I did mostly enjoy working with the staff and children, I was not really cut out for management. Looking back, I can see that I was too maverick, too nonconformist, too easily bored by bureaucracy to suit the role. And I eventually tired of the management side of the job. My predecessor had been a highly charismatic figure, who had established a uniquely individualistic culture in which the children's interests reigned and her marginalisation of managerial directives and requirements were tolerated as a result. One consequence of this, early on in my appointment, was that I had to spend an entire night attempting to trace invoices for unsupported expenditure statements. This included my discovery of some invoices in tiny Wellington boots in one of the office cupboards.

This was a short-stay children's home, which accepted children throughout the entire age range 0-18. Few of the staff had any training in child care, but my predecessor had been trained in the renowned Caldecott Community and imbued the staff with those values. Every child had one designated male and one female 'special person', a concept which anticipated that of 'key workers' by many years. Most of the children had been rescued from highly dysfunctional homes and some had witnessed homicides or been subjected to serious physical and sexual abuse. Their stories were all but unbearable, and I know that I could not possibly do that kind of work today. But there were amusing moments. We had a wonderful character as cook.

In the days before health and safety policies strangled such initiatives, the staff closed the home for a fortnight every summer and took the children camping to Sheringham in Norfolk. Everyone slept under canvas – except the cook. The deal was that she would have her own caravan and a decent supply of whisky. Imagine such a scenario today. But the camping holiday was repeated for years without incident.

On one memorable morning back at the home, Cook came blazing into my office, demanding that I accompany her to the kitchen, where I was instructed to 'Get that fucking aeroplane out of my toaster!' I complied, of course, because not to comply would have been inflammatory – and because I adored her, with her purple face and the permanent fag drooping from the corner of her mouth. I have never understood the hysteria about smoking in kitchens, since cigarette ash is, after all, perfectly sterile.

Another vivid recollection concerned the parking of my car. We were living in an area of high crime, and I learned that the home had a designated garage somewhere on the estate. My colleagues, especially my deputy, were strangely vague as to the precise location of 'our' garage, and it took time to extract the truth from them. The fact was that the garage was full – of puffed wheat, in industrial sized cartons, bearing a sell-by date which had passed several years previously. My predecessor, whose many gifts did not include accuracy in paperwork, had ordered what she thought were individual packets of the cereal and had for some reason parked the problem in the garage rather than go to the trouble of returning the colossal crates to the wholesaler. Something similar had happened when she had ordered a special favourite of hers, tinned guavas, and we enjoyed them for Sunday dessert for several years.

Life at New Place Square certainly had its benefits in so many ways: congenial accommodation which was cleaned for me – a huge boon to a chronic obsessive – a pretty dedicated staff team, very generous 'perks': each week, I was entitled to order whichever joint of meat I might care to enjoy at the weekend. But part of me hankered for something more. The home was running well, despite occasional volleys from the neighbours, but the part of me which begins to twitch when there are too few challenges or novelties had begun to flutter – and I suppose there was a creeping sense of regret that I had abandoned my legal studies so abruptly at Oxford. And so I discovered that the City College in East London was running evening classes in Bar Parts One and Two, on two evenings a week, from 6.30 to 9.30. I duly enrolled and joined Gray's Inn as a student barrister. In addition to the formal legal studies, students were required to dine at their chosen Inn of Court on a minimum number of occasions – twelve, I think – before call to the bar could properly occur.

As far as I can remember, Part One of the Bar studies consisted of Land Law, Criminal Law, Tort and Constitutional Law, but I am now hazy about the last of these. My fellow students were mature adults, typically established in other professions: one, I recall, was the buyer of films for the BBC. The subjects themselves were, on the whole, utterly absorbing, although I suspected that the study of Land Law would eclipse any night sedative in efficacy. My favourite memory is of the occasion when a clearly neonate barrister, under the rubric of Tort, was discussing the case of a UK citizen who went to Canada on business and, within hours of his arrival, succumbed to an acute infection whose severity was such as to require emergency hospitalisation. Predictably, the case involved the attempt by an insurance company to resist a claim, on the ground that the infectious agent had been contracted in the UK prior to the traveller's departure, and that he ought to have been aware of the symptoms and delayed his trip. So the case turned upon precisely *where* the infectious agent or 'pathogenic micro-organism' had been contracted. To our enormous, but well-contained, amusement, the young lecturer consistently referred to the infectious agent as the 'micro-orgasm', and we were sufficiently insensitive to leave the error uncorrected.

The dinners at Gray's Inn were simultaneously enthralling and awe-inspiring. Fine wines were served with each of the rather less inspiring courses, and luminaries of the legal world arrayed in sartorial finery at the top table. I acquired a sober black trouser suit, and borrowed the customary black robe before entering the dining hall. The usual practice was, of course, to return the borrowed garment to the robing room before leaving the Inn at the end of the dinner. On one occasion, however, having as usual enthusiastically imbibed the prescribed libations, I arrived back at the children's home in Bermondsey extravagantly attired in an inadvertently appropriated black robe, contrary to Section Something of the 1968 Theft Act.

But the combination of a relatively time-demanding day job, two densely informative evening classes and the associated hours of private study was beginning to prove rather demanding, even for me. Of greater significance, however, the Bar Council was in the process of delineating new rules for trainees, which would inevitably involve the requirement of a preliminary LLB degree for would-be barristers as well as solicitors. And, having exhausted my educational grant entitlement, and being on a relatively low salary in residential social work, I reluctantly discontinued my studies at the end of Bar Part One.

During the early months of my time in Bermondsey, I continued to 'see' Margaret, driving down to Horsham on my days off. I can no longer recall quite how it happened, but eventually Margaret left her husband and came to live with me in my little flat in the children's home. It is still difficult to analyse the nature of our relationship, but it is fair to say that I was generally ambivalent about it almost from the beginning. When we met, I was perhaps at the lowest point in my life, and consequently vulnerable to the approach of anyone who seemed to care about me. Margaret was extremely bright; far brighter than I, or so I was convinced. But I felt that she was strangely uncritical of, and surprisingly susceptible to, any new idea she encountered, especially in philosophy or religion. She went through one belief system after another at almost dizzying speed, hoping, as she sped enthusiastically along, that I might share her enthusiasm. All these years later, I can only recall a few of her attachments: theosophy, Sufism, New Age, co-counselling, primal therapy and immortalism. This last aroused both intense irritation and a sense of despair that we might ever 'connect' about anything. Immortalism involved the conviction that we could somehow live forever if we chose to do so.

Meanwhile, I began to regret having again abandoned my interest in the law, and we decided that I would leave the children's home and that we would buy a little corner shop – with attached accommodation – in Plaistow where I would work part-time in the shop and study law at the then Queen Mary College, University of London. Margaret would continue with her editorial job in a tiny publishing company in Leytonstone.

The usual legal enquiries prior to purchase of the shop lease had failed to disclose the imminent arrival of two supermarkets in the vicinity of our little corner shop and, virtually from the start, marginal profits segued relentlessly into losses. My perpetual solace – alcohol – accelerated to the point where I began each day with a dose of Whiskey Mac. We realised that we had to dispose of the shop, somehow, and that I would have to get a 'proper' job in order to restore our income. In fact, I had become almost phobic about going into the shop at all: the empty hours of no customers, and the end-of-day tally of 'receipts' and VAT. Eventually, we managed to sell the lease to a Chinese food wholesaler at a knock-down price.

We simply could not afford the luxury of my continuing full-time law studies at Queen Mary College, and I withdrew from the course – my third abortive attempt to study the subject. No doubt psychoanalysts and Buddhists would have something to say about that, but I myself was simply resigned to the fact that I was a serial failure.

With the meagre proceeds of the sale, we bought a tiny downstairs flat in Forest Gate, and I got a job with the Alcohol Recovery Project, based in Camberwell. Having decided that alcohol was my nemesis, I resolved to abstain altogether and to work as a 'recovering alcoholic' with the project. I was responsible for the day-to-day non-resident management of a home for male recovering alcoholics in Catford. The residents were former down-and-out alcoholic men who hoped for resettlement into independent accommodation and employment. Once again, working with males made me acutely uncomfortable. My discomfort was exacerbated by two further factors: one of the residents asked me, in a house meeting, if I was a 'lezzie'. I 'confessed' that I was, and was thereafter regularly taunted by some of the men. But what led to my finally seeking another job was my mistaken belief that one of the men had been drinking. The strictly applied rule was that any man who resumed drinking immediately lost his place in the house. As it turned out, the man *had* resumed drinking – but had not drunk on the actual day I wrongly accused him.

Another failure. I then applied for and got a job as counselling advisor with the London Council on Alcoholism. I was open about my alcoholism, and was appointed on the basis that I would remain abstinent. In spite of the debacle at the Alcohol Recovery Project, I had actually managed not to relapse. There were only three posts at the LCA, that of director, her secretary and me. My principal tasks were to counsel 'special cases' where individuals felt they could not turn to the conventional agencies because of their sensitive status, to organise training courses and seminars on alcohol problems and to supervise a voluntary counsellor who also dealt with 'special cases'. The one-off seminars seemed to go well, but I was criticised for not using sufficient 'visual aids' on one of the training courses I ran at a London college. I had had no teacher training and was totally unaware of the developing fondness for high-tech educational tools, having been brought up in the era of lectures and note-taking.

I had quite a few 'sensitive' cases. One involved a seminar for representatives of BALPA, the British Airline Pilots' Association, in which I discussed the recognition of alcohol problems and the then available treatment resources. Since I was then, and to a great extent remain, a 'fearful flyer', the thought of inebriated aircraft captains made my blood run cold.

And then there was the case of the gorgeous ballerina, hugely successful but desperate about her drinking which, she felt, was beginning to affect her reliability in turning up for rehearsals any time before lunch. She was divorced, with two small children, living in an Ideal Home in east London. When I enquired about her typical day, she revealed that she began each day with strawberries and champagne. As a 'dry' lush myself, I considered this an enviable start to anyone's day, and hope that my eyes did not glisten as she made her confession. I doubt whether I helped her much, as she ended up in hospital following an unsuccessful suicide attempt.

Whatever the government of the time may say, alcohol has its bright side. A senior executive from an insurance company came to see me about a colleague who clearly had a major drinking problem. The 'problem' man practically never rolled up to work on time, had lengthy lubricated lunches after which he was good for very little, and had all but exhausted the goodwill of his colleagues. A difficulty was, however, that, in the course of the liquid lunches, he sold more policies than anyone else in his division.

But things went sharply downhill when we received a request from a small organisation of gay professionals who were seeking an alternative to AA and whose jobs would be compromised if it became known that they were gay. When this request was discussed in our weekly meeting, the director's secretary declared, 'We don't want homosexuals wandering about the building!' I could hardly believe my ears. To my huge dismay – and considerable surprise – the director made no response. After a pause, I – once again – 'confessed' that I was gay and that I could foresee little harm in allowing gay people to 'wander about' the building.

After this awful encounter, the director's secretary hardly spoke to me, and, on several occasions, I subsequently discovered she had erased messages for me from the answering system: one example involved the change of venue for a talk I was to give, so I went to the wrong place. The atmosphere in the office became deadly. I was so distressed that I sought a meeting with the chair of the LCA's executive committee, Lady Chalfont, who acknowledged that the director was somewhat 'sour' and 'negative' but asked that I ignore that and carry on. But I was by this time far too demoralised and insecure to do so.

TEN

In late 1979, and out of the blue, my former manager at the London Borough of Southwark, Fred Bloomfield, contacted me to say that he had been appointed principal of a Community Home with Education (formerly known as an Approved School) in Surrey. He virtually offered me the post of head of care at the Princess Mary Village Homes in Addlestone. PMVH consisted of a campus with a circle of cottages, a school, a chapel and an administrative block.

Margaret and I rented out our tiny flat in Forest Gate to an actor, and we moved into a cottage on the PMVH campus. We redecorated our cottage – at my insistence, in somewhat Gothic colours, chiefly Etruscan and black. Margaret's enormous library was conveyed by Pickfords, those top-of-the-market removers, who, on discovering on removal day the extent of her library, and the fact that it was to be located on an upper floor, resorted to up-ending the tea-chests from shoulder height so that the books crashed to the floor, cracking more than a few spines of vintage works in the process.

Margaret continued to commute to her publishing editor's job in Leytonstone, while I settled in to my new role. The principal, my former boss, had trained as a transactional analyst and was convinced that those

90

principles could be applied to the care and rehabilitation of 'delinquent' adolescent girls. It took less than two years to show that he was radically wrong in this conviction, and little longer to see the entire operation closed down.

Meanwhile, my experience at the Young People's Unit in Edinburgh had persuaded me that openness, honesty and consistency were key to establishing any kind of rapport with young people. I did my utmost to exemplify those principles in my work, and I think it paid off.

The principal, on the other hand, was steadily losing ground to the established staff at PMVH, who, insofar as they understood the theoretical framework of transactional analysis, were implacably opposed. There were virtually nightly riots on the campus, frequently requiring the attendance of Surrey Constabulary. A visiting friend observed one evening, as several girls were carried shoulder high by policemen into waiting vans, 'I guess that's called resisting arrest!'

My relationship with Margaret was steadily deteriorating. Our interests hardly coincided, and her daily commute to Leytonstone must have been a strain. And I was developing a real fondness for Judy, the deputy principal, who had been on compassionate leave following the death of her mother when I was appointed. Judy was divorced with two children, one of whom was clearly ill at ease with himself and the world. Paul was 15 when I first met him, an exceptionally handsome, muscular boy, heavily involved in body-building and taekwondo. His father, Judy's ex-husband, was a Tanzanian barrister, with whom there was at the time no contact. Paul was given to menacing stares and unpredictable rages. He did once tell us, years after the event, that he had killed a 'squaddie' late at night at Woking station, but he never actually inflicted physical harm on either his mother or sister. Judy managed to enrol him in several prestigious private schools, supporting this through her own meagre income and by means of charitable grants, but Paul never settled happily in any school, and his remarkable artistic and musical talents were somehow insufficiently recognised or encouraged until long after he left school altogether.

Because of my growing friendship with his mother, we decided to move in together – Margaret, Judy, Paul, his sister Juliet and I – to an unoccupied mansion at the back of the campus. The idea represented an attempt to defuse some of the tensions between Paul and his mother and sister. I offered to befriend Paul, and, to begin with, I think there was a brief rapport. Looking back, I can see that he and I had a lot in common. We were both misfits in the conventional world, both unaware of any talent or redeeming feature we might possess, deeply insecure and never knowing quite when we might next be bitten on the bottom. But the experiment in communal living at the mansion house was, in the end, a failure. Matters were not helped by a new addition to our eccentric household, in the form of Judy's elderly father, who could no longer manage his flat in Battersea, and to whose dying wife Judy had promised to look after him following her demise. Margaret and I had a room in the main house, as did Judy and Juliet. Paul had his own wing in the enormous house, and his grandfather was housed at the opposite end of the main corridor.

Initially, the odd little household managed to coexist without too much overt drama, but Judy's father's equanimity was sharply extinguished one morning when belches of pungent smoke wove their way into his bedroom through the open window. Grandfather appeared in the corridor, complete in billowing nightshirt and cap, spluttering and gasping that he was being poisoned. We rapidly made our way to the source of the tear-wrenching conflagration, which turned out to be a mattress on fire in the garden immediately beneath his bedroom. Given the pungency and blackness of the smoke, I decided to call the fire brigade, indicating that our chief concern was to establish whether the fumes were toxic, since the fire itself was beginning to burn out. To our dismay, three huge fire appliances rolled up, preceded and followed by blue-flashing police cars.

The embers of the fire were rapidly quenched, the fumes judged to have indeed been toxic. But the most incendiary aspect of the episode was not so much the fire itself as the insistence of the firemaster and two police officers upon seizing Paul and subjecting him, publicly, to a blistering dressing down. That did so much more damage than the incineration of an old mattress.

The point of burning the mattress in the first place was disclosed only after Grandpa had been restored to his room and the police and fire officers to their respective depots. What Paul was trying to do was melt the plastic mattress covering in order to obtain some waterproofing material for a boat he was attempting to construct in the back garden.

Judy, while warmly disposed toward Fred, the principal, foresaw the demise of the whole establishment and wisely bought a house in Bexhill-on-Sea. She and I had got along well in the mansion house, and, as the disturbances at the campus degenerated into unholy farce, she invited me to come and share her home in Bexhill when the inevitable end came. Which it did, in 1979.

My relationship with Margaret also came to an end, and she moved back to London. I can no longer recall the critical points along the downward trajectory of our demise. But I can acknowledge that I must have become increasingly difficult to live with. Quite apart from my alcoholic intemperance, I was intemperate in my debates with her about philosophical systems, psychological and psychiatric treatment models and so on. I was inflexible and discourteous in argument, and refused to countenance the possibility that current theories and practices in the therapeutic world were, in so many respects, deeply flawed.

Up to this point, I had avoided facing my own inner demons and peccadillos, despite the six months of group analysis at the Royal Edinburgh Hospital and my spell working in a therapeutic community at Dingleton some years before. I was aware that I had a long-standing drink problem, and that I was unequivocally gay. I was also conscious that I been, since adolescence, obsessively tidy and ordered, borne out by Margaret's observation that living with me was like living in an operating theatre. Such equanimity as I could grasp was predicated entirely on an orderly environment. But I had no coherent conception of who I really was as a whole person. This may seem strange, in view of my interest in what made people 'tick', but is, I have discovered, by no means unusual in people of the psychologistic or psychiatric persuasion. Perhaps I was, with very good reason, afraid to look at myself, for what would I have found?

At that point in my life, how *would* I have seen myself? From the very beginning, an anxious, solitary individual, much given to temper tantrums and overeating; preferring bus conductor's outfits, guns and shorts to nurse's uniforms, dolls and dresses; constantly 'on guard' and generally out of place in the world. I was frequently bored, deeply frustrated and aggressive, not knowing what was ever actually bugging me. Unlike my younger sister, Frances, I was physically unprepossessing – chubby and, by adolescence, frankly fat, and with what a fellow pupil at Perth Academy described as a 'bun face' – and temperamentally volatile. Apart from recognising, very early on, that I was drawn to women rather than men, I could never discern what it was about me that somehow abstracted me from 'normal' life. There were just fragments of what we would now call 'feedback' from my environment. A school teacher telling my mother, 'If Allison only worked half as hard as she worried, she'd be top of the class'; my mother telling me 'all you do is fuss, fuss, fuss' and calling me at a high point of exasperation 'an ungrateful wretch'.

My father's attitude toward me was hardly that of a father to his child. In the early years, especially in Shetland and Paisley, he seemed to take a kind of interest in me, not in the conventional parent-child relationship role, but more of a younger associate and confidant. He discussed people's marital difficulties with me, exchanges in which I was his sounding board. He took me with him in the little fishing boats to the Skerries in Shetland, where he took early services and holy communion. I don't know whether others saw me as an adjunct to the minister, or a strange little outcast who had no tangible role to play. Later, when I was still a child, he talked to me about his financial worries and about how he occasionally contemplated suicide. I felt desolate and helpless, but it did not occur to me to tell anyone about all this, least of all my poor mother.

Given the degree and effects of my father's Asperger's, there must have been inevitable questions about his odd behaviour: his lecturing style of speech, in a higher than his normal voice; his awkward attempts at 'ordinary', empathetic speech and inability to look anyone in the eye; his startling introduction of non sequiturs in the course of serious discussion. Others must have noticed his stiff posture and awkwardness in engaging with people. On inappropriate occasions, and at quite the wrong moments, he might unexpectedly launch into a lengthy joke whose obscure conclusion bore little or no relation to the matter under discussion.

But for my sisters and me, Father was a tall, booming, authoritarian figure who was constitutionally incapable of showing us direct affection and approval. If we attempted to discuss anything with him that we knew something about, he would demolish our arguments by reference to pre-war policies and theories: what we were learning at school or university was often dismissed as 'bosh!' In fact, my mother and sisters, having more sense than I, tended to avoid entering debate with Father, as they recognised that they were on a hiding to nothing.

And, perhaps because she had become chronically depressed and tired, Mother had little energy to resist or countermand her husband's loud and frequent diktats about what was true and what should be done. A particularly painful example of this I discovered only after Mother's death, when I saw correspondence showing that Mother, having spent four miserable years in Unst, would go on to another parish in Whalsay 'over my dead body'. My father consulted Uncle Charlie about this, and the end result was that we moved to Whalsay in 1946, and stayed there for four years.

Yet I remained, in effect, a closed book to myself. It just seemed that my somewhat chequered life had consisted of a series of reactions to external circumstances and events. I was simply aware that I was generally ill at ease with the world, and subject to continuous, extreme tension. Although I was deeply ashamed of, and embarrassed about, my excessive resort to alcohol, I kept imagining that, when the circumstances were right, all would be well.

And it did look as if all would be well. With the painful and ignominious collapse of the Princess Mary Village Homes, and my move to Bexhill with Judy, Juliet and Judy's father, a promising future beckoned. Paul had by this time moved, at our insistence, to a YMCA hostel in Guildford and subsequently to a series of 'squats', where he continued body-building and, unbeknown to us until many years later, was introduced to the world of illicit drugs.

Since Judy and I have remained close friends for over 30 years, I owe it to us both to say more about our domestic life in Bexhill, where we moved in 1981. Judy, Juliet and Judy's father, nicknamed 'Bruno', decamped from the now defunct Princess Mary Village Homes in Surrey and settled into the quiet seaside town of Bexhill-on-Sea, described by Spike Milligan, who was stationed there during WWII, as 'the largest above ground graveyard in the world'.

Juliet had her own room, Bruno his, and Judy I shared a twin-bedded room. Bruno was 90 years old by now, even shorter than I, and with a girth to match his height. He invariably wore pinstripe suits and a bow tie, having worked in the City for most of his life. He had begun as a lowly clerk in Lloyd's bank at Finsbury Circus and, despite his keen intellect, had never advanced in that institution. It would seem that he was insufficiently deferential or conformist to be offered promotion, and in this, perhaps, he and I had something in common. On his retirement from the bank, he had gone to the highly esteemed legal firm of Herbert Smith in some form of accounting capacity, and hence had worked well beyond retirement age.

His consuming passion was money. His regular trips to the library were to procure the life stories of eminent financiers: he was particularly fascinated by biographies of financial giants such as Charles Clore and Henry Boot, for example. Regardless of how a conversation with him might begin, it soon wove round to the making of money, specifically to stocks and shares. Eyes glistening, and the spittle of excitement trickling from the corners of his mouth, he would repeatedly advise us to 'listen to the sound of money pouring into cash registers – then invest'. And, for Bruno, no cash registers filled more rapidly than those of Marks and Spencer and Boots the Chemist. Although he could never have had much of an income, he bought as many of their shares as he could.

Which immediately reminds me of the terrible day when Sophie, my Newfoundland dog, managed to get to the front door letter box first and enjoyed a pre-breakfast snack of share certificates addressed to Bruno. He had never been keen on Sophie, having on several occasions protested that 'We don't *need* another dog – we've already got Shandy!' This incident clinched his argument, and constituted one strand of my developing ambivalence toward him. While she was still a puppy, Sophie occasionally projected the contents of her gastrointestinal tract into the house and, if we were unable to dispose of the evidence in time, Bruno would howl with a mixture of triumph and an oddly scatological glee that 'There's a bloody great packet in the hall, girls!'

The chief source of my mixed feelings about the man, apart from the fact that he *was* a man, derived from his obviously inappropriate attachment to his daughter. Overtly, his interest seemed merely proprietorial, and any request of her issued forth as a command. But it was evident both to Judy and to me that Bruno had come to see her as a wife rather than a daughter, and this inevitably heightened the tensions in the household. From time to time, especially if I had had a couple of Pils lagers or was in clear need thereof, I would confront him about his peremptory demands. On one occasion, when we were seated at dinner, Bruno instructed Judy to bring him more 'gippo' (gravy) when we had already begun to eat. I rose to my feet and bellowed at him that Judy was not his slave. To which he roared in reply, 'She's my daughter, and I'll speak to her as I please!' Unusually, words failed me, and I threw my dinner at him. Whether I intended to miss him, I know not; most of it hit the wall and oozed down onto the carpet.

I did try to behave toward him in a civilised manner, and we occasionally managed to have conversations about the few mutual interests we had, such as the works of Mahler. As soon as the adagietto of the fifth symphony somehow spliced into a discussion of the progress of his Boots shares, however, I would ease myself from his presence. Had he not been so preoccupied with investment and the world of finance generally, I think he could have been an engaging conversationalist. Part – if not most – of his persona derived, I was certain, from the fact that he had married 'above his station'. Whereas Bruno was a mere bank clerk, his wife came from an upper class family which had 'fallen upon hard times', and Judy's recollection was that he often seized opportunities to mock her superior antecedents and early lifestyle. This took the form of provocative vulgarities in his speech and conduct which were clearly intended to belittle and to distress her.

Bruno's days began with a hearty breakfast, then a walk up the fairly steep hill to the local shops – quite a feat, since he not only had the physique of a butterball, but had become severely arthritic. On his return from the shops, he would have a large mug of packet tomato soup before walking down to the Sovereign Light Café on the seafront for his customary 'elevenses' of two steak and kidney pies and a cup of tea. If Judy and I were away for any reason, he would cover the dining table with newspapers and prepare a generous 'fry-up' for himself. In those days, GPs were not paid to conduct regular cholesterol tests on patients, and it is perhaps just as well: an unnecessary worry – if not to Bruno, then perhaps to Judy.

Bruno and Judy's mother had had a boy, Geoffrey, but unspecified difficulties with the birth had prevented her from having more children by the conventional means. They had therefore decided to adopt Judy who, she only recently discovered, had a Scottish mother who was working as a servant in a London house. Her father was named on the abbreviated birth certificate, but relevant records had been destroyed in a fire during the Second World War. She consequently knew very little of her early life, but became aware that a prevailing 'expert' view of infant care apparently involved having as little intimate contact with the baby as possible. One cannot now imagine what on earth the rationale for that entirely counterintuitive advice might have been, but Judy's very early life seems to have been one of isolation and insecurity. It also seemed as if her mother was, almost literally, wrapped up in her biological son, Geoffrey. Indeed, Geoffrey, now in his eighties, is able to acknowledge that, and to say that, throughout his life, 'Mother was clearly in love with me.'

Geoffrey's own life is a sorry tale. An obviously bright boy, he went to an independent school and, at some point, took up the violin. His practise of this instrument at home drew scornful abuse from Bruno, and Geoffrey discontinued the lessons. At the end of his schooling, Geoffrey trained as a ballet dancer. He had a petite figure, and was eventually 'spotted' and recruited to the Royal Ballet, evidence of which is probably still on film as he played a mouse in a Frederick Ashton production of Cinderella. In the course of five years with the ballet, he did quite a bit of filming, including *The Tales of Hoffman*, and he toured the United States with the company. But his career with the Royal Ballet ended, for reasons which are unclear to me, but which were given as Dame Nanette de Valois' assessment of his diffidence as a bar to his professional progress. This broke his heart and his spirit, and he spent the rest of his working life in various secretarial jobs. For years he hired the Wigmore Hall and commissioned various professional pianists to transcribe orchestral pieces into piano – poignant reminders of the long-gone days of ballet practice.

Judy's childhood relationship with Geoffrey was one in which she was in awe of him, seeing him as a godlike figure. Their mother compared them unfavourably, constantly telling Judy how wonderful Geoffrey was; whereas Judy was 'always a mess, no matter how I dress you', Geoffrey 'always looks as if he's stepped out of a bandbox'; telling Judy 'You're plain now, but you may grow up to be beautiful'. Their mother consistently gave Judy the impression that Geoffrey was 'terribly clever', implying that Judy was not.

For some reason, Judy was sent to a French convent school at an exceptionally tender age. She describes herself as an unprepossessing little soul with a squint, National Health spectacles and a permanently runny nose. The school was run by Roman Catholic nuns. At the age of six, Judy was caught by one of the nuns playing the usual 'nurse' game with another pupil, who happened to be Catholic. Judy was summarily expelled from the school, but her Catholic friend was not. A condemnatory letter was sent to Judy's parents. One need hardly ruminate on the consequences of this for Judy who, like me, predictably developed an abiding sense of inadequacy and badness. That was undoubtedly a potent component of our drawing together as friends.

The remainder of Judy's school career was somewhat turbulent, with neither her parents nor her teachers considering the possibility of higher education for her. As a matter of fact, as was subsequently demonstrated, she had enormous talent in English and in art and, on her early retirement from East Sussex Social Services, took up botanical drawing and painting with such distinction that she has been invited to exhibit her work at several significant exhibitions. Like me, she was a (very) 'late developer'.

She had a few uninspiring jobs after school, one of which was as a filing clerk in a paint factory. With her brain and complex personality, she rapidly tired of her duties, and took to filing documents behind the filing cabinets instead of inside them. This misdemeanour was eventually discovered, and her employment terminated. And then, at about the age of 17, Judy, whose family were nominally Anglican, was drawn to Catholicism and, after the statutory period of instruction, was received into the Roman Catholic Church. In retrospect, she sees this as a then unconscious attempt to redeem herself in the eyes of the Church which had so harshly judged her some 11 years before. She then entered holy orders as a novice in a further strategy to obtain redemption. Of the five years in the Order, Judy says she 'endured' the rigorous discipline, and felt herself to be 'a square peg in a round hole'. She became Sister Cecilia, was sent to a maternity unit in Wimbledon, and was then posted to West Africa, where she experienced more freedom and where she nursed patients with tuberculosis. She spent five years there, on several days a week driving two-ton trucks containing medical supplies and foodstuffs organised by Bruce Kent of later Campaign for Nuclear Disarmament fame to some of the remotest villages in the Northern Territories of Ghana. Here, with the help of a young orphan boy as interpreter, she ran leprosy clinics and held maternal welfare classes wherever a group of women gathered.

She had hoped to return to the maternity hospital in Wimbledon, but the novice mistress thought that Judy needed a quiet period away from active work, and in due course she was sent to St Thomas's Hospital for interview with a view to training as a radiographer. The prospect of having to study physics appalled her, and the project was abandoned, but not before Judy had arrived at the conclusion that she had been mistaken in her belief that she

102

had a religious vocation and, perhaps to the relief of the longsuffering novice mistress, she returned to secular life.

On leaving the Order, Judy decided to train as a specialist TB nurse, and embarked on a two-year training course at the Royal Brompton Hospital in London. At the same time, she developed an interest in African politics, in particular the African National Congress (ANC), and occasionally went to talks at the Commonwealth Institute and at London House near Marble Arch. Her future husband, Felician, was reading for the Bar at the time, and was resident at London House. And it was here, at a social event, that she met him.

Felician was a tall, extremely bright Tanzanian who attended the University of Makerere, where the future President of Tanzania, Julius Nyerere, was his tutor. Judy and Felician married in London, and their son, Paul, was born at St George's Hospital. He was clearly a distressed baby from the start, and cried incessantly. He was diagnosed as having a hiatus hernia, and throughout his babyhood he was treated with Largactil (a major tranquilliser), phenobarbitone and fortnightly injections of iron. He had regular blood tests because of some internal bleeding, and had to sleep propped up to prevent projectile vomiting.

After Felician was called to the Bar, he worked in chambers in the City and simultaneously studied for a doctorate. Judy having abandoned her training at the Brompton Hospital when Paul was born, they had little income apart from Felician's educational grant. They were extremely poor, and lived in a tiny flat with only an oil stove for heating. Felician was, in spite of their privations, invariably cheerful and optimistic. They moved to Tanzania when Paul was about ten months old. Soon after their arrival, Felician found Judy a job as assistant to the general secretary of the Tanzanian Red Cross, where among her duties were the repatriation of refugees from Zanzibar and the provision of callipers for poliomyelitis victims – the callipers being cast-offs donated by the UK and US, but the only hope for patients hoping to walk again.

Juliet was born in Dar es Salaam, but her parents' marriage became decidedly strained when Felician took a mistress. Today, Judy believes that she herself contributed to the collapse of the marriage, chiefly by refusing to learn Swahili and her reluctance to entertain on the scale expected of the wife of a senior state attorney. Judy left the marital home, went to live with the family of American Peace Corps workers, and began proceedings against her husband on the ground of his adultery. Felician, complete in robes and wig, conducted a counterpetition. After the hearing, and in an understandably emotional state, Judy stormed into the former marital home, there to find Felician and his mistress having a celebratory meal – at a table set with the silver and crystal glasses which had been a wedding gift on the occasion of Judy and Felician's marriage. In a state of heartbreak and despair, Judy rushed into the kitchen, turned off the oven and threw the chicken into the outer yard. Seizing a carving knife, she then chased the unfortunate cook round the garden with it.

Judy returned to the UK with her children and, for a time, experienced the horrors of poverty, homelessness, emotional exhaustion and an intense fear of losing her children. After several unsuccessful attempts to find suitable employment, Judy applied to the Richmond Fellowship and was accepted by their training college in Kensington for the newly established two-year diploma course in Mental Aftercare and Rehabilitation. In conjunction with her studies, she was posted to one of the therapeutic communities in Sevenoaks. After a year of this, the staff accommodation allocated to her was withdrawn, and she resigned from the organisation. She eventually succeeded in obtaining family accommodation, completed her training in Mental Aftercare and Rehabilitation and rejoined the Fellowship. She subsequently left the Fellowship and got a job as a house mother in a Community Home with Education in Chertsey, and eventually became deputy principal at the Princess Mary Village Homes in Addlestone, also in Surrey. Which was where our paths crossed.

Life with Judy in Bexhill was a kaleidoscope of domestic drama, diversion and fun, notwithstanding my continuing wrestle with alcohol dependence. The fact that we remain firm friends after 30 years attests to this.

Without at this point elaborating on the semantics of addiction, the truth is that I drank too much and too often. I very much doubt whether any expert in addiction can satisfactorily explain why an individual addict becomes a slave to a particular substance, or even why anyone should become an addict in the first place. There are so many other ways of dealing with life's vicissitudes. And I do not believe that only 'troubled' souls fall into dependence. Nevertheless, I recognise that, given my continuous tension, anxiety and sense of inadequacy, I was vulnerable to the ephemeral but soothing effects of alcohol. No doubt, had I been born at a different time in a different place, I would have succumbed to the less calorific effects of illicit drugs such as amphetamine or even heroin.

The jobs to which I was appointed when we moved to East Sussex were after a while the source of agonising ennui and frustration, and my work dissatisfaction had an inevitable effect on domestic relations.

Judy's unhappiness with my weekly intake of alcohol units caused regular explosions of rage on her part and defensive petulance on mine. I did from time to time become sufficiently moved to attend local meetings of

Alcoholics Anonymous. But, during the early eighties, these were still dominated by men and unfiltered cigarette smoke. The continual, repetitious accounts of members' descents into alcoholic doom struck me as competitive: whose descent had been deepest? This, and the reference to a higher power as an interventionist force in helping the addict toward recovery, invariably led to my AA attendance being short-lived. Although I had a somewhat tenuous belief in a 'higher power', I was unable to believe that he, she or it was inclined to assist me in this matter, since I had prayed so earnestly, and so often, for deliverance.

Judy briefly attended meetings of Al-Anon, where relatives or friends of alcoholics obtained advice and support in accordance with the 'twelve step' approach of AA. On one occasion, Judy was advised to deliver an ultimatum to me according to which, if I were to have a drink in 'her' house, she was to eject me immediately, whatever the time of day. The legality of such a procedure was questionable, since I paid Judy rent to live in 'her' house. It was also, arguably, a non-therapeutic move. At the time of my inevitable ejection, which occurred late at night in winter, I had a little mini-van, and lay shivering in the back until Judy relented and released me in the early hours. The incident did not deter me from drinking, but it did cause poor Judy remorse from which she has never fully recovered, despite my reassurance that she was simply following the advice, in good faith, of supposedly knowledgeable third parties.

In those days, I was also frequently imbibing at lunch time. There was at the time no prohibition on the taking of alcoholic refreshment during working hours, and I would often meet with colleagues in the Turkey, a shabby hostelry a few yards down the road from Thornwood, where I was appointed officer-in-charge in 1981. The proprietor of the pub was a gloomy, wheezing, purple-countenanced man and

106

we were frequently his only lunch time patrons. Whilst my colleagues would confine themselves to a half pint of shandy or 2.5% bitter, I would merrily guzzle my way through several Pils lagers. Pils was my drink of choice at the time, because it claimed to convert a high proportion of sugar into alcohol, thus mitigating my concurrent weight problem – or so I hoped. On other occasions, I met social work colleagues in a Good Pub Guide listed establishment a few miles away in the village of Netherfield, where there were splendid salad sandwiches as well as superb real ales. It did not occur to me that my enthusiastic fluid intake might be noticed or, worse still, reported: or, if it did, my need overrode caution. The result of these lunchtime refreshments rendered me tremulous about mid-afternoon, longing for the tedious hours to pass until I could go off duty and have further refreshment.

One especially awful instance of alcoholic recklessness occurred when one of my drinking social work colleagues and I had to attend a 'protection of property' meeting in rural East Sussex, where the departmental protection of property officer and we were to conduct an inventory of a client's possessions. This miserable, rather heartrending business occurred wherever a client in the council's care was deemed too incapacitated ever to return home. Not only had their property to be protected, but its estimated value would, sooner or letter, enter an equation in the calculation of the fees which the client would be charged for the privilege of residing in our care.

The client's large house and contents indicated both that she had enjoyed a luxurious lifestyle in her earlier days and that she had not been enjoying it for some time. The house interior was lavishly festooned with cobwebs and the detritus characteristic of years of neglect. In the course of the inventory, we noted a magnificent walnut cocktail cabinet whose interior disclosed an impressive array of

107

liqueurs, many of which none of us had previously encountered. Whether by means of some subtle interpersonal signalling I do not know, but we three were soon seated upon a dusty chesterfield sofa, sampling the contents of the exotic liqueur bottles. We may each have sampled them all, as we subsequently discovered that none of us could recall our individual journeys back to base. This episode did trouble me for some time afterwards, as even I realised that our conduct would incontestably constitute grounds for immediate dismissal.

But there were some pleasant, even exciting times for Judy and me, involving hazards of a different order. Both she and I were deeply committed to animal welfare – so committed, in fact, that we invited the glamorous but infamous chief figure in the animal activist movement, Ronnie Lee, to our house to tell us more about the Animal Liberation Front, which he had founded, and how we might play a part in furthering the ALF's objectives. Part of this project involved my driving backwards and forwards to Cambridge, where I joined an ALF 'cell' devoted to liberating dogs from an experimental laboratory run by Cambridge University. At the time, there was enormous controversy about experimenting with cats and dogs in the pursuit of advances in transplant technology. Parts of the sensationalist media were running stories of cats to which a second head had been surgically attached, but 'my' group was concerned exclusively with rescuing dogs.

The rescue exercises were carefully planned and executed – chiefly in the darkness of night. We were well equipped. I, for example, was the group's photographer, whose task was to picture the animals in their cages prior to release. Another member would carry and employ industrial strength bolt-cutters; a third would have the responsibility for disabling the complex alarm systems, and so on. On the occasion I remember most vividly, our efforts were focused on a laboratory which was located in the middle of a large, ploughed field on the outskirts of the city. In addition to photographing the incarcerated dogs, I was required to facilitate the liberation of one of the beasts, in this case a magnificent Rhodesian Ridgeback. The exercise was carried out according to plan; I took the photographs and collected my dog. However, as we exited the building, I was unable to see any of my companion liberators. There we were, dog and I, alone in the middle of a ploughed field upon which it had recently rained heavily, and on a carefully selected moonless night.

I was in my Catholic period at the time, and, subduing my panic as best I could, prayed to St Francis, as I was sure that the Ridgeback and I were travelling round in circles, our boots and paws increasingly clogged by mud. Almost immediately, we found ourselves on the correct route to where our liberation vehicle was waiting. Here, it would seem, a 'higher power' *did*, indeed, intervene.

Soon after this, Ronnie Lee was imprisoned and a large number of activists likewise gaoled following a series of raids in Essex. I discovered that, were I myself to be similarly sentenced in future, I could not regard my period in custody as annual leave, but would instead be considered to have frustrated my contract of employment. My activities were thereafter less adventurous.

Another animal story concerns a trip to the countryside for Judy, Juliet and me. I had become interested in photography and, when we were about to pass a barn, noticed that there was a cow lying in the doorway, apparently in the act of giving birth. I set up my SLR in readiness to record the event. We hovered about for an hour or so, then, with growing impatience, took to taking short walks round the barn, waiting for the delivery to take place. All that was eventually delivered was the afterbirth, the newborn calf having been removed elsewhere. But at least I had the satisfaction of a well shot series of images of the glistening, bluish birth sac.

It may also have been a useful introduction to Juliet's subsequent study of medicine. When we moved to Bexhill, Juliet attended the local grammar school on Turkey Road – on the opposite side of the road from Thornwood, where I was officer-in-charge. Having previously attended first-class independent schools, Juliet spoke beautifully and had the poise of a model. She was, however, rather diffident by temperament, and tended to worry about school examinations – which she invariably passed with flying colours. She distinguished herself in her A-levels, and won a place at the Royal Free Hospital in London to study medicine. Having grown into a strikingly beautiful young lady with a winning smile and delightful laugh, she would bring home various boyfriends to visit us on her time off from her medical studies. One was the son of an international operatic soprano, another became a leading forensic psychiatrist.

In addition to gardening, Judy had developed a growing interest in sheep and shepherding while I became increasingly absorbed by photography and, for several successive summers, we rented cottages in the southwest so that I could attend Exeter University photographic summer schools and Judy could visit famous gardens and wander round sheep farms in the area. Juliet came with us on at least one of those holidays, and Judy's brother, Geoffrey, on another. The photography summer schools were highly instructive, fellow enthusiasts interesting: one was the trainer of the Red Arrow pilots. In the darkrooms, we learned how to process black-and-white films. I became sufficiently confident and – I thought – proficient to try developing two 36-frame films simultaneously. In the course of the process, involving the films' immersion in

110

successive chemical trays and alternating water tanks, I missed a critical link in the procedure while chatting to a fellow enthusiast. The result was the ruin of 72 photographic images. Since I did not know my conversational companion terribly well, I was constrained to say something along the lines of, 'Oh, gosh! Look what I've gone and done…!'

The dogs came with us on holiday, and generally seemed to have as much fun as we, although I remember one amusing moment when we all strolled into a pasture where some cows were gently grazing – and eventually noticed that my Newfoundland, Sophie, was not with us. We looked behind us, toward the gate by which we had entered the field, and observed only Sophie's fluffy head, peeping nervously round the gatepost. She was not the bravest of dogs and, on another occasion, when a visiting friend's dog choked on a stolen chicken bone and the vet was summoned, Sophie disappeared behind a sofa, only the top of her head visible, eyes wide with apprehension.

One of the many joys of owning a Newfoundland was hearing the excited observations of children as we passed by. 'Oh, Mummy, look! There's a *bear!*' or 'Look! There's that woolly dog again!' Some were obviously familiar with the story or the film of Barrie's *Peter Pan*, where the family dog was a Newfoundland. Adolf Hitler was also reputed to have had Newfoundland dogs, but that was never referred to.

There were, however, drawbacks to having a Newfoundland. I was at one point referred to the local rheumatology clinic for shoulder and neck pain, and was required to answer an exhaustive list of questions designed to elicit the probable cause of the symptoms. One of the questions concerned the handling of large, strong dogs. And it must be confessed that neither Judy nor I had mastered the art of getting our dogs to walk obediently at heel. The

111

results were periodically damaging, dangerous – or both. Once, when Sophie and I were walking on one side of the main road from Bexhill to Eastbourne, Sophie spotted a squirrel on the other side and, in a moment, I was travelling horizontally across the road in her jet stream. This was some achievement on Sophie's part, because I weighed only slightly less than her 168 pounds. On a similar occasion, when she spied another squirrel on the wrong side of the road, her disregard for other road users caused her to collide with a VW Beetle, after which she shot up the road away from us. I was convinced that she had sustained a brain injury, and ran up the lane after her while Judy dealt with the Beetle driver. When I finally caught up with my mortally wounded animal and discovered only a minor laceration above her right eye, I returned to the accident scene to discover that the Beetle, on the other hand, had sustained a significant dent in its bonnet.

One of her favourite tricks was to run toward an innocent passer-by, stop just short of her victim and bounce on the spot, presumably in order to startle them. When she did this once, quite near our house, the subject of her prank, a diminutive elderly woman, was left leaning on a garden wall, panting with fear and shock. It was at this point that I insured Sophie against third party damage for half a million pounds.

Long before I learned that the sort of chocolate favoured by humans is positively toxic to dogs, I was in the habit of giving Sophie a Mars a day to help her 'work, rest and play'. That she lived to the age of nearly 12, well beyond a Newfie's allotted span, merely confirmed the adage about exceptions to general rules. She was also partial to ice cream and once, when I was walking with her on a summer's day in the Arlington woods near Hailsham, we came upon an ice cream van. I ordered a double vanilla cornet and was asked whether I wanted a chocolate Flake

112

with it. When I explained that I wasn't sure whether Sophie would appreciate that, he refused to charge me a penny, on the ground that my treating the dog in this way constituted sufficient recompense.

Judy's dog, Shandy, was presumably less oblivious to traffic than Sophie and, on Judy's days off from work, would disappear at lunchtime and make her own way up the hill to Thornwood − a distance of half a mile − to have lunch. When we had lived at Princess Mary Village Homes in Surrey, Shandy had learned that, when she managed to escape from our mansion in the grounds and make her way to the local police station, the officers there would share their evening fish suppers with her before leading her on a string back to us.

Judy's health problems began when we had moved to Bexhill in 1980, no doubt exacerbated by the tensions caused by my drinking and her anxieties about Paul, whose life in Surrey had become so chaotic that Judy suggested he move down to Bexhill so that she could communicate more easily with and support him. She experienced rather idiosyncratic lapses of memory and concentration which convinced her that she might be suffering from some form of pre-senile dementia, as early Alzheimer's was then described. Exhaustive testing by neuropsychologists disclosed a profile which had never previously been described, but which did not suggest a conventional form of dementia. Over 20 years later, when she had become even more concerned that she was suffering from dementia, the same baffling, equivocal picture emerged, with the same reassurance that she was not suffering from an identifiable dementia. Juliet, by this time a qualified doctor, was convinced that Judy's psychological difficulties were the product of anxiety, and I still believe that she was right.

Bruno's stay with us in Bexhill for the four years preceding his death at 94, his continual demands of her as his quasi-wife, his antipathy toward Sophie and his references to Paul as a 'drone', combined with Judy's tensions about my drinking, must have maintained a fairly unremitting anxiety in the poor woman. Paul was by this time living in a flat in Bexhill, taking a range of illicit drugs and subsisting on welfare benefits. As he was unable to keep appointments made by various health and social services professionals in a series of abortive attempts to identify and ameliorate his constellation of problems, it was not possible to arrive at an accurate assessment of his health and social care needs and, to this day, a comprehensive assessment has not made its way either to him or to Judy.

For Paul, a range of diagnostic theories have been postulated over the decades, but the only one to which Judy herself gives credence is the possibility that he has Asperger's, a diagnosis which for various reasons has never been confirmed by an appropriately accredited professional. Some years ago, when he was in his early forties, he abandoned the use of 'hard' drugs such as heroin and 'crack' cocaine and was somehow considered to be a suitable candidate for counselling training, an opinion entirely at odds with the possibility that he might be suffering from Asperger's, which is now generally recognised to have as its predominant characteristic a fundamental inability to read 'social cues'; to empathise with or imaginatively place himself in the shoes of another – a critical requirement of the counsellor. He was denied the certificate of satisfactory completion of the course on the ground that he had failed to complete the fieldwork placement requirements. It had also presumably been noted that he had isolated himself from his fellow counselling students.

As far as managing 'the activities of daily living' was concerned, Paul was unable to understand, and therefore to fill in, forms associated with his benefit applications – or any other questionnaire associated with his housing, income, employment or training opportunities. Matters were not helped by his insistence to a long series of professionals and 'support' workers that he could manage his life perfectly satisfactorily. Meanwhile his poor mother's own frustration and anxiety about completing bureaucratic algorithmic mazes heightened Paul's frustration and Judy's impotent anxiety – and reignited the circularity of any given problem.

If pseudo-dementia represented a continuing descant to Judy's insecurity and anxieties, the treble line consisted of a series of acute bodily malfunctions, most painfully the growth of gallstones whose appearance and dimensions were all but indistinguishable from chestnuts on removal. But the bass line undoubtedly lay in the development of diverticular disease when she was in her early fifties, and from which she continues to suffer. The disease periodically flares into acute diverticulitis, accompanied by extreme discomfort and distress. She was consequently admitted to hospital from time to time for investigations and treatment.

On one of these acute episodes, she was admitted to the Royal East Sussex Hospital in Hastings, where she was nursed in a single room. When I visited her, she told me that, during the previous night, an obviously confused elderly woman had climbed into bed with her, thereby dislodging Judy's intravenous drip.

On another, Judy was admitted to the new Conquest Hospital, also in Hastings. As usual, she was subject to the 'nil by mouth' rule until investigations were completed, and was thereafter permitted to drink high-protein 'meal replacement' cartons. But when I visited her, she told me that she had had nothing whatever to eat for two days.

Perplexed, I approached the nurses' station and relayed my concern. The nurse to whom I had conveyed the concern replied that 'She should have told us she was hungry'.

Juliet successfully completed her medical training but, for reasons about which I am not entirely clear, gave up her post-qualification training while still a junior doctor, and made the radical career switch to garden design, for which she underwent a three year, full-time degree course. She went on to become a successful garden designer with an impressive portfolio of completed projects and a series of awards at national level.

When Judy and I had settled in to her house in Bexhill in early 1980, I was appointed officer-in-charge of Haldane House, an East Sussex County Council old people's home near the sea front. The home was gently moribund, staffed by a benign group of people who had been there for ever. There was a pervasive smell of stale urine, not helped by the practice of cutting incontinence pads in half as a rather misguided economy measure. The deputy officer-in-charge was a chronic alcoholic, whose tenure at Haldane House came to an end when she was discovered rolling helplessly on the floor of the front hall with an elderly resident whom she had been attempting to escort somewhere.

Having come to this charming little seaside town and secured a permanent job, living in this beautiful little house, I believed that I was embarking on the second half of my life in a state of stability and security. I was 36 years old.

I attempted to introduce a little vitality to Haldane House where, as in so many 'rest' homes in the country, the residents sat in 'their' chairs in a circle round the main lounge, not watching televisions permanently tuned to the same commercial channel. The home was not far from the architecturally renowned de la Warr Pavilion, where there were regular shows featuring past-their-best artists. I decided, against the advice of the care staff, to take a group of long-term residents to see a show there, and accompanied them in a small coach. The show – something like old time music hall, I think – seemed to go down well, although there were one or two amusing moments provided by our party. One dear soul carefully removed her dentures at the start of the show and placed them on the backrest of the seat in front; another enthusiastically accepted a chocolate ice cream and popped it in her handbag, while a third remarked on the lovely big screen.

Bexhill-on-Sea was twinned with a small town in Germany and, every year, council dignitaries visited each other's twin town. And so it came to pass that a group of German councillors arrived at Haldane House, escorted by the lady mayor of Bexhill-on-Sea. The event passed in dignified peace until one of our blind residents, to whom I was explaining the nature of the visit and the composition of the visiting group, suddenly leapt to her feet, brandishing her walking stick vigorously above her head, screaming, 'I won't have no bloody Germans in my house; they killed my husband! Get the bastards out of here!' I swiftly led the visiting party out of the French doors and into the rather magnificent garden.

But there were too few entertaining moments to ameliorate the soporific routines and rituals entailed in the monotonous life of the home. The residents and their carers had been there so long that institutionalisation had set in. The long days were punctuated by the early morning round of washing and dressing the residents, changing wet beds, gently escorting people – some in wheelchairs – to the dining room, assisting those who required help to eat and administering the morning round of medicines before anyone managed to escape. In those days, there were no regular medicine reviews, and many of the residents had been on the same medicines for years.

By the time all 50 residents had finally been deposited in their chairs in the various lounges, it was time to distribute the post and to read out letters to people who needed help. Remaining staff prepared morning coffee, producing the homogenous grey, milky sweet drink that passes for coffee in hospitals and care homes. Domestic staff set to mopping vinyl floors, vacuuming carpets and cleaning sinks, toilets and baths. The laundress plunged soiled sheets into an industrial washing machine, gathered 'personal' laundry into bundles before throwing them into the smaller machines from which the woollens would emerge, matted and reduced.

The television sets in the lounges got hotter and hotter, so passing them at close range evoked a burst of static. No one was watching. Most residents were sleeping; those awake were able to savour the early aromas of lunch. The care staff clanged four sets of cutlery onto each table, then moved swiftly into the lounges to walk or wheel their charges toward the dining room. Lunch was served, during which 'Matron' made any necessary announcements, such as an evening concert by the local church choir, a game of bingo in the afternoon – or the death of the resident with whom they had breakfasted the day before.

Lunch time medicines were dispensed. Those who 'needed assistance with toileting' were conveyed to the appropriate facilities. Care assistants heaved stiff, heavy residents on to toilet bowls or unfurled the men at urinals. No health and safety training in these times; just the 'lower back pain' most staff regarded as an occupational hazard.

Boredom is said to be 'numbing'. I have never found it so. On the contrary, I have experienced it as having a unique, agonising ache of its own: a haunting, dispiriting form of debility which makes one feel demoralised and guilty about feeling so detached and uninterested. My recollection now is of cloyingly scented, warm rooms, of dust swirling in the sunlight; white, expressionless faces drooped on chests and a general air of stagnation. Staff appeared generally benign, but on automatic pilot: there was so much to be done, and within traditionally hallowed temporal parameters.

Meanwhile, barely a mile away, a new complex of services for elderly people was being built on the other side of Bexhill. The architect, Kate Macintosh, was charged with creating a place in which three discrete functions could be accommodated: 'supported' self-contained flats, a large day care centre, and a rehabilitation wing. The building itself was designed so imaginatively, and was so aesthetically appealing, that it won a RIBA award and was featured in professional architectural journals. Both the internal and external colour schemes were chosen to create a mood of restfulness and peace. Even the surrounding grounds were laid out in such a way that residents or day care clients could cultivate a patch of their own.

So 1981 represented a fresh challenge, a new start, when I was appointed officer-in-charge. I had the privilege of selecting many of the new staff team, and being given a relatively free hand to establish the ethos of the development. Mercifully, I had a sympathetic line manager, who supported me in setting the tone of the project. For one thing, I was determined that there should be as few 'rules and regulations' as possible, and the absolute minimum of notices posted about the place, beyond the mandatory fire exit signs. I have always loathed door signs reading 'Private' or 'Staff Only' – as if our clientele were a species apart. Mrs Thatcher's administration had been in power since 1979, and the era of paradoxical bureaucratisation had not yet begun. Nor had the culture of obsessive Health and Safety legislation been inaugurated.

A further departure from the norm in those days was our invitation to residents to bring in their pets. There was certainly some consternation expressed about this, not least by some of my own staff. An accommodation was reached, however, by which those of us who were in favour of helping people to look after their pets committed themselves to doing so, and those who were not in favour were excused the duty. The policy was tested most acutely when we admitted the retired headmistress of a prestigious girls' school, who was also a keen amateur ornithologist – and keeper of a small, private sanctuary in her garden in a nearby village. She had begun to develop Alzheimer's, but would not countenance joining us unless she could bring with her several of her asylum seekers – including an owl, a kestrel and a dog, among others: I can no longer remember exactly how many of God's creatures accompanied her on arrival. We decided to lay a heavy-duty layer of Perspex to protect the carpet, and drew up a rota of willing cleaners to keep the room to a basic minimum standard of hygiene lest we be subject to an unannounced inspection.

I hope that, as my own cerebral powers continue to decline, I shall never forget the delight we experienced when in Mrs E's room, attempting to hold a conversation with her. Her owl – rescued from Hampden Park in Eastbourne and consequently called 'Mrs Hampden' – established her quarters in the shelf above Mrs E's wardrobe and sharply turned her head toward whoever happened to be speaking. It was as if she were a spectator at Wimbledon.

We got into a spot of bother for harbouring the kestrel, which was evidently of a protected species which should not have been living in an old people's home. I cannot recall how the matter was resolved, but I have a feeling that an exception was made. Little did we realise that we were living in the closing era of flexibility, common sense and humanitarianism.

It was while I was at Thornwood that I acquired Sophie. I had no intention of doing so but, one Sunday afternoon, Judy and I had popped out for Sunday lunch at the Lamb at Hooe. On the way, I had noticed a sign saying 'Newfoundland Forge: puppies for sale'. After lunch, and a few intoxicating beverages on my part, we decided to 'pop in and just have a look' at the puppies; perhaps for nostalgic reasons, since I'd met a few 'Newfies' in Newfoundland and adored their huge fluffiness and soulful eyes.

And so Sophie had entered my life, marking her arrival by peeing straight into the boot of Judy's car before we had even driven out of Newfoundland Forge. Which turned out to be the least of the damage she visited upon that poor vehicle. On a subsequent occasion, when Judy and I had spent too long doing something in an industrial estate just outside Hailsham, Sophie took a dislike to the interior upholstery of the estate car, and stripped out the entire door and ceiling lining, costing £600 to replace: a lot in the early 1980s.

Sophie's deconstruction extended far beyond car upholstery. She was especially partial to brickwork pointing she considered about ready for replacement, and helpfully picked out and ate the crumbling mortar. She was also partial to the skirting-board in the dining room. But her *coup de grace* was surely the silent, secret and systematic gnawing of the webbing beneath the cushions of our Ercol cottage sofa. We were entirely unaware of the effects of this until someone sat on the sofa – and immediately sank swiftly and painfully to the floor.

Sophie came to work with me every day until her death, shortly before her twelfth birthday, on February 7, 1994. Dates such as these are remembered poignantly and permanently. Until then, she had been a popular member of the Thornwood community. She and Shandy, Judy's Labrador, were regularly washed and shampooed in the day centre bath, a procedure which Sophie hugely enjoyed, having to be removed at the end of the proceedings by two of us. Shandy was less impressed, but resigned.

Sophie attended residents' six-monthly care reviews. No amount of preliminary reassurance to the elderly victims of these statutory performances – and pointing out that these meetings were intended to discover whether *we* were treating people properly and meeting their interests and needs as far as possible – alleviated the anxiety many residents showed as they were invited into my office. The sight of me, key workers, social workers and sundry other service representatives must have been daunting to any sensible soul. But, on their spotting Sophie, lying in the middle of the room with her legs in the air, the creases of worry transformed into smiles.

Sophie was also an excellent timekeeper. When, usually after about half an hour, she thought that the deliberations had gone on for long enough, she emitted a lengthy, luxurious yawn, at which point the review became immediately more focused and headed more purposefully toward a conclusion.

Dogs are no longer allowed in hospitals and homes unless they are specially approved as 'therapeutic' visitors. Why? For reasons of health and safety. You never know whether a patient or resident might be 'immuno-compromised' – which, it seems to me, constitutes a compelling case for exterminating the entire canine population, just in case. And the question remains why 'therapeutic' dogs (temperamentally screened as suitable to visit hospitals and homes) should be free of the capacity to compromise people's immunity.

Thornwood had a huge, state-of-the-art kitchen, from which the delicious smells of food preparation emanated from mid-morning, creating part of the comforting feel of something resembling homeliness in the place. But, in the

122

early 1980s, with the gradual but inexorable eclipse of the public sector ethos – the notion of service to one's fellows as paramount – by market values, we were threatened with the advent of 'cook-chill' food preparation and distribution from central depots. Our residents and staff objected vociferously, as Cook and 'home' cookery were an integral part of Thornwood. The strength of our protest was sufficient to entice one of the assistant directors of social services to make a rare appearance before our assembled objectors. He attempted a jocular introduction by referring to the intimidating presence of Sophie, at the front of the throng, staring mercilessly and menacingly at him. Had she not been on her lead, she would probably have nudged him affectionately. But we were not to be mollified, either by the attempted humour or by the unconvincing justification for the change. Direct democracy was a failure, however, and the dreaded technology was introduced. Huge trucks delivered trays of meals, which were to be reheated in special ovens – replacing thousands of pounds' worth of conventional ovens – and brought to critical temperatures. At key points, electronic temperature probes were inserted and, if the temperature was not precisely as it should be, the food was to be destroyed. So much for public sector economies. On one occasion, a huge tray of chocolate sponge was tested and found wanting. Cook, frustrated at having effectively lost her original function, angrily cast the contents of the container into the garden behind the kitchen.

Sophie became the only champion of 'cook-kill', as it became popularly known, when she discovered and devoured 52 portions of chocolate sponge in the back garden. The only sequel to this glorious picnic was, perhaps, an unusually frequent emission of flatus for the remainder of the day.

One of her favourite resting places while on duty was lying across the top of the staircase just a few feet from my office door. On one occasion – at least, one that I know of – an elderly resident fell over her and rolled halfway down the staircase. I was horrified, helped her to her feet, and apologised profusely and sincerely. But the slightly shaken lady recovered herself smartly and instructed me not to tell anyone and not to 'fill anything in' as she didn't want Sophie to be banned from the premises. I could have hugged her – I probably did – and, of course, gratefully respected her wishes.

But Sophie was far from the only 'character' of another species at Thornwood. For some reason, a chinchilla, which we named 'Manuel', was donated to us and lived in a splendid cage on a table at the top of the staircase near my office. He, too, was a source of great interest and amusement to residents, staff and visitors alike.

Our enlightened architect, Kate Macintosh, had incorporated a bar inside the front entrance to Thornwood and, shortly after our grand opening, residents were canvassed as to whether they would like us to apply for a licence to sell alcoholic beverages. Not just for the officer-in-charge, who did not normally drink on the actual premises, but for residents. In those days, only a few daring residential establishments allowed residents to have a modest sherry on special occasions. This was an innovation of great interest, not only to our residents and staff, but also to the wider community via the local press. The result of the canvas was that the Nays succeeded by a couple of votes. And so the potential bar was converted into a shop, selling the sorts of wares you get in an average WRVS shop in a general hospital but with, I think, a few concessions to the special requests of residents – one of which was a special brand of dark chocolate.

But it came about that, when volunteers opened up the shop for business, they regularly discovered that several of the chocolate bars had been opened, with a few squares missing. What was particularly odd was that the tooth marks on the remaining squares were unusually small and sharp. It took us many weeks to discover the cause of the problem. Since the shop was carefully locked at the end of each day's trading, we could not fathom how anyone could have breached the fine-meshed shutters indicating that the shop was closed for the day. Eventually, the problem was solved. A vigilant member of the night staff observed one evening that, when the building had settled into quiet twilight and residents were in their rooms preparing for bed, Manuel had dexterously undone the latch on his cage and quietly descended the staircase, scuttled over to the shop, and disappeared through the gap between the counter and the shutter into the interior of the shop, where a series of cupboards, containing the shop stocks, were located. How he knew exactly which cupboard contained the chocolate bars, we could never determine: perhaps the aroma was strong enough to be detected by his acute olfactory apparatus. At any rate, the astonished night care officer observed Manuel opening the cupboard, nibbling off a few squares of 85% dark chocolate, replacing the bar and closing the cupboard. Being of a sporting nature, the officer took a day or two to report the heist, and the consensus among the staff, reluctantly concluded, was to place a padlock on the relevant cupboard.

We arranged as many entertainments for residents as we could. On one occasion, we held a party for residents and staff at the local pub, the Turkey, and invited Judy's son, Paul, to perform a reggae number. He had become a gifted and original musician, composing his own material and playing guitar accompanied by backing from an ingeniously programmed synthesiser. It went down very well indeed. I myself, invariably acutely anxious about social events of any kind, had hired a complete mouse's outfit, to conceal myself as far as possible. I had also consumed a fair quantity of strong drink, and was a lively participant – and probably mistress of ceremonies – at the event. At the end of the – evidently successful – evening, I drove home, drunk and in an all-enveloping blue, furry mouse's outfit. Had I been apprehended, the headlines would undoubtedly have stalled, if not terminated, my so-called 'career': *Matron in Mouse Outfit Caught Drink Driving...* These 30-odd years later, I still tingle with embarrassment.

Another of the more memorable times at Thornwood was our selection to be a sort of 'show' home to a group of Japanese visitors. This was quite an honour, as I subsequently learned that we were the only older people's service in the county to be selected. In due course, an unexpectedly large contingent of Japanese dignitaries arrived, each bearing what turned out to be extravagant gifts wrapped in gorgeous fabrics. We were quite unprepared for this, and had not been briefed that the gift-giving was traditionally expected to be reciprocal: all they took from Thornwood was a warm handshake and our latest brochure.

I think by this time I was regarded as an unpredictable loose cannon which could, if carefully contained, prove an asset in demonstrating innovative, progressive service provision to the outside world. But in the long run – and with the coming of managerialism in the public sector – I became a subversive, unrestrainable critic of the developing asphyxiation of public service.

One of my most controversial decisions was to appoint a black ex-prisoner as a care officer. We had developed the practice of introducing people from the local prison to work as volunteers in the day centre. These men were being prepared for release. We encouraged them to use whatever – legal – interests and talents they had in working with our elderly guests. The scheme as a whole was a marked success. One of the men being prepared for freedom was an attractive Guyanese, Roosevelt or 'Rudi', who, I

126

instinctively felt, was a natural if unconventional potential care officer. His laughter was infectious, and his human warmth and intelligence considerable. I interviewed him, in the properly prescribed manner, along with other candidates for the post of basic grade care officer, and considered him the best candidate for the job. The other members of the interview panel evidently agreed, and he was duly appointed. Having worked in London for some years, I was not prepared for the outcry which greeted my announcement of Rudi's appointment. This was the first time – in the early 1980s – that a black member of staff had been appointed, as far as I knew, in the area. One of my senior care officers said to her colleagues, 'What does that make *us*?' As if it were self-evident that blacks were inferior to whites. The headmaster husband of a care officer was so outraged by the appointment that he threatened to withdraw his wife from Thornwood.

We had a 'comforts fund' fed largely by the profits from the shop, despite the literal erosion of these by Manuel the chinchilla, and the purpose of the fund was, of course, to supply 'extras' – Christmas presents and so on – on special occasions. The fund was usually in a pretty healthy state, and there were then no regular audits of the balance sheets. Rudi, having recently emerged from prison with one suit of clothes, a train warrant back to London and a tenner 'resettlement allowance', needed to have access to a car in order to take residents out for appointments and outings. Other members of staff had managed to obtain bank loans in the ordinary way, and travel expenses were then sufficiently generous to maintain the vehicles on the road. But Rudi was prohibited from opening a bank account immediately upon release from prison, and was at a singularly embarrassing disadvantage – quite apart from the racial tension to which he was subjected – at the time. I decided to lend him £600 from the comforts fund so that he could purchase a real bargain of a car, which could only be found in a place like Bexhill, with its enormous population of careful, elderly drivers. The car was a pristine blue Vauxhall, about ten years old, ordinarily garaged and with precious few miles on the clock. Irresistible. I knew Rudi would repay the fund, and he did indeed do so – in less than the agreed time. Those of us who knew about the transaction considered it a prudent investment, and our faith in Rudi was fully vindicated. Today, it would be called embezzlement, and I would have been summarily dismissed for gross financial misconduct.

Following an in-house seminar on the principles and practice of rehabilitation, it was clear that Rudi had absorbed the message when, during evening duty, one of the residents asked him to change TV channels. Aware of the need to encourage people to do as much as they reasonably could for themselves, Rudi responded by saying to the woman who had requested the switch, 'What's the matter with ya? You got legs, ain't ya?' His stock with our clientele was sufficiently high for him to get away with this, and his point was taken with good grace. I am happy to say that, when I encountered him many years after I had left Thornwood, he was working at a senior level as a mental health support worker in Uckfield, and was married with a son.

I was based at Thornwood for ten years and, despite some of the aforementioned highlights, I inevitably developed my usual sense of grinding boredom and frustration. The early innovations had become embedded in our work, and I was better at instituting than maintaining projects. One of our early service diversifications consisted of developing links with the local NHS mental health services. My own background – and chief interest – had always been in psychiatric work, and we were increasingly asked to consider referrals of people with unusual problems which were not quite acute enough to merit the intensive clinical environment of hospital, yet who were not sufficiently independent to manage at home. Our age range parameters grew steadily more flexible, with a proportion of referrals of middle-aged people who did not quite fit the criteria for other services, but who were in need of gentle re-entry into the community. At the time, we were not receiving enough referrals of elderly people to satisfy the increasingly demanded 'occupancy levels', so the surreptitious extension of our remit satisfied all parties. We took to referring to our two rehabilitation units as 'extended short stay', and no one seemed to spot the paradox.

But I began to dread going to work, and seized every opportunity to distract myself from the daily operations. By this time, the erosion of the public sector ethos of service to others was evidenced by Mrs Thatcher's infamous declaration – which she subsequently denied – that 'There is no such thing as society'. With many others at the time, I took this to imply that individual effort and self-sufficiency were all that mattered: the Malthusian principle that 'the weak should go to the wall' and rely upon charitable alms rather than the bloated, grossly inefficient and overmanned welfare state. Resources were not infinite, and the proverbial bottom – financial – line had to be drawn somewhere. The effect of this profound sea change in social and economic policy was exacerbated in East Sussex by the appointment of Ken Young as director of social services. I believe that he had been brought up in care, and that his Scottish upbringing may have been tough. And he himself had become, perhaps inevitably, tough and abrasive. He loathed what he perceived to be the professional preciousness of qualified social workers, and elevated the status of residential social workers by sending them en masse on less rigorous, more 'practical' part-time training courses. The predictable result was that social workers became marginalised and demoralised, while their lesser-trained residential counterparts acquired an overblown sense of their worth and competence.

Inevitably, workers at the service front became less reflective about their work and less able to discern what was happening to the social policy landscape. Increasingly, non-professionally trained workers now foresaw opportunities hitherto denied them to ascend into managerial positions. The males among them took to adopting similar sartorial styles − black leather jackets and the beginnings of 'designer stubble'. The long-established practice of social workers having professional supervision was derided variously as 'wet nursing' or 'flea upon flea' mentality. Managers at all levels engaged in displays of the ruthlessness they thought would impress the upper echelons of their commitment to the new 'macho management'. And the women were not immune to the increasingly overt expressions of what eventually came to be called 'managerialism'.

Ken Young publicly announced that he wanted to stay one step ahead of Mrs Thatcher, and in this I believe he succeeded. Despite Mrs Thatcher's repeated attacks on excessive bureaucracy, the 'target' culture of the late 1980s and early 1990s anticipated that of the 2000s in East Sussex by an explosion of paper trails, management checks and policy documents sufficient to paper the whole of County Hall. One example of many pointless paper trails which I personally researched concerned the weekly and painstaking manual recording of establishment menus on pink sheets which were countersigned by several layers of management and ultimately sent to County Hall, where, I discovered, they were unexamined and consigned to a large skip at the rear of the building.

Whereas I had briefly been valued in the early 1980s as an enterprising manager with original, enlightened ideas, I rapidly became a nonconformist pariah, rarely shortlisted for modest promotions, and, in one case, learned from my manager that I was 'too client oriented' to be considered for the new post of complaints officer. My frustration and fury escalated, and I resorted to writing the odd critical letter to the social work journals – none of which was printed. My ennui and personal desperation affected my relationship with poor Judy, whom I had persuaded to apply for the post of deputy officer-in-charge at Thornwood, and who shared an office with me for years. Although Judy was a truly imaginative manager of the day centre, she was much too disorganised and chaotic for me – and she shared my office. Whereas I took to polishing my desk and telephone when feeling particularly bored or frustrated, Judy's relaxed ordering of paperwork tended to spill over into 'my' space and slide over into the wastebin.

We reached the point, one awful day, when my agitation accelerated to such a degree – her corresponding resentment rising to a parallel pitch – that she resorted to throwing plants at me. Feeling that the situation had got rather out of control, I telephoned my line manager to apprise her of the unusual crisis. She duly appeared, and I have no idea how she handled matters at all, but by some means peace was ultimately restored. Because of our dramatically divergent management styles, we often rubbed each other up the wrong way, and this obviously percolated into our relationship at home.

Meanwhile, I was becoming rather fond of the line manager whom I'd asked to help us stop the plant-throwing, Jean Carruthers. She had been a staff officer before becoming team manager of Bexhill West. We had virtually nothing in common, and she took to calling some of my ideas 'outrageous', which did not augur well for our relationship. But there was something about her that I liked. Her smile, for instance. And her rather endearing way of teasing me without actually inflaming me to verbal retaliation.

Jean was obviously straight, but had never had a satisfactory relationship with any man. I eventually moved out of Judy's house and into Jean's in Eastbourne. She, too, hated my fondness for strong lager, although I do not recall that I caused any actual damage beyond going to bed with my Doc Martens on once. For all that, we hobbled along for a few years until I formed an attachment to another Jean, and moved to her house in Hailsham.

When I look back over my relationship history, I feel embarrassed, ashamed and inadequate. The one thing I have in common with Elizabeth Taylor is that I 'married' – or formed a live-in relationship with – all my lovers. Of whom there have been seven in total. However, now that I am heading for 70 – years in age as opposed to number of relationships – I try to convince myself that more influential and successful people than I have vastly surpassed my score.

In retrospect, I think I conducted a campaign of emotional attrition as far as Jean Carruthers was concerned. If anything, Sophie was actually the lure which drew Jean into letting me move in with her. Long after we had parted, and after her death in 2000 from colon cancer, the priest conducting her funeral revealed that Jean's greatest joy in life was dog walking – and the only dog she had ever walked was, as far as anyone knew, Sophie. Looking back, I dearly wish that I had left Sophie with her when I eventually moved out. But somehow I doubt whether I had the sensitivity to recognise the depth of her attachment to Sophie – or the degree of selflessness I should have possessed in order to leave Sophie behind.

ELEVEN

The days at Thornwood seemed endless. There was nothing further I could contribute, and the hallmark of departmental virtue was metamorphosing from 'personal social service' to 'bringing in the budget'. The director of finance became the arbiter of moral worth in every section of the organisation, verbally assassinating 'underperforming' units of service in monthly bulletins. The virus of managerialism began to infest the department, and by 'managerialism' I mean the elevation of 'macho management' to a virtue-in-itself; the replacement of altruism by budgetary control. 'Underperforming' homes or day care centres were closed down or sold to private companies, 'dinosaur' professionals sidelined or made redundant. Old-style professionals took early retirement wherever possible.

My growing unpopularity with senior management was aggravated by my reluctant involvement with a local AIDS 'case'. A few colleagues knew that I had once had a partner who was 'gender reassigned', and a social worker who knew of my interest asked me to meet a client of his who was not only the first officially known victim of AIDS in Eastbourne, but also a male-to-female transsexual to whom domiciliary social services were at the time being denied for 'risk' reasons. I was persuaded to meet this unfortunate soul, who was well over six feet tall, living alone in a suburb of Eastbourne, her male partner having died some months earlier of AIDS. My limited encounters with male-to-female transsexuals had led me to believe that they tended to be rather cruelly endowed with above average height, enormous hands and feet, prominent Adam's apples – and a deep bass voice. Carol was no exception to this admittedly sketchy stereotype. By the time I met her, she was fairly well advanced on the wretched journey to death, having done a round or two with PCP (an AIDS-related pneumonia) and with a hair-transplant wound which refused to heal, leaving a suppurating, bloody V-shaped scar on the top of her head.

This was the mid-1980s, when the government was engaged in the gruesome campaign Don't Die of Ignorance. At that point, the fragility of the human immunodeficiency virus (HIV) was reasonably well known, as were the routes of transmission – essentially by means of the exchange of body fluids. I resolved never to exchange body fluids with Carol.

The house was in a state of chaos. Carol, too weak to wash soiled sheets and duvet covers, had been refused any form of domiciliary care. And so it came about that I acquired *de facto* home help duties. The department graciously allowed me to drive to Carol's home before and after work at Thornwood each day, a distance of 13 miles each way, so that I could carry out the home help duties which I had acquired by sheer default. I have never been the most practical of people, and the laundering by hand of mounds of soiled sheets and duvet covers I found nauseating and exhausting – especially after a full day's work at Thornwood.

The local MP for Eastbourne at the time, Ian Gow, somehow got wind of the case, and systematically applied pressure on my department to provide some assistance. I am no Conservative, but admired his tenacity and the regular enquiries as to Carol's welfare. Whether the leak of Carol's plight to the national press was in any way attributable to Mr Gow, I shall never know, but the media cottoned on enthusiastically to the awful story. On one occasion, when Carol became acutely ill, I had to badger the authorities to send an ambulance for her, as she was too collapsed to convey in my car. To my astonishment, when an ambulance eventually materialised, the paramedics were attired in what I can only describe as astronaut suits, and they somehow manoeuvred Carol by gloved fingertip into the waiting vehicle.

Mr Gow's persistent pressure on the department eventually forced the concession that meals-on-wheels might be delivered to Carol's home. I was once with her when I happened to notice two conveyors of the little foil containers scurrying away up the incline of Carol's lawn, having suspended the package on the handle of her front door. Mr Gow was, of course, subsequently assassinated by an IRA explosive device attached to the underside of his car, but I remain eternally grateful to this man, whose concern for an early AIDS victim could have earned him little political kudos.

In the course of three frighteningly short weeks, Carol became completely blind – due, I imagine, to the onset of cytomegalovirus or CMV, which wreaks havoc on brain tissue. A friend of mine in the department, a rehabilitation officer for the visually impaired, volunteered to visit Carol with me, and produced from her case a whole cornucopia of devices for helping blind people retain as much autonomy as possible. There were specially constructed devices enabling them to sign cheques, make telephone calls, navigate their way round rooms, and so on – Carol was, by this stage, too weak to go outside her house where, in any case, there was frequently a media presence. Some reporters even took to shouting through her letter box, 'You might as well give us your side of the story, Carol – all the nationals are printing the negative side...' Carol declined to respond.

Having reached the end of her presentation of appliances and adaptations, my ROVI friend announced, warmly, 'But the last thing I want to do is fill your house with aids...' It was too late. The words had been uttered, and my friend, immediately realising her double entendre, could think of no remedy. Neither could I. And, by now, Carol had utterly lost her ability to appreciate the irony of the situation. She all but threw my friendly ROVI out of her house.

I think it was the Spectator which printed an article about the East Sussex Social Services Department's 'sick' treatment of Carol, which flew in the face of current knowledge of the nature and transmissibility of HIV. The thrust of the piece was that the department was in danger of allowing a client to die prematurely because of the social services' ignorance. The assistant director – the erstwhile champion of cook-kill – objected to me that the article was 'scurrilous', and implied that I was somehow responsible for its publication. In fact I was not, but I knew who was. He was a gay senior social worker in Brighton, whose partner was a freelance journalist. The 'informant', whom I got to know reasonably well, had been passed over for promotion to team manager on several occasions, and had been told by a slightly inebriated colleague at a staff leaving 'do' that it was simply because he was gay. Although this was never made explicit, it preceded anti-discrimination law by many years. When he died – of AIDS – his funeral service was held in a large Brighton church, his coffin festooned with single white roses. The otherwise intensely moving ceremony was rather marred by the attendance of several senior managers who had been actively involved in blocking his promotion and abdicating their responsibility for helping the victims of this terrible epidemic.

Perhaps the most distressing feature of Carol's dramatic decline was the radical change in her personality. At our initial meetings, we had managed to have lively conversations about politics and classical music. But our meetings degenerated sharply in the weeks and months of our involvement with each other. She stopped washing and dressing, languishing in a heavily stained dressing gown day in and day out, draped in the same high-backed recliner chair, and receiving me as one would a recalcitrant servant. At each visit, she presented a list of chores for me to attend to, tasks frequently beyond my meagre ability to perform. One of the most challenging involved her instructing me to install a new electrical pump in the tropical fish tank, a procedure which I undertook with a level of apprehension which could only be described as sustained panic. Carol barked orders, reiterating them at progressively shorter intervals and with increasingly withering criticism. It took hours to achieve the installation – and I still had to deal with the washing-up and soiled laundry.

Jean insisted that I have a lengthy shower when I got home, mentally and physically drained, in the late evening. She felt, as did the line manager who succeeded her, that I was running a personal crusade for my own satisfaction. If they could have been privy to my real thoughts and feelings throughout this dreadful period, they would have thought differently. I was in fact deeply resentful that I had been persuaded to step in where others had refused, had grown to loathe the client, who became more imperious, demanding and critical by the day – and I was absolutely exhausted.

A brief period of respite presented itself when Judy's ex-husband, the Tanzanian barrister, invited her, Juliet and me for a holiday on his farm near Arusha in Tanzania. The home help organiser in my team, Mary Pearson, had become sympathetic to my dilemma and offered to send in a small, dedicated team to look after Carol in my absence, quite without the department's knowledge. This felt like a miraculous deliverance. And so Judy, Juliet and I flew to Nairobi, where her tall, handsome ex met us and drove us to his home. Fuel was severely rationed at the time, following the war with Uganda, so we were unable to do as much touring of the country as we would have wished, but did manage a mini-safari to the edge of the Serengeti. The weather was extremely hot, and I acquired the best suntan ever, although my freckles were outnumbered by mosquito bites.

The charismatic, altruistic former president of this one-party state, Julius Nyerere, had just resigned as the first President of Tanzania in 1985. He was born in the former Tanganyika and trained there as a teacher. He went on to study at Makerere University in Kampala, and thence to Edinburgh, where he read economics and history. In 1967, he issued the famous Arusha Declaration, setting out his socialist concept of Ujamaa, which became the dominant theme in Tanzanian politics. While at Edinburgh University, Nyrere had been introduced to Fabian thinking, and it was there that he developed his unique vision of marrying socialism and communal living. He went about the country speaking to ordinary people and tribal chiefs, trying to gather support for movement toward independence. He addressed the UN, and his gift for oratory and obvious integrity advanced the cause for independence without war or bloodshed. He was responsible for the incorporation of Zanzibar and Tanganyika into the new state of Tanzania.

It was odd to be sitting in the Arusha Hotel in 1985, where the famous Declaration had been signed, and we were hungry and hot from a 'stroll' in the mid-day sun, eyeing a solitary cheese sandwich in the food cabinet, its edges curling upward, over which hovered a predatory fly. Nyerere's belief was that Africans were constitutionally socialist and that all they needed to do was to revert to their original way of life and reject capitalism in all its forms. But, as is so often the case with charismatic utopians, Nyerere's dreams were ultimately shredded by the realities of war (with Uganda), and years of drought. As a result, agricultural output nosedived, and the deficit in cereal grains amounted to in excess of a million tons between 1974 and 1977. The World Bank and International Monetary Fund rescued Tanzania from bankruptcy, thus attenuating Nyerere's dream, as Tanzania, once the largest African exporter of agricultural products, became the largest importer. Conditions entailed by the IMF and World Bank effectively compelled the introduction of free market principles to the Tanzanian economy. Nyerere announced his retirement in 1985, and our holiday coincided with the arrival of a new president – and the inevitable, parasitic incubus of widespread bribery and corruption.

So our stay in Tanzania coincided with a period of uncertainty and unease for the citizenry. On the whole, we found that the people were everywhere disposed to smile, and to greet us warmly. The one taboo was to attempt to take photographs without prior permission – and failing to make the payment of a few shillings to the persons or properties to be photographed. The 'properties' concerned were, with the exception of Judy's ex-husband's grand farmhouse, principally mud huts. We were deeply fortunate in finding that there were several Masai settlements within easy distance, and they permitted us to take pictures of their elegant figures dressed in traditional cloaks and jewellery. These tall, slim, beautifully dignified people were said to subsist exclusively on blood and milk.

My bedroom window looked out to the top of Mount Kilimanjaro, at that time capped all the year round with snow. It felt so odd to be lying, perspiring in temperatures in the nineties, surveying a peak of dazzlingly white snow so near – and yet, in altitude, so far.

AIDS, which it was thought had originated in Africa, had begun to decimate the population of the Kenyan town of Mombasa where, it was claimed, all the prostitutes were infected. Some UK tourists to this popular resort on the coast of the Indian Ocean, just north of Tanzania, got more than they had bargained for and imported the virus to Britain, where increasing numbers of heterosexuals became infected. In due course, the entire, enormous African continent was affected. Appropriate responses were mired in the twin difficulties that most African nations were in no economic position to finance the necessary palliative drugs to postpone the inevitable deaths, and that there was a widespread myth – promulgated by a future president of South Africa among others – that HIV was not, in any case, the cause of AIDS.

When we got back to the UK a fortnight later, we were on the very first plane to land at the new fourth terminal at Heathrow. I proved I was the first passenger to use one of the new toilets, as I sat on a sheet of polythene covering the seat. As soon as we arrived back in East Sussex, I telephoned Mary Pearson to discover how things were with Carol. Predictably, she had become sicker than ever. The core evil of the disease is that it devastates the body's immune response: its capacity to resist infection. Victims are consequently prey to 'opportunistic' infections at any juncture and in random order. Some infections seem more likely to occur than others. CMV and PCP I have already mentioned, but one of the most common stigmata of this appalling disease is Kaposi's sarcoma, a form of skin cancer which manifests itself in highly visible purple lesions all over the body, including the face. Carol escaped that, but had enough alternative pathologies to contend with. The blood and pus oozing from the wound of her failed hair transplant became daily more offensive, ameliorative measures less and less effective. The entire length of her gastrointestinal tract was infected with *candida albicans* – a form of thrush which, again, was unresponsive to conventional fungicides.

She grew visibly thinner by the day, and progressively weaker. Her memory had begun to fragment, her irritability and grandiosity to increase. No doubt her imperiousness was a perfectly understandable response to the rapid and profound loss of autonomy she was suffering. Or it may simply have represented an organic personality change wrought by the CMV on her poor brain, once so bright and rational. This etiolated, cadaverous soul, leaking noxious exudates from virtually every bodily orifice, remains the most pitiable sight of another human being I have ever laid eyes on. Now that she was blind, she insisted that I read the daily newspaper to her, and I had to take care to edit out the quotes from fundamentalist Christians who were insisting that AIDS was God's punishment for gays' defiance of biblical teaching. As southern US Baptists repeatedly pointed out, homosexuality was a freely chosen perversion of nature, and AIDS was as effective a way as any of meting out the appropriate punishment – with the double benefit of eliminating gays from human civilisation. A popular bumper sticker of the time in the southern states read 'Kill a Queer for Christ'.

Carol eventually developed a recurrence of PCP, the AIDS-related pneumonia. Antibiotics had no effect, and her breathing became laboured and painful. She was, by this time, doubly incontinent and suffering from the inexorable shutting down of her body systems. It took time, persistence and immense patience to persuade the local health authorities that she really did now require full nursing care, and she was eventually admitted to St Mary's Hospital in Eastbourne.

It was fortunate that she was isolated in a private room, which simultaneously protected her from unnecessary ghoulish attention and facilitated private conversation with her visitors. Actually, I think I may have been her only visitor. I had to steel myself to sit by her bed every few days; by this time her poor frame had become skeletal and her face was gradually becoming engorged with a yellowish fluid which from time to time oozed out through splits in her skin. Her unseeing eyes became deeply embedded in their sockets, and her voice reduced to a hoarse whisper. I tried to ask her whether there was anything either I or anyone else could do for her, but was invariably met with terse refusals. It seemed that she had become distinctly and generally suspicious of anyone and everyone involved in her care. I dreaded every visit, but a part of me hoped, perhaps Quixotically, that my presence might convey to her that she mattered.

The truth was, of course, that I hoped for her death, for both our sakes. It had been a wretched chapter for us both, and the intimate encounter with the effects of the human immunodeficiency virus an excruciating challenge to the few shreds of religious belief which I had at the time.

Carol's funeral was held at Eastbourne crematorium, officiated by a local vicar who had obviously suffered a nosebleed shortly before the start of the service, and whose presumably white cassock was badly in need of laundering. The dignity of the occasion was not enhanced by the poor cleric's regular mixing of gender in describing the deceased's prospect of eternal life.

And so it was over.

TWELVE

In a very important sense, Jean Carruthers saved my life.

The few remaining shreds of my sanity were themselves splitting by the time I moved in to her house. By 1986, she was clearly tired of my ranting and raving, fulminating about the department and its moral turpitude. She was certainly tired of my swilling Pils and going to bed with my boots on. And so she presented me with an advertisement in the Guardian, announcing the start of a new MA in Public and Social Administration at Brunel University, starting in the autumn. The course would run for two years, and require attendance at the university campus in Uxbridge one day a week. Although I had studied Social Administration at the LSE from 1970 to 1972, time and policy changes had intervened, and social policy and administration was still a subject of considerable interest to me.

It would also mean a heaven-sent weekly break from the increasingly jaundiced department. Mercifully, the department and I had not yet reached the stage of outright hostilities, and I was given permission to attend Brunel on Wednesdays, a round trip of 170 miles between Eastbourne and Uxbridge.

I attended for interview, regrettably sober on this occasion, unfortified by alcohol: anxiety glued my tongue to the roof of my mouth, rendering answers to the interviewers' enquiries difficult. God knew I had had more university interviews than most: this was my sixth. But self-confidence is not one of my most notable characteristics.

I began the course in the autumn of 1986. Those Wednesday drives were the highlight of my week, the tedium of negotiating rush hour traffic on the M25 mitigated by the sight of Concorde soaring up from Heathrow toward New York. Talking with other disaffected employees of public sector health and social services; increasingly understanding why – as well as how – social and health economic policy was being driven away from the ethics of public service toward those of the market. It had seemed inconceivable not only to me but also to the academic world at the time that the moral imperative of full citizenship could be eclipsed by budgetary parameters.

The creation of the welfare state after WWII embodied the principle of mutual care, of institutionalised altruism, of care for citizens 'from the cradle to the grave'. The state came to have an incontestable duty to provide for the poor, the sick, the elderly and the generally disenfranchised. I can still recall lectures at the LSE in the early seventies arguing not only that there was a cross-party consensus as to the necessity for a comprehensive welfare state, but that this consensus was irreversible.

But this is an autobiography, not a polemic, and I shall confine myself to the basic themes of my concern. There are two principal views of human nature: one is that people are innately good, altruistic or 'perfectible'; the other that people are fundamentally self-centred, competitive and seeking their own welfare above the welfare of others. I see the first view as conducive to *communitarianism*, the drive to cooperate with one's fellows in seeking mutual wellbeing; the second as *individualism*, the drive to seek one's own wellbeing prior to the interests of others.

144

The Thatcher and Reagan administrations were, I believe, fairly extreme examples of what came to be called 'neo-liberal' individualism. Thatcher's infamous declaration that 'there is no such thing as society' appeared to me to embody the political philosophy that 'the weak should go to the wall'; that government had no fiduciary duty to provide for the poor, the disabled, the sick or the elderly. Instead, the furtherance of capitalism and of monetarism – control of the money supply in the economy – would inevitably lead to a 'trickle down' of wealth to the socio-economically disadvantaged members of the citizenry. There was consequently relatively little need for 'paternalistic' or 'big' government to continue the byzantine labyrinth of welfare benefits which had proliferated from the creation of the post-war welfare state.

The practical result of all this was that ever-increasing charges were imposed for hitherto free or subsidised health and social services, and threshold criteria of eligibility for services were systematically raised so that people who would previously have been entitled to services were advised to engage private, independent or 'for profit' companies.

What dumbfounded me in the eighties was that my own department appeared to be endorsing the prevailing political ethos with wholesale enthusiasm. I could not then understand why so many of the professionals on the front line were evidently capitulating to these immoral imperatives; why they were not protesting in the vigorous terms with which Mrs Thatcher's hated poll tax was defeated. It was obvious that 'coal face' workers striving for promotion to the managerial ranks might subscribe overtly to the ethics of managerial economics, but I failed to comprehend the reluctance of the operational staff to object to the erosion of the ethos of public service and the steady transfer of domiciliary and residential services to the private, 'for profit' sector.

Managers of direct services were increasingly subjected to senior managerial initiatives and instructions; middle managers were seen less as supportive, encouraging mentors and more as purveyors of budgetary checking mechanisms. Good professional practice gave way to 'coming in on budget'. Instances of supervening financial imperatives abounded. I recall becoming apoplectic when a memorandum from the director of finance ordered that, when a lost elderly person was brought into a residential establishment by the police for emergency care while their identity and immediate care needs were established, we were somehow to seek payment for their temporary stay, even if it had only been for a few hours. I objected vehemently in a return memorandum, refusing to implement such an instruction, and do not remember any repercussions, but no doubt my 'card was marked' then, if not before.

Whereas residential and 'field' social workers had, prior to the eighties, been regarded as honourable people doing honourable jobs, some of us began to feel as if we were now regarded as potentially subversive functionaries. We became subject to 'stick and carrot' management, to be beaten by poor showing in financial league tables or rewarded by promotion to more senior managerial posts.

I experienced the moral metamorphosis as hurtful at two levels: on the one hand, excellence in care practice was subordinated to 'success' in budgetary control, and on the other, there was an underlying presumption that ground level workers could not see through the new 'management speak'. The department's managerial mission represented a microcosm of the national political mission, and we, the operatives, were either too stupid to detect the progressive inversion of moral values or too oppressed or cowardly to resist.

146

Wednesdays at Brunel were opportunities to ventilate these frustrations and to develop an understanding of how political systems could be manipulated by the construction of new vocabularies: new language in which previously neutral or negative moral judgements could be transmuted to become positive. This still seemed to me to represent a massive insult to the intelligence of the populace, but it simultaneously seemed to be a tide that could not, for whatever reason, be turned back at that time.

My master's dissertation focused on the contrast between 'professional' and 'managerial' perspectives on the rise of 'macho' management in the personal social services. To my surprise, my supervisor suggested that I might develop my research into a doctoral study. In some trepidation, in 1989, I registered for a PhD at Brunel. I applied to my department for study leave in some part-time form, but my request was rejected – hardly surprising, in view of my reckless opposition to the trajectory of its policies and practices. Undeterred, I took to setting my alarm for 4.00 am each day, and managed three hours' study and writing during the gentle onset of dawn. For inspiration, I played rousing organ music, mediated by powerfully cushioned earphones.

Needless to say, the early morning bursts of academic energy were undertaken in a state of sobriety. After three hours of intensive study, followed by a full day's work, I rewarded myself with Pils lager because, of course, I had earned it. Jean did not attune herself to my thinking, and there were regular tense exchanges about this matter.

Candour requires that I explain a little about the nature of our relationship. Jean had never been, nor was ever likely to be, gay. She had had very disappointing relationships with men, and had settled for a single life. I do not believe that she ever fell in love with me, and I am sure her offer to give me a home where I could keep Sophie was an expression of sympathetic generosity. However, since I had romantic sentiments toward *her*, I convinced myself that they were to some extent reciprocated. At the time, I could not see why she was so reluctant for us to be seen as partners, to introduce me to significant friends and relatives in her life. Perhaps I thought that she was simply shy. She was certainly not homophobic or conservative in principle.

Jean was a fully trained teacher of Hatha yoga, and taught evening classes at various schools in the area. I attended a few of her lessons, but decided it was not for me. And, apart from walking Sophie together, the sad fact is that we had little in common: too little to form the basis of a fruitful friendship. As she died in 2000, I am unable to consult her about how she really felt then, but there were certainly regular, acute tensions about my drinking and ranting about the department. On several occasions, we visited a couple of gay friends to enlist their aid in helping us to reconcile our differences, but the reconciliations were temporary.

Somewhat lacking in self-confidence, she worked extremely hard for the department, often bringing work home or going into the office at weekends. Her chronic diffidence was poignantly illustrated by her habit of over-writing words which were already appropriate and correctly spelt. I felt that she was in awe of her superiors, and was highly anxious about my regular outbursts about the department – especially when they were translated into written memoranda to chief officers. Only now that I am retired and – slightly – mellowed can I appreciate her angst on my behalf. In 'career' terms, my conduct was suicidal.

Eventually, I decided to move out, and bought a flat near the seafront in Bexhill. I would be closer to my place of work and to Judy, with whom I had remained on friendly terms. There was no prohibition on keeping animals, and there were fewer staircases to climb.

But then I let my heart run away with me again, this time with a social worker who lived in Hailsham. She and I had met on a few occasions, and she knew that I had studied bits and pieces of law in various places. I think that her question concerned a dispute over a boundary wall at the foot of her garden, and I presume I delivered a satisfactory opinion because she invited me to dinner and then into her bed. I eventually moved in with her, but we were ill-matched, and the arrangement did not last.

Despite our differences and the lopsided nature of our relationship, Jean Carruthers was disturbed by my departure, although I still wonder whether it was really the departure of Sophie which distressed her more. At any rate, she severed diplomatic relations for a time. Jean not only had encouraged me to apply for the MA course at Brunel which I had enjoyed so much, she even paid one year's tuition fees for me. That is how good a friend she was.

And then along came another change in my life. I was offered a sideways move to run a psychiatric rehabilitation home in Bexhill, which was, coincidentally, next door to my own flat. Apart from the fact that no increase in salary was involved, I was the only social services employee in the area with a psychiatric qualification and many years' management experience. So it was no promotion. On the other hand, I was grateful for the chance to leave Thornwood behind. The days of setting up the new service in a highly innovative new building had been stimulating and rewarding, but the maintenance of a 'steady state' service was not, and especially not in the changing political climate.

Albany Court was an enormous detached house in Bexhill town centre, possibly built at the turn of the twentieth century, with labyrinthine, narrow corridors and small, dark rooms. I was a heavy smoker in those days, but even I was taken aback by the reek of stale tobacco smoke

149

which permeated the entire building. Whatever their original colour, the walls in every room were stained a deep yellowish brown by the smoke of many years, the carpets riddled with cigarette burns from time immemorial. I could not believe that the décor, fixtures and fittings could have been so neglected for so long.

And the staff matched their environment in key respects. The longest-serving staff members themselves were smoky, long neglected and impregnated with gloom. I did not realise it at the time of my appointment, but it gradually dawned on me that I was there to preside over the closure of the establishment and the relocation of its residents and staff to other destinations. I cannot recall what had become of my predecessor in the role of officer-in-charge, but was faced with a hostile deputy and an assistant officer-in-charge with what we would now describe as 'personality issues' and a drink problem to match my own. From the very outset, they placed every conceivable obstacle in my way as I attempted to get the place redecorated, the overgrown garden tidied and a therapeutic programme for the residents established.

I discovered that a significant proportion of the residents were not, by any stretch of the imagination, mentally ill. How they had fetched up in this God-forsaken cul-de-sac was largely undisclosed to me, as accurate record-keeping had not been a priority at the home. Several of the residents I remember most vividly were not remotely mentally ill. One was a severe epileptic whose grand mal fits had been so bad that a consultant to whom I took him speculated that his brain must by then have had the consistency of scrambled egg. The young man had not a trace of psychiatric morbidity about him, and was invariably cheerful and optimistic despite his miserable circumstances. No one in the world appeared to care about him, and I seem to recall that he had no named next-of-kin. With the help of a local GP, I managed to get him referred to a national

150

epilepsy association which ran homes for people with severe epilepsy, and we were successful in obtaining a place for him there. I visited him there several times in his airy, fresh room and was invited to inspect his programme of activities. The staff told me that his favourite treat was Malibu liqueur, and I took him a bottle at each visit.

The resident with whom I had most direct contact was a particularly handsome young man, Nigel, with impeccable manners and amiable disposition, who stood out from the rest of the residents in many respects. His divorced parents were involved and concerned for his welfare, but were constantly distressed by the management of his care. He displayed none of the symptoms of mental illness that I could discern, but was discriminated against by both fellow residents and staff because of the perseverative nature of his conversation: he reiterated, over and over again, any question that concerned him. He was also subject to repetitive routines and habits; attempts made to distract him from these resulted in disproportionate distress. His consultant was a specialist in learning disability who was unable to enlighten us as to how we could best manage him and improve his quality of life. I could not understand for the life of me why he had come under the care of a learning disability consultant, since, apart from his eccentricities and routines, Nigel seemed to have at least average intelligence.

By sheer chance, a visiting student psychiatric nurse who had read an article about Asperger's thought that Nigel's behaviour conformed to some of the criteria and we managed to get an appointment for him at the Bethlem Hospital where, after a residential assessment, he was diagnosed as suffering from Asperger's. He was thereafter placed in a residential home in London under the auspices of the National Autistic Society, where he flourished. His mother and I visited him on several occasions to attend reviews and to make sure that he was happy.

Another resident who was clearly not mentally ill was a youngster who had sustained a severe head injury in, I think, a road traffic accident. He also had a cheerful disposition despite his environment and the restrictions placed on his liberty by virtue of his disinhibited, reckless behaviour. It was impossible not to like the lad, whose occasional questions such as 'Are we still in England, Allison?' made us smile. After a series of case conferences, we managed to pave the way for him to be transferred to a brain injury rehabilitation unit.

At the other end of the spectrum, however, were people whose psychiatric disorders were so severe that I thought they should be either in hospital or in a specialist NHS unit. I can honestly state that one young man, in particular, was the most psychotic individual I had ever encountered – and certainly the most handsome. He had a beautiful face and the deepest blue eyes. Despite his illness, he was unfailingly polite and honourable. Every now and then, his psychosis flared up so dramatically that he had to be admitted to hospital. On one of these occasions, as he was escorted out of Albany Court to a waiting ambulance, he made his escorts turn back so that he could give me three cigarettes in return for some I had given him the day before.

Raymond believed that he lived in a different galaxy and moved in and out of different time zones. He was mostly unable to conduct a conversation with anyone, and spent most of his time in his gloomy little room. From time to time, his galactic masters would whip him into a frenzy of guilt over imaginary offences and convince him that he ought to destroy himself. These were the occasions when he was sectioned under the Mental Health Act and admitted to the local psychiatric hospital.

During his last admission to hospital, I visited him before attending a discharge case conference convened by the consultant in charge of Raymond's case, who considered him fit for discharge back to Albany Court. When I remarked that I had just found him more disturbed than I had ever seen him, the consultant said that 'He has been most cooperative with treatment; I can't hold him any longer'. I explained that Albany Court did not have the resources to supervise and care for a man so terribly ill, but was overruled. Raymond was duly returned to Albany Court and, within days, was found hanged in his room.

In addition to Albany Court, I was responsible for the management of a day centre for the mentally ill a few streets away in Bexhill. That, too, had been a moribund establishment with 'industrial therapy' the main activity undertaken. When the officer-in-charge retired shortly after my appointment as line manager, her place was taken by the thoroughly enlightened, lively and deeply caring deputy Margaret Moss. It is people like Margaret Moss who can make an otherwise wretched job bearable. She transformed the centre, created a programme of absorbing activities, and even arranged holidays for some of the centre members in Walberswick each summer.

The third service under my management was the Mental Health Accommodation Team, initially housed in an old people's home closed down by the department. As the name implies, the team's chief responsibility was to identify accommodation for people with mental health problems and to support them in maintaining themselves and enhancing their daily lives. Most of the flats the team acquired were in the private sector, and landlords were, on the whole, only too pleased to let their properties to people from whom the rents were likely to be regular and by whom the properties reasonably cared for.

Since I myself had moved out of my own flat and into my new lover's house in Hailsham, I offered this to the accommodation team in the belief that it was consistent with my principles, and that there was a sporting chance that the relevant accommodation team officer would oversee the care of the actual premises. This worked well with the first tenant, who happened to be an obsessional girl whose need for order exceeded even my own. When she subsequently moved in with a boyfriend elsewhere, I was asked to transfer the tenancy to another girl who would be no trouble at all. And she herself probably *was* no trouble. The difficulty arose when she let her drug-addicted boyfriend move in with her. Clearly dissatisfied with the décor of my property, he took to painting some of the walls a luminescent pink, and, to add insult to injury, sploshed the paint onto the ceiling and carpet. When I finally regained possession of the flat, I found that the carpets were saturated with vomit and urine as well as the pink paint.

Altruism has its limits, and mine had certainly been reached. All of the furniture and crockery had been destroyed, and I decided not to let the flat to anyone else with mental health difficulties. Not long after the tenant had moved out, she was found murdered, her assailant the man who had desecrated my flat. I admit to wishing, at the time, that the assailant had been the victim.

The closure of Albany Court was gradually achieved, the residents individually reviewed and dispersed to group homes or independent flats. One simply prayed that their new homes introduced them to a better quality of life than that they had known at Albany Court. Shortly before I assumed management responsibility for the place, it was reported to me by a shocked social work visitor to Albany Court that, while she was sitting in the staff office, a seasoned care officer had said, 'Well, we'd better go and feed the pigs.' Which says more than I ever could about the regime.

My office was based in a former bedroom of an old people's home which had been closed down, and which also housed the Mental Health Accommodation Team. A fault in the antiquated heating system meant that the home was overheated during the day, regardless of the temperature outside. If I had not kept my office windows permanently wide open, I would have expired. As a former bedroom, my room held a fitted wardrobe with a space between the top of the wardrobe and the ceiling. A family of white doves decided that this would be an ideal spot to raise their young, and proceeded to build nests in that cosy space. I had no objection to their doing so, and, as I repeatedly had to point out, precious little choice. The products of the doves' digestive systems – and stray twigs and feathers from their nests – inevitably accumulated on the carpeted floor, and I took to clearing them up each morning as I brewed my coffee. Needless to say, however, if I had been off duty or away from the office for some reason, the detritus had a tendency to accumulate further.

It was merely a matter of time before my line manager descended upon me for a supervision session before I had had time to clear up the doves' deposits, and I was advised that the situation was both disgusting and unacceptable. And I had to *do* something about it. Since I was, after all, in charge of an accommodation-finding team, I made various enquiries about re-homing these beautiful birds, with which I had developed a close bond. The first strategy was to move them to a pigeon loft in a pub – the very pub where I had been drinking just before I met Sophie – and I enlisted the aid of the local Royal Society for the Protection of Birds to capture them and convey them to their new, custom-built home in the country.

Within 24 hours, they were back. Life and its routines resumed as before, until the matter was again raised by my line manager as a health and safety issue. Since I was perfectly healthy – physically, at any rate – and the doves were clearly thriving, I was not convinced by the argument, but was forced to adopt a new strategy. I contacted

Mallydams, a bird sanctuary out at Fairlight, beyond Hastings, and they sent out officers with enormous nets to ensnare the birds and transport them there. I think they were somehow contained there, for I cannot recall their returning to my wardrobe nest. But I certainly missed them, with their elegance, their beauty and their soaring independence of spirit.

Meanwhile, on the domestic front, 'Hailsham Jean' and I did not have an entirely comfortable relationship. She had originally been married and had two adult sons who had already had to accommodate their mother's lesbianism, as she had had several female lovers before me. She was a petite, trim silver-haired soul with a strong interest in, and impressive knowledge of, the arts, literature and classical music. My own love of classical music somewhat overlapped hers, but I was outclassed on art and literature. By the time I moved in with her, I was so deeply immersed in my doctoral research that we probably had relatively little time in which to converse intelligently. I was still rising at 4.00 am to study and write before a full day's work, and by evening was inclined to relax with a drink. Jean enjoyed the occasional glass of wine at dinner parties, of which she held many, and I still smart at the recollection of her bitterly accusing me of 'wrecking dinner parties'.

Jean had a relaxed attitude to the running of her home, and found the odd sprinkling of dust here and there a perfectly normal phenomenon and of little importance in the scheme of things. I, on the other hand, maintained a study of immaculate order in her house, daily polishing the huge antique desk and dusting my huge library – every book individually. I could not otherwise have got on with my research. When my tidying, dusting and scrubbing extended one day to clearing out her kitchen, she acidly observed that I was doing it in order to satisfy my own neurotic needs and not to please her. She was right, but it did hurt.

Another source of dissonance concerned her ecological sensitivity, as a result of which she insisted on buying 'green' products for washing up, laundering and toilet cleaning. In those days, I did not believe that these expensive solutions were nearly as effective as my preferred solution of undiluted bleach for the toilet and Sainsbury's detergents for washing dishes and clothes.

We also diverged on the matters of physical exercise and sex. Whereas Jean regularly went on long walks at the weekend with a group of gay women, I stayed at home or visited friends. I did, however, support her in her 'hiking dykes' activities, and on one occasion went along to the Canadian Donut Company shop to buy a dozen luxuriously proportioned and flavoured doughnuts for the hikers' afternoon tea when they returned. I failed to stow them with sufficient care, and Jean's little whippet treated herself to the whole lot. I watched her anxiously for the remainder of the day, praying that she would not perish from bloating, but she seemed unaffected.

It is easier to confess to sloth than to the possession of a low libido, but honesty compels me to do the latter. The truth is that I do not find it easy to be touched at all, sexually or otherwise. In my old age, I have come to suspect that I have inherited some Asperger's features from my father. But early experiences of physical and sexual abuse were no doubt a contributory factor. Throughout my life, I have dreaded the moment when friends or relatives make moves to hug me. There was no real hugging in my immediate family: the best that Mother could manage was an occasional light pat on the back, while Father was rigidly aloof and stiffened when attempts were made to hug him. Jean revealed early in our relationship that she had a 'robust' sex drive, which naturally intensified my apprehension and awkwardness.

Really, we were doomed. There were too many differences between us, and, after a year or two and a couple of brief separations, we terminated the relationship and I moved back in with Judy. By this time, Bruno had died in a nursing home at the great age of 94, a testament to the triumph of self-indulgence over Department of Health guidance. I was therefore able to have a room of my own at last.

THIRTEEN

A fresh opportunity arose in 1994, when I was offered a secondment from social services to manage community mental health services in the Hastings and Rother NHS Trust. I expect the social services department were pleased to have some respite from me, and the period of my secondment was not specified. The trust comprised an in-patient unit and community services for people with mental health problems, or what we now term 'mental health issues'. I was responsible for the management of the psychiatric social workers, community psychiatric nurses, a day hospital and a case management team. This last service constituted an 'assertive outreach' service, in which the case managers had strictly limited caseloads of people who were chronically and severely mentally ill but who, with intensive support, might be kept out of hospital unless or until their behaviour became impossible to contain in the community.

I have little idea of how I was initially regarded by my new colleagues, but I suppose that I was at least partly accepted on the basis that I had trained as a psychiatric nurse, albeit 30 years before, and that I had undergone more advanced psychiatric training almost as long ago. On the whole, I think I went down well with people who had similarly sceptical views about overbearing management, and especially about the 'purchaser-provider' split introduced by the Thatcher government whereby health services were to be purchased or commissioned by health authorities and GPs from 'provider' service units, such as hospitals and community nursing services. This was the principle of 'internal markets', a principle which was intended, in practice, to create a climate of competition among service providers with the overt intention of forcing competing service providers to increase the quality of their 'product' but also to 'drive prices down'; that the two were incompatible aims was fairly obvious to the service providers. Thus the National Health Service ceased to be a unitary body with the common purpose of providing high-quality health care.

Neither my line manager nor his had any training or experience in psychiatric work, and this obviously created the potential for interface tensions for me as the manager of frontline service providers but implementer or 'enforcer' of increasingly dictatorial senior management directives. Needless to say, the senior management tiers were subjected to increasing pressure from the chief executive to 'deliver' the kind of service now demanded by the 'purchasers', namely the health authorities and the new GP fundholders. The chief executive himself was appointed on the basis of a time-limited contract, one which would be terminated if he did not perform to the satisfaction of the new holders of the purse-strings. Contractual relationships and obligations were inadequately articulated in the new culture – a seismic change in the NHS – and former partners in patient care inexorably became adversaries in the new health economy.

A new vocabulary of discourse evolved in the implementation of the 'internal market', wherein hitherto unacceptable policies and practices were introduced and enforced. Regular reorganisations of service structures designed to eliminate 'poor performers' were termed 'rationalisation' or 'restructuring' to give an impression of neutral efficiency. Annually ordered 'cost savings' were actually directives to cut services, the clear implication being that the previous year's services had been run inefficiently. 'Overoccupancy' – too many patients requiring beds in the in-patient unit – implied that patients were being unnecessarily referred for admission, or that their stays in hospital were too long; what the drive to decrease admissions and to shorten in-patients' stays actually meant was that people with acute episodes of illness were kept in the community, to the increasing distress and subsequent embarrassment of the 'clients', and the case managers were expected to manage ever more psychotic and behaviourally disturbed 'cases'. My 'career trajectory' – such as it was – was abruptly severed when I exposed a racket involving the employment of an underqualified agency locum psychiatrist to 'empty beds' in return for an inflated salary (see p.176).

In tandem with the drive to keep people out of hospital, the myth of the 'worried well' or the 'walking wounded' was propounded. These were individuals who did not qualify as sufficiently 'disturbed' for treatment, either in the community or in hospital. The criterion for 'disturbed' metamorphosed into the degree of disturbance *to the community* rather than the degree of distress to the patient, or the paralysis of their work, family or social life. In fact, the 'worried well' or 'walking wounded' were often far more subjectively *distressed* than those with psychotic disorders. They were people, for example, who might be suffering from extreme anxiety with panic attacks or obsessive-compulsive disorder, who would clearly have benefited from hospital treatment but were increasingly 'managed' in the community. They were left to limp along, partially paralysed by their inability to lead constructive, fulfilling lives.

Perhaps one of the most pernicious neo-concepts was the notion of 'risk management' – an oxymoron if ever there was one – which has persisted to the present day. This intrinsically illogical notion carries with it the presumption that accidents and other untoward events may be eliminated; that 'something' could have been or should be done to avoid undesirable events. The media, predictably, continue to have a field day on the more extreme examples of 'risk management' strategies requiring children to wear goggles when playing conkers, police community support officers to stand back and watch children drown because the officers have not had the necessary training in health and safety to protect themselves from danger, and so on. It is all very well to laugh at these instances of 'health and safety gone mad', but the 'risk management' obsession has had the effect of distorting criteria for hospital admission of people who are thought to be at risk of self-destruction. Fortunes have been spent on the compilation of predictive indicators of suicide, but there is only one accurate predictor of this, which is 'has the person committed suicide before?' The more philosophical question also arises: are there circumstances in which a person should be permitted – even assisted – in the termination of their own life?

The question has a particular resonance for me. A common argument against voluntary euthanasia is that people who have 'mental health issues' are *ipso facto* irrational and consequently unqualified to make the decision. A case which will remain in my mind forever concerns a patient I nursed at the Murray Royal Hospital. Mrs B was a former theatre sister, married with twin daughters, who developed what was then diagnosed as 'intractable' or 'refractory' schizophrenia. Mrs B was a tall, imposing figure who, when she was at her most 'disturbed',

162

possessed the strength then attributed to 'the insane'. When she was acutely ill she was prescribed a tranquilliser by injection, and a minimum of four nurses were instructed to hold her down while the drug was administered. And then along came a new drug – probably chlorpromazine, in the early sixties – and in a relatively short time Mrs B became steadily calmer and more 'rational' than she had been in 20 years of confinement in a mental hospital. Her marriage had long ago been terminated on the then legal basis of 'five or more years of continuous insanity', her husband had remarried and her daughters were grown and pursuing successful lives: Mrs B had had no contact with them from the time of her admission. After 20 years of Mental Health Act detention, Mrs B became an 'informal' patient while plans for her rehabilitation were formulated. So she was still a patient in a mental hospital when she took a walk up to the top of Kinnoull Hill, a short distance from the hospital, and threw herself off. She was found impaled on a fir tree at the bottom of the hill. I was transfixed by the shock of the event itself, by the form it took – and by the fact that I had been very fond of this woman who, in spite of her serious illness, had something noble and admirable about her. No one knew precisely why Mrs B, who was 'recovering so well', decided to take her life. But I surmised that, as she had regained what is called 'rationality', she had realised what she had lost through her lengthy illness – a professional career, a husband and children – and had decided that, in late middle age, her future looked too bleak to contemplate. I thought at the time that perhaps her decision was one to be honoured in retrospect, and I dearly hoped that there might be some form of restitution or compensation for her in an afterlife.

The notion that suicide is invariably 'wrong' and that not only is it to be prevented but, where it does occur – which it always will – someone must be held accountable is simply unintelligent. It is a philosophical – and practical – nonsense. But it is a striking example of how semantic manipulation and distortion can skew social policy to the detriment of 'clients', frontline professionals and conscientious managers alike. Indeed, the very term 'clients', applied as it is to people whose legal rights have been peremptorily removed, for example, is perhaps the most telling example of linguistic perversion imaginable, for what is a 'client', after all? The connotation of the word, in ordinary speech, is surely that the client is someone who voluntarily engages the services of a professional, such as a lawyer or an accountant. There is nothing voluntary about a person who is compulsorily detained under a Mental Health Act or whose children have been taken into care against the wishes of the parents or whose affairs are in the hands of the Court of Protection.

The distortion of the English language is not merely an aesthetic offence. It can and does lead to the inversion of policy imperatives and dressing them in moral overcoats. Thus it is implied that it is *morally wrong* to expose 'clients' to elements of risk or to permit them to expose themselves to such elements. In the seventies, when I was working in health and social services, there was a 'quality of life' argument for risk-taking to certain levels: 'patients' or 'residents' could not expect to have a richly textured life experience if they were 'wrapped up in cotton wool'. Hospital wards and residential homes installed little kitchens where people could boil kettles to make themselves hot drinks between meals or during sleepless nights. Present-day managers would faint at the very thought.

Most of the CPNs with whom I had the privilege to work were highly committed professional people who attempted to provide the best possible service to the people on their caseload. One of these was a French specialist in family therapy who had immense experience and expertise as well as considerable intelligence and a mordant sense of humour. Posted above his desk was a cartoon whose caption read 'Brief Therapy' and whose illustration showed a therapist striking his client sharply across the face. But I shall remember particularly his observation that 'Life is inevitably risky – and invariably fatal'. There is more wisdom in his witticism than in most social policy initiatives in the eighties and nineties. The wit's name was Jean-Pierre Parmainteny, and it was an incident involving him that exacerbated my frustration and downright outrage at the way consummate professionals were being marginalised or 'disrespected'. I was showing my line manager round the community mental health centre, when we came to the newly refurbished family therapy suite over which Jean-Pierre presided. When my manager asked him what he thought of the new suite, Jean-Pierre politely pointed out a few defects, such as the wrongly angled cameras and inadequate space for observers behind the one-way screen. No sooner had we left the suite than my manager remarked on the 'negative', 'whingeing' attitude of my colleague.

Another of the many illustrations of managerialism trumping professionalism concerned the imposition of a new form to be completed by psychiatrists at every out-patient clinic encounter. The items on the form concerned administrative data which the organisation required for completing aggregate returns on information which had no bearing on the patient's treatment. The psychiatrist who later became my partner – and still is – noted the average time taken to complete the forms at every patient appointment, and found that this amounted to nine minutes. She then requested of the departmental manager that the out-patient appointments be extended to compensate for the loss of therapeutic time, and this was firmly refused.

Life as a manager of community mental health services was by no means one of unrelieved gloom, however. I especially enjoyed the weekly CPN meetings, where part of the agenda consisted of my reading out the latest managerial instructions to about 20 intensively trained and experienced nurses. So many of these directives were risible in their essence and unimplementable in practice that they were met with successive rounds of laughter. I have to confess that the manner in which I read out the edicts probably lit the fuse of fun, but I was expressing my own frustration by allowing my colleagues to vent theirs. I was reassured by some of the CPNs that being able to 'take the piss' out of the latest obstacles to professional discretion and good practice enabled them to discharge their distress and get on with their jobs.

I was deeply impressed, also, by the enthusiasm and commitment of the Case Management Service, whose members I supervised directly. Because their 'cases' were typically 'psychotic' to a very marked degree, the case managers were expected to form as close and supportive a relationship as humanly possible with them. It was anticipated that, once a bond of trust and mutual respect and understanding had been carefully established, the case manager would be in an ideal position to negotiate agreements about the behavioural and cognitive changes that would bring about the best outcome for their people, and minimise the likelihood of involuntary hospital admission. By 'cognitive' changes, I mean alterations in the way people think about things: the familiar 'half full or half empty' whisky bottle being a paradigm case of diverging perspectives on life in general.

In some respects, the case managers had the most interesting jobs of all. Experienced psychiatric professionals often profess a particular fondness for working with 'psychotic' individuals; there is a really wonderful moment when, by dint of sheer skill in human relationships, patience and persistence, the worker 'gets through' to the person whose camouflage of hallucinations or delusions can be impenetrable to professionals who have little natural contact with them.

One admirable case manager, Hazel Brooks, stands out in my memory for her powerful commitment to her 'cases', and her colourful, adventurous and idiosyncratic lifestyle. Supervision of Hazel often consisted of her recounting true stories about her people. Some I still remember after all these years, and enjoy telling others. I think my favourite tale concerns Hazel's home visit to a woman with 'severe and enduring mental illness' who was being maintained in the community largely as a result of Hazel's affection for and dedicated support of her. In the course of one visit in particular, Hazel noticed that the woman's washing machine was in operation, and that, amidst the suds, what appeared to be a solitary tomato was rotating vigorously round the drum. When Hazel tactfully enquired whether this was, indeed, a tomato, the woman confirmed that it was, and added: 'You're supposed to wash fruit before you eat it, right?'

On another occasion, Hazel escorted a woman to the local post office to collect her new welfare benefit book and to cash the first payment. The cashier searched in vain for the book, explained that it did not appear to have arrived and acknowledged that this was in fact the due date. Whereupon the aggrieved woman erupted in a frenzy of rage, tearing down notices, knocking display stands sideways and, in the process, pushing other customers aside. Hazel managed to manoeuvre the lady out of the post office, where, sweating and breathless, she said to Hazel, 'It's just as well I didn't lose my temper in there, isn't it?'

Yet another of Hazel's adventures in case management began with an urgent call from one of our consultant psychiatrists' secretary's office in which Hazel's immediate attendance was demanded, as one of her 'cases' had pinned the rather diminutive consultant against the wall of his office. Hazel, herself a tall woman, strong in physique and personality, strode into the unfortunate consultant's office and sternly instructed the patient to 'Put the doctor *down*, dear' – which, of course, she did.

The Case Management Service was eventually disbanded, after I had left the service, undoubtedly on cost grounds. The idea of 'limited caseloads' had apparently become a luxury which the trust could no longer afford. Prior to its demise, the case managers had been forced to take on more and more cases, with the result that there were more frequent admissions to hospital and more complaints from the community of dangerous lunatics running about the streets. And this, in turn, justified the termination of the service.

The written case records of community psychiatric nurses were now considered inadequate reflections of their work, and an electronic recording system was imposed which required the CPNs to 'input', *inter alia*, the time they had spent with each patient, the purpose of each visit and the overall 'care plan'. Of course there was some merit in requiring the nurses to account for their time and practice, and of course there were – as there are in any organisation – workers who enjoyed prolonged contact with patients they liked or lengthy coffee breaks between client visits. But electronic recording systems – introduced at colossal expense in terms both of hardware and training – could be manipulated as easily as written case records by intelligent operators. I have no idea what the cost of designing, piloting, hardware and training actually was, but I do know that it carried a high cost in terms of resentment amongst the nurses and, most importantly, increasing alienation of the professionals who felt – rightly – that their professional integrity was being challenged. Many felt that it took longer to input the data than to make case notes.

The Day Hospital was run for years by a highly competent, committed psychiatric nursing sister, Elisabeth Gimblett, another French import. She was assisted by Cheryle Sifontes, and the programme for patients was full, rich – and effective. At one point, shortly after I had retired from the NHS, the closure of the Day Hospital was proposed. The proposers involved made the mistake of widely consulting the service users and providers, with the predictable result that the Day Hospital was saved. I never understood the rationale – other than sheer desperation – which underlay the proposal: after all, the day service was saving the very high costs of actual hospitalisation.

My impression of the in-patient unit – which, mercifully, I did not manage – was that it was downright inadequate, and I made the mistake of saying so in meetings with senior management and, at least once, in the presence of the chief executive. The charge nurses who ran the two wards were suspected of having an intimate relationship, although both were married. I had occasion to visit the unit from time to time, either to attend meetings or to see individual patients where particular problems had arisen with community-hospital liaison. The atmosphere on both wards was oddly dull and tense. When I mentioned my concerns to my line manager, who was responsible for the unit, he told me firmly that the unit was in 'safe pairs of hands'. The charge nurses were, much later, suspended and dismissed.

Criticising medical staff is a high-risk activity, and one is necessarily circumspect in this delicate territory. By not naming the consultants or staff grade doctors, and by mentioning characteristics of their practice randomly, I hope I can convey the poverty of clinical practice. One of the psychiatrists clearly suffered from Asperger's, although this was not recognised at the time. Actually, it was not he but his patients and colleagues who suffered from his Asperger's. Patients and colleagues suffered from his rudeness and inconsistency, his inability to understand and adhere to mutually agreed care plans. He was incapable of reading social cues or empathising with people, interpersonal skills which are absolutely essential in mental health work. When I was subsequently demoted to become a member of one of the four services I had previously managed, I took a deeply depressed 'client' in to see him. She was so miserable that tears streamed down her face, and she was barely able to speak, so I tried to explain to him the source of her unhappiness. He sat back in his chair, extended his legs forward, crossed at the ankles, and clasped his hands behind his head. Closing his eyes, and with a beaming smile, he said, 'Let us celebrate bliss…'

Another of my clients, who had been in and out of hospital − chiefly in − had become a patient of his in my time. She had 14 volumes of case files − a 'record' surpassing those of the old days of lengthy institutionalisation. A brother of hers had murdered their maternal grandfather in gruesome circumstances in a drug-induced, psychotic state. My client was so traumatised that she developed various psychological symptoms, some mimicking psychotic features: extreme stress can cause such symptoms. Instead of being referred to a sensible psychologist for work with her trauma, she was admitted to hospital and, in the course of many years, was labelled with an impressive array of diagnoses as a succession of psychiatrists 'treated' her. There was no evidence that I can recall of 'pre-morbid symptoms'; that is, she had appeared to be a perfectly normal young married woman with a tiny son.

When the pressure on in-patient beds became overwhelming, she was discharged into the care of the Case Management Service; I became her case manager. Initially,

170

she and I would sit on the steps behind the community mental health centre, smoking. For many of these first meetings, that was all we did – smoke together. Sharon was virtually mute, and, from time to time, I made observations that I rather desperately hoped might somehow comfort her or pave the way to some common understanding of what she had been through. We eventually managed to establish contact, and then slowly constructed a plan for the immediate future. She had been allowed little contact with her young son, so we negotiated exhaustively – and sometimes exhaustingly – with the people responsible for the boy's care, including the boy's father, who cared for him most of the time. We were allowed to take the boy out with us for gradually increasing periods. We went to funfairs and putting greens and even managed a day trip to France. I had left the headlights on in my car at Dover and, on our return from rather a marvellous day in Calais, the battery was dead. I swore, and Sharon laughed – the first laugh from her I had ever seen.

Anyway, I bravely arranged a meeting with the Asperger's psychiatrist and, as tactfully as possible, suggested that, at least for a time, she disengage from him as, it seemed to me, Sharon was making more progress outside formal psychiatry. I suggested that the involvement of the formal psychiatric service had done her more harm than good, was in fact exacerbating whatever it was she was suffering from. To my astonishment, he replied, 'I couldn't agree more,' and we established a care plan agreement whereby Sharon would gradually be re-introduced to 'normal' life and receive psychotherapy from a psychologist, focusing on the original trauma.

Sharon later remarried her husband, resettled at home with him and their son, and went on to have another baby. I have maintained contact with her ever since, and, as far as I know, she is surviving the ordinary ups and downs of life. If

171

only she had been referred to a mental health professional who could practise reflectively, look at the history involved and fathom how this young woman might have been feeling from the time of the murder of her grandfather. From my own experience with Father, I knew only too well how men in powerful positions but completely lacking common sense or sensitivity could run roughshod over lesser mortals, oblivious to the effects of life's wounds and sorrows – and to the effects of their own lack of human understanding.

Another psychiatrist spent much of his time conforming his practice to the principle of whether he could be 'criticised', in paradoxical consequence of which he was, of course, regularly criticised. This was the man who was pinned against the wall of his own consulting room by Hazel Brooks' client. I happened to be present when he was interviewing a new patient who suffered from severe bulimia and a chronic alcohol problem. In the course of the meeting, he asked the patient the usual questions involved, but in a manner which could hardly have elicited the correct answers. For example, he asked the routine question about alcohol intake, framing the enquiry as 'Do you drink alcohol?' and, when she answered in the affirmative, went on to say, 'Moderate, yes?' Before she had time to reply, he had ticked the 'moderate' box on the assessment form. I remember that her eyeballs were yellow, a pretty sure sign of liver damage.

I was present when yet another psychiatrist asked the patient, 'Have you been having any paranoid ideas?' A paranoid idea is, of course, one which the patient does not recognise as irrational or delusional: he does not know he is paranoid. This kind of encounter between patient and doctor led to my conviction that many of the senior community psychiatric nurses could run the out-patient clinics far more effectively than some of the psychiatrists. The only possible practical difficulty would consist in the prescription of

172

medicines, which I thought could be solved by having the doctors discuss and agree the appropriate drug regime over a few minutes at the end of the session. This is routine practice in the training of GPs. I made the suggestion on several occasions, but was invariably met with astonished stares and blank incomprehension. I remain convinced that the idea should have been piloted. Doubtless it would have been regarded as a dangerous encroachment upon medical territory: after all, psychiatrists earned much more than other professionals – a matter of some resentment among highly qualified clinical psychologists, many of whom were obviously brighter and intensively trained in psychotherapy, which most psychiatrists are not. I expect that the introduction of the highly controversial European Working Hours Directive, which restricts the total weekly hours junior doctors may be required to work to 48, and the gradual extension of nurse prescribing will attenuate the force of the argument sustaining the case for the marked salary distinctions between doctors and the allied professionals.

I am no racist, and indeed marched against the National Front in 1977 in London, and saw NF members spit at black passers-by. Along with millions of others, I was sickened by the apartheid system in South Africa. I believe that the more interracial marriage increases, the greater the potential for peaceful relations between nations and races. What continues to perplex me has nothing whatever to do with skin colour but concerns *linguistic* and *cultural* differences. Communication between patients and their doctors is especially critical in psychiatric practice, where the words the patients use and the culture from which they come are essential to understanding their situation. I have seen and heard so much evidence of misunderstanding of language and social mores which potentially or actually affected accurate assessment and treatment.

A new patient was presented to a doctor whose use of English was appalling. An early question in the interview consisted of the doctor enquiring about the patient's painting. The patient, puzzled, explained that she did not paint at all. Whereupon it was the doctor's turn to look puzzled, and he said, 'But letter from doctor says you painting.' It turned out that he meant 'fainting'. I took a Case Management patient to see him for an out-patient appointment. She had been prescribed a new antipsychotic drug at a previous appointment, and was extremely distressed that she had put on several stones in weight since starting the medicine. The normal response would have been to acknowledge her distress, explain that this was a recognised side effect of that particular medicine, and explain that the benefit of the new drug was intended to be the reduction of distressing symptoms and the severe side effects associated with the more traditional antipsychotics. This is basically a question of cost-benefit analysis, a discussion which crucially involves the patient. Instead of which, his succinct response was: 'You must exercising more.'

The appointment of a new general manager of the trust's mental health services promised to introduce a fresh appraisal of the prevailing professional and cultural standards within the trust. He had trained as a midwife, was very bright and well-informed about management theory and practice and, in his previous post, had sometimes popped into my tiny office for a fag and a cup of tea. I rather liked him, and I believed that we had a common perception of the politics of central government and our local management system. He was a rotund figure, with a boyish, smiley face, and, although he was incontrovertibly male, I felt relatively safe in his company. As far as I knew, he was happily married and apparently not homophobic.

Every barrel contains the proverbial rotten apple; my preferred expression is 'there's one in every group'. The 'one' CPN who was troublesome was a married chap who was notoriously flirtatious with especially naïve young student nurses on placement with us. More worryingly, he was reported to have made suggestive remarks to some of his younger female patients. I considered the complaints against him, and judged his conduct to be inappropriate and unprofessional. When my former fag-sharing colleague had just been appointed general manager of the mental health services, I mentioned to him that I believed I had enough evidence to 'nail the bastard', expecting him to understand and approve. I assumed that he, along with everyone else, would be pleased at the news.

To my dismay, I was summoned to the chief nurse's office, where I was castigated for the deeply unprofessional remark I had made to my erstwhile friend and fellow smoker. This was a significant disappointment – but not nearly as disappointing as the subsequent dismissal of my complaint against the CPN. Chickens do come home to roost eventually, and the man was dismissed after police investigations proved him to be the stalker of a woman who worked near the CPN's home. His stalking was carefully planned, as he always borrowed a friend's car in which to await the passing of his victim so that his identity could not be traced.

So it can readily be seen that I was at best a 'loose cannon' in the organisation, an expression which was applied to me by one of my social work admirers, and at worst a potential or actual saboteur. One of the managers I unintentionally but occasionally exasperated when I was in social services, Graham Shuttleworth, told me that I was 'attractive, exhilarating – and dangerous'. It was the best reference I have ever had, but was not intended as such at the time. I still strongly regret having upset poor Graham, as he was one of those essentially decent people whose management style clearly reflected his genuine commitment to high-quality services, but did not fit with the increasingly 'macho' management culture.

The scene was set for my extrusion when a new locum arrived at the in-patient unit. At the time of his appointment, the unit was bursting at the seams. 'Overoccupancy' was at its height, and intense pressure applied to the clinicians to shorten patient stays or prevent admission altogether. Very shortly after the appointment of the locum, who ran his own agency and was consequently able to charge agency fees as well as his locum salary, it was observed that the overoccupancy problem was resolving quite dramatically. The locum started attending the team meetings of the community services, and took to instructing my CPN colleagues, in particular, to take on cases which clearly required in-patient care or where the psychiatric services were obviously inappropriate. He did not discuss; he did not request – he gave orders.

Unsurprisingly, the CPNs so instructed were outraged, never having been treated in this manner before. These community meetings became ever more confrontational, and I tried repeatedly to mediate without success. I attempted to explain to the locum how the system worked and to point out that, if the CPNs were to take on all the cases he insisted they take, they would be grossly overloaded, and patients who really needed their time and attention would deteriorate. Things went from bad to worse and, on a particularly awful day when he had been abominably rude to one of the medical secretaries, I requested a meeting with my line manager, with whom I thought I was on reasonably good terms. I had mentioned the locum's behaviour before, but now felt that some formal action was required.

176

But when I arrived at my manager's office, I was astonished to find that not only was the general manager present – but also that the locum about whom I needed to complain was present. I had had no notice of this, and was momentarily nonplussed. I nevertheless recovered sufficiently to refer to my list of concerns about the man, giving instance after instance of inappropriate practice and insulting behaviour to mental health colleagues in the Community Mental Health Teams. I was not responsible for the management of the in-patient services: all I knew was that the occupancy levels were declining wondrously.

To my utter amazement, both my line manager and the general manager repeatedly *apologised* to the locum for my complaints, and expressed the hope that he would be generous enough to forget them. At the conclusion of this surreal encounter, the general manager stood up, pointed his podgy finger a few inches from my nose, and loudly announced, 'Doctor X is staying with us until at least the end of March, and you had better get used to it!' The end of the financial year was many months away.

It turned out that the locum about whom I had complained, and whose professional judgement many of my colleagues had questioned, had been offered an unprecedentedly high bounty in return for 'solving' the in-patient overoccupancy problem. The deal was confidential, clandestine – even the medical director was unaware of it, and subsequently erupted when it was disclosed. It also emerged that the locum was not even a member of the Royal College of Psychiatrists…

I was shocked and, for the first time, really certain that the game was over and that I would soon be metaphorically terminated. This proved to be the case when my collateral managers and I were called to a meeting at which it was announced that a 'restructuring' of services would require the elimination of one post – mine. In compensation, I was to have a protected salary and continued employment – as a case manager. One of my case manager colleagues had the decency to come over to my flat in Bexhill and tell me that he had overheard a conversation with senior managers in which it was clear that I was to be 'taken out'.

Despite the embarrassment of being demoted, in some respects I quite liked the case management role, and was glad of the respite from the strain of management. The most rewarding case was that of Sharon, whom I mentioned earlier. Most of my 'cases' were males with longstanding psychotic disorders, whose illnesses – it was hard to describe them as 'issues' – took a hectic, unpredictable course regardless of medication 'compliance'. One was an exceptionally handsome former policeman whose schizophrenia had ruined his young life, who had 'got religion', and who, beneath his unending struggle with evil, was a thoroughly sweet man. On occasions, when I was due to visit him in his tiny basement flat, he was playing religious music so loudly that he could not hear my ringing and banging on his front door. His one pleasure in life was to treat himself to a generous English 'fry-up' in a café on the sea front. Which may – or may not – have contributed to his sudden death at the age of 35.

Another was an engaging young man, formerly a gifted photographer, whom I met sometimes in the Pig in Paradise, a popular seafront pub with a reputation for high-quality doorstep sandwiches. There he rolled up straggly cigarettes with a trembling hand and sank a couple of pints of Guinness as we – or, rather, he – talked. It did not occur to me to lecture him on the inadvisability of drinking alcohol on top of industrial-strength antipsychotic drugs, and anyway it didn't seem to make much difference to his mental state. He talked non-stop, invariably smiling, and, on one occasion, asked me if I wanted to know the winning numbers of the forthcoming lottery. I indicated that I was keen to do so, noted the numbers and relayed them to my colleagues back at the office. When they turned out to be quite wrong, I challenged him as to the source of his erroneous intelligence. 'The fridge,' he replied.

Most of my 'clients' were men, and not all were as endearing as those I have described. I was inevitably uncomfortable about visiting some people in their own flats or bedsits when they were seriously, sometimes aggressively, disturbed. The coalescence of several strands of social and economic policy during the eighties and nineties, especially the resulting community care legislation, led to the closure of the large mental hospitals and the relocation of long-term patients into low-grade accommodation in the supposedly 'caring' community. In my previous management role, I regularly dealt with angry letters from members of the 'caring' community about the behaviour of our people. So here they were, isolated in fuggy rooms, trying to figure out how to maintain their tobacco supplies and get enough food while on 'welfare' benefits. It seemed to me that their quality of life was often close to zero.

Eventually, I grew tired and angry about the poverty of the system, the inadequacy of my contribution to the happiness of my clients. I decided to retire. But not before my personal life had undergone a transformation which altered the course of my life permanently.

(The general manager with the pudgy finger moved to a new post in the southwest of England, where he was subsequently convicted of downloading child pornography, was struck off and compounded the felony by attempting to blame his own son.)

FOURTEEN

Prior to my demotion, and in my role as manager of community mental health services, my frustration with the resource level and quality of the adult psychiatric service had led me to approach the medical director to plead for more psychiatrists. I had heard of, but not met, a psychiatrist in the psychogeriatric service who was highly regarded by patients and colleagues alike. Heaven knows where I got the courage, but I arranged to meet Dr Gillian Smith in her office in the psychogeriatric unit. It was common knowledge throughout the mental health services that she was the most competent and approachable psychiatrist in the entire department. I had not expected her to be quite so tall, nor to be quite so friendly: she was both. In retrospect, I remain surprised by my courage in approaching her – but my despair at the poverty of psychiatric practice in the adult service undoubtedly played a part.

When I explained the purpose of my visit, she expressed some enthusiasm. It turned out that she had just had a bit of a tiff with her boss, the medical director, about her on-call commitments: he had evidently wanted her to undertake duties beyond those to which she was contractually bound. I, of course, was not aware of this, and was pleasantly surprised when she showed immediate interest in joining us on the adult side. And so I was equally surprised, when I asked the medical director if he would agree to second Dr Smith to the adult service, that he seemed pleased to do so – he who had once refused to 'throw good money after bad' by augmenting the current group of adult psychiatrists.

Unlike most of her psychiatric colleagues, Dr Smith preferred to be known to both patients and colleagues by her first name. Before the formal secondment began, Gill took to popping into my office for informal chats and, initially, I felt mildly uncomfortable about these *ad hoc* encounters. I suppose this was because I am innately shy. On one occasion, when I glimpsed her coming along the corridor toward my office, I hid in my secretary's office until, on finding my office unoccupied, she went away. I soon discovered that no one was more egalitarian than Gill Smith.

From a strictly professional point of view, achieving Gill's transfer to the adult service was the best – perhaps the only – achievement of my own secondment to the NHS from social services. It did not, of course, mitigate the effects of the poor quality of service supplied by the other psychiatrists, but it certainly raised the spirits of many colleagues – and Gill's caseload of patients.

Gill continued to pop into my office for the odd moments she was free. She did not seem to mind the fug of smoke from my More cigarettes, nor the swarms of flies which buzzed around my office window, hovering over the waste skips immediately below. Gradually, I began to feel at ease in her company.

By this time, Jean and I had separated, and I was single again, living back at Judy's house in Bexhill. Her father had died, and I was therefore able to have a room of my own. Gill gradually revealed the difficulties she was having with her husband, another doctor. If things did not go exactly as he wished or planned, he might not speak to Gill for days on end. A ridiculous – but typical – example of this consisted of her being accused of piling newspapers against the freezer in such a way that the lid did not close properly. She occasionally invited me round to her house for coffee, and told me about the 'all picture, no sound' episodes – and how she was contemplating separation, becoming 'a single mother'.

Her overriding concern was that there were three young children of the marriage, boys aged twelve, ten and six. They were strikingly beautiful boys, and I gradually got to know them as Gill and I became friends as well as colleagues, and we went for walks in the park and on the seafront with them. I also got to know the next-door neighbour, Sarah, with whom Gill and her family were on such close terms that they constituted a miniature community. And it was through an unlikely link between Sarah and my old friend Judy that The Scandal began – paradoxically, before there was any factual foundation for it. Judy happened to be seeing a Christian counsellor who was married to a former professional partner of Gill's husband. Judy was confiding in the counsellor how worried she was that I was getting close to Gill, a wife and mother of young children. I had told Judy about my feelings for Gill, never for a moment suspecting that she might disclose any of this to anyone. Given the golden rule of counselling, namely confidentiality, we were astonished – and deeply shocked – when the counsellor breached that rule and warned Sarah, who promptly warned Gill's husband.

Gill came to work one morning, asking to see me as soon as possible. She explained that Judy's counsellor had conveyed her anxiety to Sarah, who had immediately relayed it to Gill's husband. Whereupon he had enquired of Gill, 'Are you a lesbian?' At the time, I think he regarded the counsellor's warning as more amusing than foreboding.

In any case, neither Gill nor I had given each other the slightest indication that we had other than companionable sentiments for each other. Nevertheless, Gill was clearly perturbed as she told me about it.

Not for the first time in my life, I was torn apart by deeply conflicting feelings. My love for Gill grew more intense as each day passed. Simultaneously, like a repetitive auditory hallucination, the biblical warning 'Better that a millstone be hung about his neck than that he hurt one of these, my children...' resounded in my head. Part of me felt that, if ever my love for Gill were reciprocated, I would be party to one of the greatest sins of all. Wrecking a marriage was iniquitous enough, but behaving in a way likely to traumatise children was infinitely worse.

Gill's marriage continued to deteriorate. Matters came to a head most dramatically when her husband was in the process of opening a new office. The interior walls had been painted, and her husband asked their eldest son to come down to the surgery to help with putting office furniture in place. The unfortunate boy, invariably amiable and cooperative, inadvertently left a fingerprint on a newly painted wall. His father evidently lost his temper, dragged the poor boy home, instructed the rest of the family not to speak to him and ordered him straight to bed. Not content with all that, he continued to harangue the poor boy as he lay there, cowering in fear. Gill became aware of the shouting, rose from her bed and, for perhaps the first time in their marital life, screamed at her husband to stop – and ordered *him* to bed. Somewhat to her surprise, her purple-faced husband did as instructed and left the room.

A turning point had been reached. Never, in 19 years of marriage, had Gill confronted her husband so directly and so forcefully. She had come from a peaceful home and had gone on to medical school, where she met her future husband, a fellow student. She found him sparky and amusing, and they were part of a group of students who socialised and made merry between studies. On one convivial occasion in a Belfast pub, a fellow student temporarily persuaded her that, in the antipodes, blood circulated in the opposite direction from that in the north. She subsequently denied this, insisting instead that she was briefly convinced that water circulated in the opposite direction when draining from a basin. I prefer the former account, whatever she may now say.

It would seem that Gill and her husband were good mates in the highly pressured setting of medical school, and that she admired his lively involvement in junior medical politics. There was no sign of his later short temper and belligerence, which did not really emerge until after the children were born. I gather that Gill did not 'fall in love' with him as such and, indeed, did not actually experience 'the real thing' until several years later when she had an affair with a male nurse. Her husband was Gill's first 'real' boyfriend and, perhaps because they had been fellow students and friends for several years, it was almost taken for granted that they would marry. Which they duly did, in a church on the notorious Shankill Road in Belfast. It subsequently emerged that at least Gill's mother had reservations about the union, but kept them to herself at the time.

Gill regards herself as having been a naïve, trusting and peaceable soul at the time of the marriage and during its early years. She had been brought up in a stable, loving home, and had no reason to suspect that her own, new family life might be any different. At first, as the children were born, her husband seemed to be a loving father and shared in the domestic tasks of the home. He and Gill were working as busy junior hospital doctors, and there was little time for the luxury of reflection on how the marriage was developing. One of the first signs that her new husband

184

might not be the mature adult she had assumed came about when he asked his wife to buy some envelopes for him. Gill complied, but bought the 'wrong' ones, thus precipitating an explosion, an early warning of how her husband might react if things did not go exactly as he wished.

In those early years, however, Gill assimilated these unpredictable outbursts and perhaps attributed them to the stresses of the work, raising children and the structure of his temperament. Whereas her husband was given to cyclonic rages in the face of adverse events, Gill was the peaceable buffer. And this was a feature throughout the marriage. When her husband went ballistic from time to time at his surgery, Gill tipped off some of his colleagues to stand clear of the locus of the storm. Blessed are the peacemakers.

This pattern simply continued up to the time she and I became friends. But a crescendo had clearly been reached by this time. The fact is that we were strictly platonic companions when Gill was contemplating ending the marriage. On our days off, we had coffee together in her garden, or went for walks with the boys in the nearby park. Her husband's tantrums, alternating with periods of mutism, had become intolerable. And I was falling ever more deeply in love with his wife.

My feelings, too, were reaching a crescendo, and, when Gill next proposed a walk in the park, I telephoned her to say, 'I really don't think that's a good idea, as I've grown inordinately fond of you.' No doubt fortified by a Pils lager or two, I waited for her reply – which came after what seemed an eternity. 'I feel very much the same way,' she said.

And so began a chapter of intense joy, pain, anxiety, guilt and a field day for the lawyers. Gill explained to her husband that the marriage had 'run its course', and that the paramount concern was the care of the children. Whereas I had a one-bedroom flat in Bexhill, the marital home in

Hastings was a five-bedroom mansion with two sitting rooms. On the face of it, the coldly logical step would have been for Gill and her husband to reach a settlement whereby they realised the value of the marital home and each would purchase a separate property so that the children would live with Gill and me, their father in his own property nearby, with easy, informal visiting arrangements.

Such an arrangement is a template for many separating couples, but it certainly did not – or could not – apply to our situation. Her husband told Gill that his new office had involved the remortgaging of the marital home and that, if any attempt were made to sell it, he and his partner would immediately become bankrupt. Gill believed him, and we sought to make the best of an excruciatingly painful situation by arranging for Gill to come and live with me in my one-bedroom flat and for her to have reasonable access to the children. An informal agreement was reached whereby Gill would have the children for one evening a week and for every third weekend. This agreement predictably proved to be a disaster – and inevitably caused the children distress. Gill asked for more time with the children, but her husband refused to vary the contact arrangements.

Simply because of Gill's request, her husband refused to let her see the children on the following week night and withdrew his consent to allow the children to have a week's pre-booked agreed holiday with Gill and me the following week. An emergency hearing was held, at which the judge described the husband's response to Gill's request as 'a gross over-reaction' and ordered that Gill have contact with her children on two evenings a week and every alternate weekend – and that the holiday should proceed as originally agreed. The boys' father subsequently put it about that we had managed, at the eleventh hour, to arrange for a lesbian judge to hear the case – a feat which, had it been true, would have indicated a miraculous power on our part. Gill's poor husband was required, unusually, to pay three quarters of the costs of the case. For him, the only consolation was that I had my handbag stolen as I sat outside the courtroom.

And so the little holiday went ahead. We had hired a caravan on a site at Mousehole, in Cornwall. Despite the horrors the boys had been forced to endure for the previous awful weeks, we managed, the three boys, their mother and I, to have some fun and relaxation. The boys probably regarded the highlight of the holiday as the moment when a seagull snatched a Cornish pasty from Gill's hand as we strolled round the harbour.

However terminal the marriage had become long before Gill and I began our relationship, the fact is that we both felt intensely guilty about the entire mess. For there was no escaping the stark fact that a man had lost his wife and part of the lives of his children. Throughout their 19 years of marriage, I gathered that Gill had been much more than a conventional wife. Her equable temperament and instinct for peace-making had helped to buffer her husband's regular tantrums from his colleagues and his children. It was she who warned his professional partner and the practice manager when he was 'on the warpath', she who spent her own holiday time doing locum work because he had failed to pay his income tax and she who attempted to mollify him when he perceived the world as operating against him.

The extent of his shock and loss must have constituted the worst kind of bereavement, and he attempted to find respite in alcohol – to which he had long been devoted – and having his poor solicitor fire off vituperative letters to Gill and to her solicitors. Two box files of the legal and personal exchanges reside in a loft cupboard in our house, should the boys ever want to consult them.

Fate suddenly intervened, and from a surprising quarter, to alleviate the situation for the children. Although I was technically on secondment from social services to the NHS, the social services department had one of its regular 'restructurings', 'rationalisations' or whatever it was called that year, and my layer of management was stripped out, leaving me with the alternatives of demotion or redundancy. I eagerly chose the latter, having at least the temporary security of a job within the NHS, and received a lump sum which enabled me to buy the long-empty flat adjacent to my own, which had the added advantage of two bedrooms instead of our one. This meant that, when the boys were with us for the evening and alternate weekends, they had their very own accommodation.

The boys' father immediately reported the circumstances to social services, claiming that the children were 'unsupervised by an adult'. In fact, the boys' front door was approximately six feet from ours, and we kept our front door unlocked and had installed baby alarms so that the boys could either come straight into our flat or talk to us from their rooms. Social services wrote to us, asking about the arrangements, and wrote back to say that they were perfectly satisfied with the set-up.

However, soon after we had acquired the second flat, the middle boy, John, telephoned his mother and asked if he and his younger brother could come and live with us. In the course of one of their father's tantrums, all the boys' toys had been thrown into a series of black bin liners with the threat that they would be disposed of; I believe that the episode had been precipitated by one of the boys' request for some new pencils for school. Gill sought to avoid the accusation of enticement and arranged, through her lawyers, that there be an acknowledgement that this was the boys' spontaneous wish. And so the two boys came to live with us, carrying their personal effects in bin bags – and a cage containing two gerbils. The eldest boy, Nick, remained with his father, but joined us on the one evening a week and on alternate weekends – until his father encouraged him to join the ATC (Air Training Corps) on the 'contact' evening, so that we had a quick KFC on the pavement before dropping Nick off at the ATC. As Gill was – and continues to be – a passionate pacifist, Nick's enlistment in the ATC was disappointing, but we suspected that it was simply another sign of his father's distress and fury.

Meanwhile, back at the workplace, if all hell broke loose, we were unaware of it. There was no concealing the development of our relationship, as Gill's husband decided to have the writ for divorce personally served on Gill at her place of work, in full view of the receptionist, half the secretarial staff and any passers-by. No one confronted either of us about the matter, and, in any case, Gill and I were not in direct contact professionally. Whereas I was responsible for managing the community mental health teams, the day hospital and the case management service, Gill was clinically and managerially outside my orbit. The two of us being frail humans, however, it would not have taken a private investigator to note the frequency with which Gill came along to my office to subject herself to some serious passive smoking. Neither would it have escaped notice that I occasionally popped into her office – on one occasion to find her fast asleep, draped over her radiator. Domestic dramas inevitably take their toll.

None of my colleagues commented on the situation, and I was unable to detect any changes in their demeanour toward me. Perhaps I was at least partly protected by the fact that Gill was immensely popular throughout the service, and I was not aware of any antipathy toward me within my own ranks. But I have no doubt whatever that there were ordinary, decent people in the centre who were aghast at the fracture of a marriage and the resultant damage to the children. It was some time before we were made aware of the extent of the bush fire of 'intelligence' about our affair and its ramifications.

All tragedies have a lighter side, and there were times of joy and amusement throughout the four or five years of war conducted largely through the poor boys. The youngest boy, Charlie, reported an announcement he had made in his Personal and Social Development class at school. The teacher had clearly been warning these seven-year-olds of the evils of nicotine, alcohol and drugs, when Charlie cheerfully told the class, 'My Mum's girlfriend smokes 20 cigarettes a day – and my father's an alcoholic.' Out of the mouths of babes...

The eldest boy, Nick, who had stayed with his father when John and Charlie had departed, was eventually thrown out by his father in the course of another tantrum whose origins are lost to me. By the time the decree absolute had been awarded, and financial matters more or less settled, Gill, the boys and I were doing our best to form some sort of cohesive unit. Gill insisted that the boys maintain contact with their father, pointing out that they would subsequently regret losing contact with him. In fact, none of the boys communicated with their father voluntarily, and the poor man wrote increasingly sad letters to them weekly for several years. These letters alternated between rage and pathos, and eventually ceased. When they became adults, both Nick and John resumed contact with their father, but Charlie never contacted his father again.

After my demotion from manager of community mental health services to a mere member of the case management service, I eventually retired. Gill grew tired of the relentlessly accelerating bureaucratisation of the NHS and saw a job opportunity in the private sector. This was a rapidly-expanding psychiatric clinic on the main road between Bexhill and Hastings. The owner of the clinic was a trained metallurgist, who, having no experience or knowledge of the mental health field, had nevertheless seen the financial opportunities arising in the independent health and social care sector in the 1980s. In order to minimise costs, he employed nurses from the Philippines, whose nurse training programmes included very little psychiatric education. There were also considerable inherent language problems. At the time, there were no mandatory checks on professional nursing qualifications or ability to speak English.

It did not take long for Gill to assess the nursing care at the clinic as bordering on the dangerous, and she felt it necessary to advise the clinic's owner that her own professional standing and commitments were being compromised by the inadequacies of the nursing care, particularly in light of proposed specialist developments which were not planned to be in line with national guidelines. The owner, who was not disposed to adapt his recruitment policy, resisted Gill's attempts to persuade him of the necessity for hiring more competent staff. Consequently, Gill began looking at locum opportunities in the area.

During Gill's turbulent period at the clinic, we attempted to settle the boys in local schools. Prior to the end of the marriage, two of the boys had been enrolled in a 'failing' school in Hastings, which subsequently became the subject of 'special measures'. Coming from a family of academic pedants, I was appalled and enraged by the poverty of education these boys were receiving. Such 'homework' as there was seemed to consist of photocopied single sheets of paper with questions or tasks which, in my antiquated view, could have been accomplished by a six-year-old. By the time the boys were reasonably settled in Bexhill, we negotiated their transfer to the former grammar school, which had a fairly decent reputation. The youngest boy, Charlie, however, was too young to be admitted to the senior school, and Gill tried to enrol him at the local Catholic school, which had an exceptional, countrywide reputation. A friend of ours was a teacher at the school. She was also gay, but not 'out'. When the boys' father was consulted about the proposed move, he wrote a lengthy epistle to the headmaster, denouncing Charlie's mother and me, and disclosing that one of the teachers was lesbian and a friend of ours. The headmaster took the not unreasonable view that he 'didn't want The Troubles' imported to his school, and regretfully rejected the application.

It is possible that this decision marked the beginning of poor Charlie's decreasing interest in schoolwork. The Catholic school had a strong reputation for scholarship and discipline, whereas the school to which Charlie was sent was, by default, somewhat relaxed in these matters. There seemed to be few consequences if pupils failed to do assignments and little meaningful contact with parents as to their children's progress – or lack of it. The only tangible result of Charlie's education was from the subject of Food Technology, when he would bring home slightly grey, high carbohydrate items such as pizza which, frankly, I rather enjoyed, but which did neither of us any good.

Following my retirement from the NHS, and a very brief period of leisure and housework, I was approached by the local Council of Voluntary Service and asked whether I would consider managing a mental health advocacy service. Initially, I refused. But, when a further approach was made, I agreed to take the job. In retrospect, it was a foolish move on my part. I had surely demonstrated to all and sundry, but insufficiently to myself, that I was a hopeless manager. My brief was to develop mental health advocacy services throughout the area, and to raise the necessary funding. There were two established advocates in the organisation, both of whom I had known quite well before accepting the post.

192

There are various models of advocacy, but the one adopted by this agency embodied the principle of representing as precisely as possible what the client actually declares to be their wishes. Ideally, the client is encouraged to represent their own wishes, but the advocate often has to speak on their behalf. Because I grasped every opportunity to work with clients myself – although I should have been concentrating on managing the advocates, raising funds and developing the service – I occasionally found myself talking sheer nonsense; conveying clients' utterly delusional and sometimes defamatory thoughts, feelings and wishes to mental health professionals. Most people with mental health 'issues' recover, and, should they become aware of what advocates had been saying on their behalf, would squirm with embarrassment. I had a similar reservation about the wholesale decanting of psychiatric hospitals when the policy of community care came into practice. People with severe, chronic mental illness were deposited in hostels, 'group homes' or ordinary rental flats in the community – where their bizarre behaviour during acute episodes of their illness could result in social ostracism and, on recovery, the person's intense shame.

Sometimes, an advocate would 'win' a case in the sense that the client's stated wishes succeeded – to the detriment of the client. One case which stands out and still irritates me when I think of it concerns a young man whose mental health 'issue' had led him to take to his bed for several years. He had a young, caring wife who had abandoned her job in order to look after him, and the two subsisted in an isolated cocoon. The client became progressively more emaciated, but refused all offers of medical and psychiatric assistance. Eventually, the consultant psychiatrist and a community psychiatric nurse formed a strategy to approach the client in as respectful and sympathetic a manner as possible in the circumstances. The CPN – again, a man whom I respected enormously – very gently and gradually established a warm and positive relationship with the client and, when he considered the client ready to consider at least a domiciliary assessment, the client panicked and appealed to the advocate for support. To my immense frustration and disappointment, the advocate 'won' – and the client remained a bedridden prisoner. I have no means of knowing how the situation resolved itself, if it ever did.

Another source of considerable frustration regarding the advocacy practice itself was that the people who, in my opinion, were least well served by the mental health services tended to be the least likely to approach our agency for assistance. On the other hand, there was an entrenched group of serial complainers whose concerns reflected their personality 'issues' rather than the deficiencies of the mental health services.

My experience of fund-raising led to much wailing and gnashing of teeth on my part. It seemed to me that successful fund-raising required either inside knowledge or a sixth sense of what precisely potential funders were actually looking for in political terms. Experienced applicants would know, by one means or another, what were the 'flavours of the month' in terms of favoured client groups or social problems, styles of working, partnerships with other agencies and so on. More disconcerting to me, however, were the headings or questions which potential funders posed. It became clear that particular forms of wording were being sought; that there was an unstated invitation or temptation to 'spin', to exaggerate – indeed, I have seen many funding applications where it was fairly obvious to me that the applicants were thoroughly reckless with the truth. Statistical projections which could not possibly have possessed a sound basis were regularly sought.

So both Gill and I had demanding, full-time jobs and, with hindsight, I can see that we gave the boys less than perfect supervision. All three were highly sociable creatures, and their flat soon became an informal social club. On one occasion, I went into their flat to find one of their friends using the boys' computer – with none of 'our' boys in sight. I ejected the young man and worried constantly about what might be going on in that flat when we were at work.

Charlie, in particular, worried me. He had acquired a band of acolytes, whom I once described to Gill as 'losers', much to her annoyance: 'How can you call yourself a Christian with an attitude like that?' As I suspected, these youngsters were experimenting with drugs. I had told Gill of my suspicion that Charlie was taking drugs, but she remained doubtful until a friend of ours reported her concerns and observations. God knows that I, then addicted to nicotine and at least psychologically dependent on alcohol, was in no position to pontificate about the evils of mood- or mind-altering substances, but I writhed with anxiety as to the effects on Charlie's future education and job prospects if he became embedded in the drug culture.

Charlie was an outstandingly handsome and engaging young man, witty and kind. When he was younger, he would spend hours constructing elaborate and intricate models of castles, Star Wars figures and machines. I thought he might have the skills and talent to become an engineer, so impressive were his endeavours. He would explain to me, at great length, the nature and potentialities of his inventions, such that I could barely keep up with him. He was also a fine mimic, and could quote extensively from comic programmes and films. My mother once described Charlie as 'beautiful', an uncharacteristically sentimental observation on her part. And 'beautiful' he was and remains. His prospects in the 'real' world of education and work have, however, been affected by his love affair with cannabis, which began in earnest when he was 13 years old.

Nick, too, was having problems of his own. He had always been a nervous, diffident and somewhat submissive boy, who sought to avoid confrontation at all costs. This may have been the reason he stayed with his father after his two younger brothers had left. But when Nick came to live with us, he did not settle into Bexhill High School at all well, and, despite the best efforts of counsellors and teachers, he made a poor showing at GCSEs and finally dropped out before completing A level studies. He did not appear remotely interested in illicit drugs, but had begun to smoke cigarettes while he was still living with his father.

John was temperamentally quite different from his brothers. After he had recovered from the shock of his parents' separation and acrimonious divorce, he emerged as a reasonably self-confident youngster with fairly 'straight' friends and interests. He played football – and computer football management games. It was customary, when one visited him in his flat, to find him playing the football management game while watching television. He was strongly attracted to a 'designer' lifestyle, and paid considerable attention to his grooming, hairstyle, clothes and accessories.

And then the garden flat, immediately beneath us, became vacant. Gill's sister, Rosie, and her daughter, Beth, moved down from Boston, Lincolnshire to this flat. Rosie was a medical audiologist, and Beth an exceptionally bright 14-year-old. Beth's father, Rosie's husband, had looked after Beth while Rosie worked, and they had formed a close bond. Plagued by depression, however, he took his own life when Beth was only seven. This tragedy may have bequeathed to poor Beth an array of fears and insecurities – especially about her own sanity. Her father had been diagnosed as suffering from depression some years before his death, and perhaps his 'househusband' role made it difficult for him to develop a robust sense of self-esteem.

By this time, then, our expanding 'family' occupied three of the five flats in the building, and we had some wonderful times. I have always been deeply fond of Rosie, and her temperament and mine chimed nicely. Rosie and Gill are as different as chalk and cheese, particularly in personality characteristics. Rosie and I, on the other hand, are temperamentally similar in some respects. I think Rosie and I are somewhat insecure souls, with short fuses. The household therefore comprised one equable and two feisty adults – and four somewhat traumatised youngsters. All four were embarking on a somewhat bumpy adolescence, and none was doing well at school. There were the usual quarrels and tantrums and, because I had no children of my own, I worried intensely about what would become of these youngsters.

FIFTEEN

On the evening of June the first, 2002, there was a concert in Hyde Park, with Pavarotti singing his heart out in *Nessun Dorma*. Diana, Princess of Wales was present, and I think there were tears in her eyes as he sang. I seem to remember that it was raining.

The telephone rang around nine o'clock. It was Cheryl, telling me that our mother had had 'an accident' – that she had been following Father along the street to go shopping and had fallen backwards and bloodied her head on the pavement and been taken from St Andrews to Ninewells Hospital in Dundee, where she died at 5.30 pm. I noticed that, all too briefly, I felt peculiarly calm.

If only shock could last a bit longer. I soon dropped into an emotional hell, all but immobilised by a sense of profound panic; a terror to exceed anything I had ever experienced. I had been involved, years before, in the setting up of a branch of Cruse, the bereavement organisation, in Hastings and Bexhill, but could not remember any reference to the unique form of terror associated with grief. I was unprepared for the agony of that panic, and it was not until I later read CS Lewis's *A Grief Observed* that I learned that this is not unique.

I found that, in a way, the world *did* stop. It was absolutely inconceivable that she could have gone, and gone for ever. There could be no possibility of a world in which she did not exist. Cheryl told me that Marion literally called Mother to come back, and I knew precisely how she felt. She and I were utterly uprooted, lost in an abyss of pain.

We went to McGregor's funeral parlour to 'view' her, and were shown to a waiting room and sat for what seemed an age. Finally, we were escorted to a room which held nothing but a simple bier upon which rested the coffin which contained a miniature representation of our mother. I had seen her only in March, when she seemed to have become thinner than before but to be of the same height, yet here she was, a tiny figure in what looked like a child's coffin. The dear face was gaunt, the skin a waxy yellow-grey. There was a very slight smile about her lips. There is a belief in our culture that it is psychologically valuable to see the deceased: the rationale is that it 'helps' the bereaved to accept the loved one's death. But it was the worst thing I could have done. I will see that precious, emaciated face for as long as I live, and I wish to God I had not seen her like that.

Frances came over from Ottawa with her two lovely sons, Scott and Blair. We all stayed in a hotel near the golf course. As if the circumstances could not be worse, we were 'bumped' out of the hotel after a couple of days because a member of staff had made a double booking. My intemperate rant at the hotel proprietor had no effect, and we were ignominiously despatched to another hotel along the road. And then poor Scott had his bank card swallowed at an ATM. It was not a good time.

On the day of the funeral at Holy Trinity, we lined up at the front door of our parents' house. The hearse and cars arrived, but had to wait until Father finished telling us a long story of no relevance to anything. We drove the few

199

yards to the church. My three sisters recalled our mother in terms of amusement and affection. I was unable to speak. And then we were on our way to the crematorium in Dundee, following the hearse. As we processed on our solemn way, an impatient motorist hooted at us, a pretty wretched thing to do on such a heartbreaking occasion. Surprisingly, Cheryl made a particularly rude gesture at him, and we went on our way.

We were met at the crematorium by my cousin Donald and his wife, Joan. Donald was my mother's sister Alice's son, a man of great height and enormous intellect, neither of which he was ever able to put to good use. Indeed, the poor man was a lifelong alcoholic who was, like my father, absolutely hopeless with money. Joan, at half his height, was equally intelligent but trammelled by Donald's deficiencies. It was good to see them, and I remained fond of them since Bobbie and I had lived with them so many years before at 163 Bruntsfield Place in Edinburgh. Donald greeted us with the reminder that Mother had always referred to him as her favourite nephew. He was her only nephew.

The crematorium service was, of course, grim. There is no way of denying or escaping the finality of the coffin's progress to the hellish inferno. On the drive back to St Andrews, the hymn *Oh Love That Wilt Not Let Me Go* resonated throughout my skull, over and over.

The evening passed, for me, in alcoholic haze.

Frances and her lovely boys returned to Canada, and Gill and I to Bexhill-on-Sea. Although I loathed my job in mental health advocacy, the sheer agony of my grief was undoubtedly attenuated by having to concentrate on work. A dear friend attempted to comfort me by saying that 'it gets better', but it didn't.

It is almost ten years since Mother went. The panic certainly did subside over the years, but I remain unable to think of her for any length of time. My intellect tells me that there are sound, compelling reasons for this admittedly pathological grief. Perhaps the account of my early life may help to explain it. My mother was unable to protect us from the unloving, irrational and violent behaviour of our father. Understandably, she was both oppressed and depressed. She had had to abandon us for a time when Frances and I were very little, when she could cope no more. But my own response, presumably, to this state of affairs was to lapse into terrible temper tantrums, to which Mother once referred, in a letter to Father, as 'her usual rages'. The word 'oppositional' seems apt: I remember making a conscious decision to hate tinned tomato soup, for example. But I do not recall so much my anger as my sense of alienation, loneliness and fear. I was, above all, terrified of war, a phobia which I have already mentioned. When we were living in Bankfoot at the time of the Suez crisis, I carved into the kitchen door lintel '*Will we have war?*' and left a space for the answer. Years later, as I began my psychiatric nursing training, the same extreme fear recurred during the Cuban missile crisis. I experienced the world as a terrifyingly unpredictable, hostile place, where one could be destroyed in a moment.

It would not take a first-year psychology student long to connect the dread of war with a dread of Father's wrath. And the school phobia which began in Shetland was reinforced by the regime at Mossvale school in Paisley where a teacher might without warning initiate a mass belting session if a wrongdoer did not 'own up' to some misdeed. Or fellow pupils might gang up on you outside the school walls. There seemed to be no safe quarter. The anxieties of the day percolated through the partition of sleep, inducing nightmares of torture, destruction and death.

Rage undoubtedly represents the futile attempt to warn off the sinister spirits that seemed to pervade my young life.

201

In reality, of course, the expression of anger entirely defeats its own purpose: it invites fresh assault. And this was precisely what happened with my acts of fury in Father's presence. It was safer to vent the spleen in Mother's presence. Which was perhaps the most potent source of the ineradicable guilt I felt as I moved through adulthood, but which reached a crescendo when I lost her. I knew in my bones that I was what used to be called the black sheep, the Bad and Stupid cuckoo in the nest, and have spent much of my adult life attempting to redeem myself. My erstwhile partner, Jean (the second), observed that, when I entered Mother's presence, she appeared to stiffen, seemed apprehensive and vigilant – waiting, perhaps, for me to do or say something awful. My own recollection is that Mother was never able to remain seated in the same room with me. There was always some little task to which she had to attend. When I mentioned this to Marion on one occasion years ago, she carefully arranged to 'mind' the homestead so that Mother and I could go for a coffee in one of her favourite coffee shops in St Andrews. I seized the opportunity to spend some uninterrupted time with Mother – maybe even to find a way to make some sort of peace with her; to acknowledge and seek pardon from her for all the terrible things I had done or been. But I was thwarted entirely. Our conversation firmly confined itself to all things safe, all things neutral.

It is a terrible thing to confess one's sins, to seek forgiveness only for the sinned against figure to turn away. But that is how I felt when Mother died. The opportunity to put things right had vanished. All these years since her departure, I still regularly wake up saying, 'I'm so, so sorry, Mum'…

When Lorna Luft was asked how she felt after her mother, Judy Garland's, death, she answered, 'It doesn't get better;

it gets different.' And that is exactly my own sentiment. Life just became different. I remained deeply happy in my life with Gill, continued to worry about the boys becoming feral, and to loathe my job. And I finally retired, at the age of 59, in 2003.

In the summer of 2004, just as I had reached my sixtieth birthday, Gill and I visited the Shetland Islands. I had never returned there since our departure in 1950, though had often dreamed of doing so. Hitherto the deterrents had been the considerable expense and the length of time it would take to get there. We drove in our little green Mini Cooper from Bexhill to Aberdeen, with our aged lurcher, Digger, in the back. We had been assured that there were kennel facilities on board the ferry, which I took to mean that there would at least be a comfortable bed and toilet facilities. Not so. We discovered that a plain cage had been booked for him, devoid of bedding or matting of any kind. And there were no toilet facilities. Animals were expected to tolerate these Spartan conditions for a journey of nearly 15 hours. Red mist descended, and I came close to throttling the ship's officer who explained the conditions. In the end, we reached the compromise that Digger would remain in our car, locked away in the ship's hold, to which we would have no access until everyone had disembarked at Lerwick. Gill is able to accommodate setbacks such as these, and was reconciled to the situation. I am not and was not.

Mercifully, the ship's bar was well stocked with excellent real ales, especially those produced by the tiny Valhalla brewery in Unst. A gloriously rich amber ale called Simmer Dim – the term for Shetland's summer nights, in which darkness never descends – helped attenuate my extreme anxiety and dark mood regarding poor Digger's confinement.

I had had so many dreams over so many years about what Unst and Whalsay might look like, and it was hard to believe that I was actually about to see for myself. It had been 53 years since my last glimpse of the islands. We disembarked at Lerwick, the 'capital' of the Shetland Islands. It took an age for us to be reunited with dear old Digger – who seemed entirely unfazed by his long night's confinement. Indeed, he did not even disgorge the contents of his bladder until we had traversed a few streets of Lerwick.

There was nothing familiar about the streets and buildings of Lerwick: I recognised nothing. Yet I was pretty sure that we had spent time here in the course of our emetic trips to the Scottish mainland. To our surprise and joy, there was a Chinese restaurant in the town, and we lunched there. Our bed and breakfast accommodation on the outskirts of Lerwick was congenial; at breakfast on the first morning, we met the daughter of a Church of Scotland minister whose parish had been in Yell, an island away from Uyeasound, where my father began his ministry. Here we both were, looking for the imprint of our parents.

The fields about us were full of Shetland ponies, gossiping away, their feathery tails waving in the wind. The Shetlanders were delighted by the sunny weather, almost complaining about the heat. We experienced it as rather a chilly, force eight gale, entirely defeating the sun's brave efforts. We strolled through the streets and along the wild shore. There was the Anderson Institute, an educational establishment to which students from the smaller islands went after primary and junior secondary school. I remembered it being mentioned back in the late forties. There was a tiny hospital, too, but people who required psychiatric treatment or specialist secondary care still had to go all the way to Aberdeen for treatment.

We began to see signs of the Shetland dialect: a café called 'Da Toon' (the town) or 'The Peerie Café' (the little café). We had coffee in an old hotel by the shore, one I was

204

sure my parents, if not Frances and I, must have visited. My mother, in particular, was renowned for her coffee breaks in dignified surroundings: not for her the occasional 'greasy spoon' which Gill and I sometimes enjoy. All the while, I was impatient to be on our way to Unst.

It is impossible to hurry to Unst. It is first necessary to drive north from Lerwick to Toft, close to the northeast tip of the mainland, and there to take the small ferry to Ulsta, on the southwest coast of the island of Yell. These inter-island ferries are smart, modern craft which, I think, were commissioned at the time of the massive oil extraction boom in the seventies and eighties. The narrow but well paved roads through the islands, too, are a product of the oil bonanza. A further drive, northeast to Gutcher, where we stopped at the Wild Dog restaurant for refreshments. And, finally, we were on the way to the island of my birth. It was a bright, sunny day as we crossed the water to Belmont, on the south side of Unst. There were several species of bird swooping over and beside us on our passage, most notably gannets and skaws, the latter being indigenous to the islands. As we approached the little landing at Belmont, we saw a house standing proudly alone on the brow of a gentle hill leading up from the shore. This was Belmont house, once grand but now about to fall down. So many houses of all sizes on these islands, uninhabited, left to die.

Uyeasound lies on the south coast of Unst. We had booked bed and breakfast in a house close to the shore, called Prestgaarten. When we had made the booking some months before, we had asked the proprietrix, Sandra Firmin, whether the old Uyeasound manse was still in existence. To my amazement and delight, she replied: 'This *is* the old manse'! I could hardly believe that I was to be sleeping in the house in which I was born 60 years before... The name 'Prestgaarten' is Norwegian for Priest's Garden.

Gill and I strolled to the shore, and there saw the row of houses which appear in an old black-and-white photograph in one of my albums. The frontages had hardly changed, but the shop whose edifice remained as it appears in that photograph was now closed and its interior disclosed a few dusty items which, for all we knew, might have lain there for decades. I took a photograph in order to compare it with the original from so long before.

The wind hardly dropped all the while we were there, and I took advantage of its low howling to camouflage the slight moaning of my own. I realised that I was really calling out to my mother for some sort of recognition; some sign that she had been there, perhaps left a clue or trace of her existence – a scrap of information that I needed to piece together a bit more of the story of the time. There was so little to go on. Little did I realise that I would soon possess a scrap which both surprised and saddened me.

There is precious little to gossip about on these tiny outposts of the kingdom. So it should have been no surprise to learn that news of my visit had spread through the island. Its only source must have been Sandra Firmin, our landlady at Prestgaarten. For it was she who told us that a certain Mary Peterson was eager to meet me. Mary was the official keeper of the key to the little Muness castle in Uyeasound: had indeed received an OBE for her fidelity in this role. She and her husband, Jamie, lived in a little cottage near the castle, and we were invited there for a meal. She turned out to be Mary Niven, who, at about the age of 18, had helped Mother with the housework at the manse. That would have been during the years 1942–46. It was a joy to meet her, and to be shown photographs of her investiture and some fine examples of Shetland 'Fair Isle' knitting.

And it was Mary Peterson who advised me that there was a very elderly soul who wanted to see me. This turned out to be Mima Sutherland, the district nurse who actually brought me into the world. I could not believe it, having understood that it was Dr Saxby who had done so. Mima was now 99 years old, living independently in a little cottage in Westing, to the northwest of Uyeasound. The meeting with Mima was a profoundly moving occasion. She was as sharp as a tack, her memory intact. She recalled that I had 'cried a lot' at birth, that I was born on the same day as a boy who later became a policeman but was now sadly dead – and that my mother 'always had her head in a book'.

Mima was an extraordinary individual. She was born and spent her entire life on the island, where she became the midwife for all the babies in the course of her career, a career in which, she claimed, not one baby was lost. She had also, at a great age, successfully completed a degree in Norwegian. Meeting dear Mima was truly a high point in my life, and I remain immensely proud of the fact that I met her and was able to kiss the woman who helped me into the world. But why did my parents tell me that I was brought into the world by Dr Saxby when it was actually nurse Mima Sutherland who had done so? Still, I was – and remain – thrilled that I had come face to face with my 'deliverer' after all these intervening years.

Then it was time to catch the ferry to Whalsay from Laxo. I was pleased to be able to recognise the harbour at Symbister, although it was now greatly extended to accommodate the massive pelagic trawlers lined up at anchor. And there was the little Hanseatic Booth which I also remembered and which represented perhaps the sole remnant of the days when there was trade with the Hanseatic League. I looked for, and probably found, the carcass of the little shop where Mother would regularly buy a Mars bar and divide it between Frances and me. Now there was a minimarket further up the hill from the harbour, where we stocked up on food and drink in preparation for our stay at Whalsay's answer to a motel.

It is almost impossible to describe the flood of feelings I experienced as we drove out of Symbister. There had been so many recollections, so many dreams over so many years. I soon recognised the road from the harbour, and, suddenly, the manse came into view. And it was exactly as I had remembered it, especially the arched window at the side of the house. The only addition at the site was a small, modern bungalow, which turned out to be the new Whalsay manse. I was subsequently pleased to learn that the current incumbent was a woman. We drove on to our accommodation, Oot Ower, a recently built group of chalets with a central lounge and bar.

We settled in to our little hut and Gill knitted while I stowed the victuals, especially the deeply dark ales from the Valhalla brewery in Unst. The 'summer' wind whistled about the timber slats, and momentarily cast me back to the time when I feared its merciless, droning power. Again, I could sense Mother's shudder at the sound. We set up the computer so that we could view the photographs taken thus far, and huddled close to the tiny electric fire.

Answering a knock at our door, I came face to face with an elderly woman whose face and form I thought I recognised across the span of over 50 years. It was Winnie Poulson, Frances's and my babysitter. I hoped she wouldn't notice the aroma of Simmer Dim, and invited her in to our lodging. In the course of conversation, she referred to 'your mother's breakdown', a revelation which made the hairs on my arms stand on end. I had no recollection of such a thing, although I was vaguely aware that Mother had been 'away south' at some point when Frances and I were very small. After Mother's death, I came across a letter in which Mother mentioned Frances's whoop of delight when she reappeared. I experienced a stab of frustration as I realised that I was unlikely ever to know more about the nature of Mother's 'breakdown', the circumstances in which it occurred and the length of time she was away from us. It certainly caused me to wonder whether a fear of abandonment formed part of the complex equation in my pathological development.

The following morning, we traced the journey from Whalsay Manse to Broch school, which I attended from the age of four. In my mind's eye I had so often traced out the route, and estimated it to be about two miles from door to door. To my gratified surprise, our little Mini Cooper registered precisely that distance. As we drove to the school, I could feel an odd sense of apprehension: here was I, sitting next to my partner in a cosy car, about to check out the territory upon which were laid the foundations of my worst nightmares over half a century. The peat fields in whose freshly cut trenches I had been so crudely humiliated were still there. And we drove on to where the loch lay, just over a hill about quarter of a mile away from the school. It was exactly where and how I remembered it, and now our lurcher, Digger, stood in silhouette on the brow of the hill over which Father had eventually appeared after I had been cast adrift in the dinghy.

When we reached Broch school, we discovered that it no longer functioned as a school, but housed a charity shop. We met the occupants of the former headmaster's house adjacent to the school, and I remembered the times when I had played there – and taken surreptitious puffs of Mrs McWhirter's cigarettes. If only I could have told her what was happening to me as I walked home from school...

We visited Whalsay Church, where Father preached for four years, and I gazed at the pulpit in which I had seen him wave his black batswing arms as he spoke; a towering, mournfully menacing figure. Mother would have sat in the 'manse pew'. I became aware that I was desperately willing the place to yield some clue: some revelation or explanation for the scraps of terror which had haunted me for so long. I talked under my breath to the headstone of my teacher, Miss Margaret Stewart, entreating her to speak, to tell me what, if anything, she might have known or suspected. Nothing.

Unless one was an archaeologist, an ornithologist or a botanist, it seemed to me that there was little to commend these God-forsaken, treeless islands. Undoubtedly, however, my perspective is deeply tainted by my experiences, both recalled and 'forgotten'. I would never wish to visit them again, but felt grateful that I had been able to view the scenes of my fear and sadness.

SIXTEEN

Not long after our return from Shetland, Gill was discussing the referral of one of her patients to The Retreat in York. The consultant with whom she discussed the case mentioned that there was a consultant vacancy there, and wondered whether she was interested. The Retreat was founded by the Quaker William Tuke at the end of the eighteenth century, chiefly because of local Friends' concerns about the care, treatment and subsequent death of a Quaker called Hannah Mills in York Asylum. Her family, who lived some distance from York, were prohibited from visiting her, and asked local Quakers to visit. They, too, were refused permission to do so, and were advised that Hannah was 'not in a suitable state to be seen by visitors'.

Not surprisingly, York Quakers ('Friends') suspected that Hannah's death was the result of ill-treatment and negligence. At the time, the care of people with mental illness was generally poor, often to the point of abuse. The 'insane' were considered to have lost their reason, the very faculty which was held to be essential to individual humanity. Hence the insane were less than human.

As a Quaker, Tuke endorsed the 'testimony' of non-violence, and brought his concern about the treatment of Hannah Mills to the Society of Friends' quarterly meeting

211

in 1792, where it was agreed to establish a place where Quakers with mental illness could be cared for, although this was soon extended to non-members of the Society. Quaker values would inform the management and care of the residents: especially the equality of all persons, based on George Fox's founding principle that 'there is that of God' in everyone, required that residents be treated with gentleness and respect.

As nonconformists, Quakers were unable to enter the professions since they were not permitted to study at either Oxford or Cambridge, the only universities established at the time. Hence many Quakers were engaged in commerce. The first superintendent of The Retreat was an apothecary. A lady superintendent was appointed, and she and the apothecary subsequently married. The Retreat came to be known as a 'family establishment', with William Tuke, its founder, the 'father of the family'. A visiting physician attended to the medical needs of the residents. The key elements of 'treatment' consisted of good food, 'a glass of wine or porter', plenty of light, friendship and meaningful occupation.

Gill had been a Quaker for many years, and expressed interest in seeing The Retreat. To our delight, we were *both* invited to visit, and were put up in bed and breakfast accommodation near the hospital. I recalled that, during my psychiatric nursing training in the early 1960s, we had learned about The Retreat's advanced system of care and regarded it as perhaps the progenitor of what came to be called 'social' psychiatry. And so it was quite an honour to be invited to see it.

Although we were not offered a glass of porter, we attended a reception with members of staff and the Resident Friend, Annie Borthwick. We were shown round the hospital, and were duly impressed by the atmosphere of the place: an air of calm throughout the wards and corridors, carpeted throughout – a change from the usual tiles and skid-marked vinyl – and magnificent old grandfather clocks and antique furniture everywhere. But the ambience was one of understated elegance rather than opulence. The grounds of The Retreat were beautifully laid and maintained, although not as extensive as in Tuke's day: much of the land has been leased out or sold to local farmers and to the adjacent University of York.

We were hugely impressed by the hospital itself and by the surrounding city. Gill was duly interviewed and appointed, and became the consultant responsible for, among other services, the Hannah Mills ward. Her speciality is the treatment and rehabilitation of people with severe, complex illnesses who have not benefited from NHS care or who have the means to finance their own care, often through health insurance. In practice, most patients are NHS referrals.

This is perhaps the moment to mention my own spiritual odyssey, a journey of fear, disappointment, occasional exhilaration, exasperation and – finally – of hope. Indeed, now I come to think of it, it is a journey whose trajectory closely matches the passage of my life. One might think that to be born and raised in the home of a practising Christian minister would be to be blessed with a secure sense of the truth of Jesus Christ's teaching and the glorious implications for believers' present and future lives. Jokes about 'the children of the manse' and their delinquency point to a different story. It seems to me that a central difficulty in having a clergyman for a parent is that whereas that parent is inevitably seen as some sort of representation of Jesus or God while in the pulpit, things may be very different in the manse. I have said before that Father appeared to be immensely tall and powerfully built and, in full black robes, presented a formidable figure. And, as soon as he opened his mouth to speak, his booming, sonorous voice with its doom-laden intonation filled my young heart with a sense of fear and inadequacy. My father's Asperger's undoubtedly imbued his proclamations with a peculiarly eerie cadence which resounds through my inner being to this day: 'Dearly beloved, we are weak and miserable sinners, and there is no health in us...'

People with a developed aesthetic sense enjoy visiting places of worship, but my own response to the churches and cathedrals of Protestantism is to shiver involuntarily, feeling their atmosphere to be cold, dusty, dead and yet threatening. And they seem to me to represent the very antipathy of what Jesus himself would have chosen as places for teaching, prayer and worship. As far as I know, he chose to do his work on hillsides, in fields, by and on the Sea of Galilee and in friends' houses. And if I have understood the Christian message at all, it is that we should love and help one another above all. To do so surely requires the application of our love and resources directly in this service, and not the erection and maintenance of grand buildings.

I wish I could remember how I thought and felt about the God business when we were in Shetland. However strenuously I try to cudgel my mind for the images and feelings recorded there, I can recall no sense of being loved by God or Jesus. On the contrary, I believe that, almost from the beginning, I had a strong sense of being outside, of not belonging to the throng of the Good. Although I perceived Father to be a frightening giant, I nevertheless believed that he was Right, a 'fact' promulgated as much by himself as anyone else. And I was certain that Mother and Frances were completely Good.

When we moved to Paisley, I already knew at some level that I was gay, although I did not realise that anyone else was. As I have already indicated, it was a matter of unspeakable shame. This undoubtedly exacerbated my sense of otherness, of deviance, and it was not long before I learned that neither God nor Jesus would tolerate such ugly, sinful perversion. Yet I nevertheless exercised myself over and over again in the attempt to fathom whether God was really like this, would actually consign me to hell. I had certainly not *chosen* to be like this, and was endlessly perplexed by the paradox which inhered in the hell versus salvation question. If God really was Love, and if I didn't *intend* to be gay, would I still be cast into hell? And, anyway, if I said I was sorry I was gay, would I be forgiven?

I have a clear memory of preaching while standing on a spindle-backed kitchen chair as my pulpit, with Mother ironing close by in the kitchen at Mossvale manse in Paisely. I must have been about seven years old. It had occurred to me that God might not reside in the conventional heaven well beyond the stratosphere, but that he might actually dwell *in our heads*. As I enunciated this revelation to my congregation of one, Mother emerged from her usual reverie and said, 'Oh, Allison, I don't think that's quite right...' Frustratingly, I cannot remember any further exchange on the matter.

It is strangely difficult to say whether, in general, I really believed in God during these years. I do know that I *hoped* for his existence and that he really did send Jesus to comfort us and reassure us of his love. But the undertow of doubt certainly persisted until I reached adolescence and beyond. When we had moved to Newfoundland, I nailed holy pictures, posters and plaques to the walls of my little bedroom in the basement: 'Be still and know that I am God'; 'I am the way, the truth and the life'. I grasped and repeated the line from the funeral service which says '...in the sure and certain hope of the resurrection...' as a guarantee of the afterlife, a preoccupation which persists to this day. Indeed, it has always occurred to me that, if there is no afterlife, there is very little point in belief in God. We might as well be humanists.

And so, for a few decades, I was at best agnostic, with short bursts of angry atheism. I certainly believed in Doing and Being Good in principle although, in practice, I invariably dragged about with me a deeply rooted sense of failure and inadequacy. It was not until I was in my thirties and living in Bexhill that I first had the feeling that I might not be entirely lost. And it is to Judy and Catholicism that I owe my gratitude for learning of the possibility of real or actual redemption.

Judy was a convert to Catholicism, and through her I heard about, and in some cases met, Catholics whose intellect, humour and compassion moved me in an entirely new way. It was because of these enlightening and encouraging encounters that I began to read about the institutions and beliefs of Catholicism. I was particularly drawn to Jesuit writings, and came upon a book by a Jesuit called McNeill: *The Church and the Homosexual*. Of course, I lent it to someone who never returned it, but I remember that McNeill, a theologian, carefully analysed all the texts in the Old and New Testaments which seemed to proscribe homosexuality and contextualised these apparent condemnations in order to show that God was not condemning gay people as such. It is no exaggeration to say that I was finally freed from the greatest millstone of my life, and remain convinced that no God of love would condemn someone who is constitutionally gay. In fact, I strongly believe that 'true' homosexuality will soon be shown to be determined importantly, if not entirely, by genetics.

And then I came upon the 'Dutch catechism', published, I think, in the late 1970s, whose official title I forget. And, inevitably, I have discarded or lost the book. But my recollection is that it miraculously managed to explain some of the most difficult Catholic dogma concerning, for example, the immaculate conception, transubstantiation and so on, in a brilliantly mystical exegesis. I am no mystic, but I began to recognise that black-and-white literalism, while necessary at various times in early civilisation, may have little place in contemporary theology and matters of faith. I must nevertheless admit that I remain slightly wary of the reckless attribution of difficult phenomena to mystical explanation.

I decided to seek formal instruction in the Catholic faith. Needless to say, I looked for a female rather than a male instructor, and found the ideal in Sister Louis de Gonzague of the Our Lady of the Missions order, based in a convent in the Old London Road in Hastings. Sister Louis was a short, rotund figure of indeterminate age who had been a music teacher. She was highly intelligent, deeply discerning and possessed of a fine sense of humour. Her wisdom and discernment led her to steer away from the conventional sticking points in Catholic theology, and I grew ever more convinced that I had found my spiritual home. This was one of the happiest times in my spiritual life – no, it really *was* the happiest.

After the period of instruction, the next requirement before formal reception into the church is what was formerly called Confession, now more commonly known as Reconciliation. I necessarily encountered a male priest for this purpose, and drew the proverbial deep breath as I 'confessed' my homosexuality and alcohol dependence. He did not seem unduly fazed by these, and I cannot remember whether I even received a penance. At any rate, I was ready to be admitted to the 'one true Church'.

A reception was held, just for me, in the convent of Our Lady of the Missions. Judy was with me, dear Sister Louis was there, and there was an enormous feast presided over by all the other nuns. On that infinitely precious day, I felt

217

convinced of the Truth of Catholicism and – briefly – knew that I was OK.

The feeling and conviction did not last. I attended Mass assiduously at the church of St Mary Magdalene for a while, but the old doubts and sense of dislocation from the world of the Good eventually returned. I stopped going to Mass. I stopped praying.

I have always had the greatest possible difficulty with prayer. It has never made logical or theological sense to me. I cannot believe in an interventionist God. When I mentioned my difficulty to a young Catholic priest once, he answered, 'The point of prayer is that it changes *us*.' This seemed at the time a pretty unsatisfactory answer. I have neither the desire nor the theological or even philosophical skills to extemporise on the problem of prayer. At a very superficial level, however, I cannot see the point of asking God to change anything. Evangelical Christians of my acquaintance have often claimed that such-and-such an event has come about as the direct result of supplicatory prayer. They cite this as evidence of God's love, a demonstration of his willingness to change things in answer to personal prayer. At the simplest level, my prayer to cure my loved one of cancer may not have the desired result. Would that mean that God wanted them to die? Fundamentalist evangelicals attempt to massage away God's apparent refusal to grant the supplicant's wish by suggesting that, in his infinite wisdom, God has other plans...

Which leads directly to the problem of suffering. Why does God allow it? There are various answers to this, one of which is, of course, that there is no God – or no God worth worshipping. Another is that God has worked everything out in such a way as to ensure that those who successfully contend with the vicissitudes of life and Keep the Faith will ultimately triumph and thereby achieve the Kingdom of

God – the afterlife. Or one may believe in predetermination; that everything is preordained and inevitably involves pain and suffering on the way. I do not understand this one, and will not dwell on it.

The problem of suffering leads inexorably to the problem of evil. Why does God allow it? I think this is known as the problem of 'theodicy'. In one of my early 'sermons', I tried to explain evil as a necessary means to test believers. I proposed that God would have been terminally bored had he arranged things so that the entire human race existed in an eternal, beatific paradise peopled by Stepford subjects lacking the capacity to do evil. There would be no merit whatever in gaining heavenly paradise. God would only be really interested if, by *free will,* his people chose to worship and follow him. It would seem to follow that evil arises from the choice not to do that which is good, and is therefore an inevitable part of the Godly scheme of things. There can be no good in the absence of evil. When I am desperate spiritually, as I frequently am, I wonder whether my childhood 'insights' serve me better than the interminable anxieties and agonies of adult contemplation.

When I was pretending to manage the Mental Health Advocacy Service toward the end of what we may laughingly call my 'career', I became an *ex officio* trustee of a voluntary organisation in Hastings with the lamentable title of Association for the Pastoral Care of the Mentally Ill. I should not otherwise have joined. A fellow trustee, Anne Bonnaud, turned out to be a Quaker. Anne was an elderly, 'weighty' Friend. 'Weighty' until recently meant a very experienced Quaker with strong spiritual roots and extensive knowledge of the Society's workings. We now refer to 'seasoned' Friends, which regrettably summons an image of Kentucky Fried Chicken to mind. When I discovered Anne was a Quaker, I asked her about it, having the sketchiest of knowledge. The more she explained about Friends, the more intrigued I became. She recommended that I read Geoffrey Hubbard's book *Quaker by Convincement*. I did so. And, in an important way, it changed my spiritual life, such as it was.

One thing I *had* known about Quakers was that they were the very first religious movement to assert that being gay was not sinful, and to issue a formal statement to that effect. Much later, in 2008 to be precise, Britain Yearly Meeting endorsed the proposition that gay partnerships be accorded equal value to heterosexual marriage. Needless to say, the Quaker attitude to gay relationships was a salient factor in drawing me to the Society.

I wrote to the Society of Friends headquarters in London, requesting what is called an Enquirers' Pack, and was encouraged even further. As a result of this, I met a Bexhill Quaker, who warmly encouraged me to attend the Bexhill Meeting for Worship, the meeting house for which happened to be in the next street to the one in which I was living. Unbeknownst to me at the time, her husband had previously been clerk to that meeting, but had ultimately resigned his membership of the Society when confronted with the formal acceptance of gay people. Ignorance, indeed, is bliss. I eventually learned that this poor, tormented man had taken to sending epistles to various members of the Society, expatiating on the evil especially of lesbianism and, specifically, on lesbians' presumed use of dildoes...

In due course, having heard that Hastings Meeting was much larger and with a much wider age range, I began to attend there. Becoming an 'attender' did not exactly represent anything like a Damascene conversion: rather, it was more like a kind of 'coming home'. All that I had read and heard about Quakers was remarkably consonant with my own long-held views and sentiments. Not only was I terrified of war, I could never see how it could in any circumstances be constructive or positively good from any point of view. And, from a very early age, I have had a passionate belief in the equal worth of all people. Furthermore, I could never see how man-made dogma and elaborate ritual could be desirable to the Creator of all. All of these considerations, which had for so long churned inside me, chimed beautifully with the heart of Quakerism as I understood it.

I cannot do justice here to what might be called Quaker theology, but I can state that the founder George Fox's preaching that 'there is that of God in everyone' is undoubtedly the central principle. All of the Quaker 'testimonies' flow from that: the equality of all, pacifism, care for the planet Earth, simple living, integrity of conduct and so on. Quakers avoid dogma and ritual and meet in simple meeting houses, where members and attenders sit in a circle round a table upon which are placed important texts: the Quaker Book of Faith and Practice, one or other version of the Bible, perhaps a concordance, a copy of Advices and Queries and some other spiritual document or guide. There is usually a vase of flowers in the centre of the table. It has occurred to me more than once that this may in itself be described by purists as a form of ritual...

If there is a Quaker bumper sticker, it surely reads Quakers Do It Silently. Far from a meditative activity, Quakers 'centre down' into a shared sense of spiritual, communal seeking for the Light or presence of God. The entire hour may be silent. Or someone may be moved or prompted by the Holy Spirit to 'give ministry'. It is today a moot point whether a given 'prompting' must necessarily be of the Holy Spirit as traditionally or conventionally understood. I have, over the 18 years of my attendance, heard a few samples of 'ministry' which were self-evidently the personal sentiments of the speaker and bore no relation to the Spirit.

I applied for, and was accepted into membership of, the Society when we came to York, having been an attender for about 11 years. Being received into membership was a very different experience from becoming a Catholic. I had no sense of transformation or salvation as such, but was instead reasonably sure that, despite my deficiencies, I was more or less acceptable as a human being. I identify strongly with the Quaker idea that we are endlessly seeking the Light, or truth... or God. We necessarily live with uncertainty, a notion which I find psychologically difficult, but intellectually necessary.

Another Quaker idea is that each moment is of supreme importance. For the life of me, I cannot recall the authorship of the concept of 'the sacrament of the present moment': Teilhard de Chardin, perhaps. Every moment matters. I try to practise this principle, most often in the ordinary, mundane situations and encounters which characterise daily life. If I go the post office to buy stamps, for example, I usually make the effort to greet the cashier in such a way as to show warm interest in the person serving me. If I see that someone looks distressed or downcast, I consider whether there is something I might say or do to demonstrate that I care about them. But I would not wish anyone to imagine that I am some sort of paragon or saint. The truth is that I have always had a short fuse, and can rush from calm to fury in less than a nanosecond. One of my moral imperatives, though, is that human flourishing or 'right living' depends upon our having some Project or Policy informing our lives. Drifting from day to day without such a principle or programme may underlie much of the depression and anxiety which are so prevalent in the materialistic West. I believe that I myself suffer from 'recurrent' depression and, when I start sliding into the pit, I invariably feel or think that life is utterly futile, pointless, and that all religious institutions are the product of humanity's collective wishful thinking.

Since my retirement, I have never sunk so deeply that I have been unable to move and take to my bed. At the first sign of lowered mood – usually heralded by extreme irritability and the sensation that I am seeing the world through glass – I do my best to live 'one day at a time'. For me, this means having a clear but simple plan for the day and sticking to it through hell and high water. It is as well that I always have a dog, as I could not fail to take him out for a walk, however my feet drag.

It is a coincidence that Gill and I are both Quakers, I having enquired about the Society before getting to know her. But it is an important bond, despite my occasional periods of apostasy. Moving to York marked the beginning of a period of closer involvement with Friends. Gill is an Elder, responsible, with other Elders, for the spiritual life of the Meeting. I am an Overseer, concerned with others for the pastoral care of members and attenders of the Meeting.

The move to York itself was somewhat complex and protracted. Gill's youngest son, Charlie, was 16 when she was appointed to The Retreat. Initially, it was agreed that he would stay in Bexhill, and accommodation with a mature acquaintance was arranged. But as the time to move approached, Gill realised that Charlie was more involved with cannabis than she had at first supposed, and she therefore insisted that he move with us to York. Charlie was not pleased.

Since we owned three flats in the house at Albany Road, it took some time to sell them all, and in a market which was somewhat sluggish at the time. So Gill and Charlie moved into a rental apartment in Monkgate, close to the town centre and the Minster. There they stayed for three months, while I remained in Bexhill dealing with the three property sales. Gill and Charlie went house-hunting, and fancied the very first property they saw. I viewed it on a weekend visit, and fell in love with it too. We moved into 59 Melrosegate during a snowstorm in February 2005.

Gill began her job at The Retreat in October 2004, and loved it from the start. Surprisingly, perhaps, she was the only actual member of the Society of Friends among the doctors, and there were only a couple of Quakers – including the Resident Friend, Annie Borthwick – among the remaining staff. It has not always been easy to communicate the Quaker principles throughout the institution, despite the fact that the directors are all Quakers. Perhaps they are too remote from the day-to-day operations of The Retreat to have enough influence. On the other hand, there is no question in my mind that the care of patients is vastly superior to that which I experienced in the NHS.

Charlie had for some time said that he would like to become an architect, and we hoped to enrol him at York College to study for the requisite A levels, but the college considered that his GCSE results were not good enough to admit him to an A level course. This was something of a setback for us, as he had been accepted on to an A-level course at Bexhill College. He was instead offered a one-year construction course, which he duly completed, and then went on to the first of a two-year more advanced course. It was hoped that, if he completed the two-year course at a high standard, this might be considered the equivalent of A-levels for the purpose of gaining entry to a university course in architecture. Sadly, he dropped out, and it became obvious that he was continuing to smoke cannabis in sufficient quantities to rob him of motivation, concentration and organisation. He got a kitchen assistant's job at Café Rouge, a position which he held until he became 18.

As soon as he became a legal adult, he decided that he wanted to return to the south coast, where he had many friends and had been happy. He had continued to resent being 'dragged' to York, and so we found a flat for him in Bexhill. It was intended that he would return to Bexhill College which had, in spite of his poor GCSE performance, previously accepted him on to the A-level stage. Sadly, he was too late in applying and set about job-hunting. Nothing materialised, and we advised him to 'sign on' for welfare benefits. This he was unable somehow to achieve, at least partly because he slept through appointments at the Job Centre. He also from time to time reported that he was projectile vomiting – a pretty sure indication of excessive cannabis consumption. All in all, it was an unsuccessful attempt at independent living, and he returned to York, leaving his Bexhill flat in such a state that Gill lost her deposit.

I have a recurrent worry that my role in contributing to the breakdown of his parents' marriage played a significant part in Charlie's resort to drugs. And my occasional outbursts of frustration and fury with him for appearing to follow in my footsteps of substance misuse and submersion of talent only exacerbate that guilt. In wanting the best for him, I risk inviting the worst.

SEVENTEEN

Father died on the second of February, 2006. The funeral took place in Holy Trinity church in St Andrews. To my surprise, I wept. The minister conducting the service referred to Father as 'a true gentleman', and I briefly reflected on the irony of this. The service itself proceeded as Father – I nearly said 'God' – had intended; highly traditional, of course, and with excellent music. I have never cried about or for him since, but he is never far from my thoughts, which swing between rage, pity and... a sort of love. For years, I have been agitating about which behaviour I could attribute to his Asperger's and which to his underlying personality. Where is the line to be drawn?

Cheryl and her husband had had a glorious, al fresco wedding ceremony at the Hermitage in Dunkeld on the second of October, 2004. This was her second marital adventure, and the signs for a happy union were, and continue to be, favourable. Now that they were mature in years, they were keen to multiply as soon as possible. And, despite the repeated torment of five miscarriages, Cheryl gave birth to a healthy little blond boy on March the first, barely a month after Father's departure. Being Cheryl, she had read a library of books on childbirth and aftercare, but not of the orthodox variety. Thus my tiny nephew was

226

swaddled, massaged and comforted at the first cry. Cheryl was of course determined to breastfeed the little soul, but, despite her best attempts, she did not succeed. I know that this was a matter of some distress to her, but the fact is that, now nearly six, Finlay Ramsay McIlwraith is a very fine figure of a boy, confident, happy, sociable and very, very bright. Since both his parents are frighteningly so, this is unsurprising.

There was a brief, early blip – perhaps in the second week of Finlay's life – when Cheryl had a crisis of confidence and turned to me for help. Which indicated the degree of her desperation, since, of course, I have only ever had puppies and, despite my running a children's home in the mid-1970s, had little idea of what to do with a baby. Anyway, I dashed up to Edinburgh and did my best to breathe confidence into the new parents. Since I was not the infant's mother, I did not experience the anxiety which beamed out of poor Cheryl's eyes. I simply plucked up the little bundle and plopped him onto my left shoulder, where he happily clung. It was a deeply gratifying feeling, holding this dearly awaited child. There is something quite blissful about the smell of babies which seems to trigger a biological switch, drawing one as close to the infant as possible. Until they need changing, of course.

We all wish that Mother had been alive to meet Neil and to welcome Finlay into the world. I hope that, somehow, she knows them. Father always claimed that he was not particularly interested in babies, because they couldn't speak. Perhaps his Asperger's prevented him from feeling that he could communicate with little people by other means.

I have already referred to the radical differences in temperament, disposition and interests of us four sisters. Cheryl is highly intelligent, and obtained a first at Edinburgh University, a fact I did not know until

227

comparatively recently. She has a lively, positive personality and is dauntingly sociable. Marion, Gill and I are amazed and amused by her rich social life, which seems to consist of one long series of tea parties. As Miss Jean Brodie famously observed, 'For those who like that sort of thing, that is the sort of thing they like.' Perhaps we envy her: she clearly has a remarkable gift for friendship, and I doubt whether there is a much greater gift. For myself, I have to be at least four sheets to the wind before I can force myself to 'mix' socially: it has a lot to do with the problem of 'small talk', the difficulty of changing tack every time one encounters someone else in a social gathering. Now that I am old, I find it generally less challenging to say, 'Sorry – I don't do parties.'

Meanwhile, over in Ottawa, Frances has had a long 'battle' with cancer. One day, I should like to see a reference in the media to a cancer victim who capitulated to the disease on the day of diagnosis instead of bravely Battling it with Courage and Humour. Frances's response has been highly complex, due, at least in part, to her 'battle' with depression. She has been ambivalent about life for 20 years.

Early in 2003, Frances noticed that the nailbed of her right index finger had turned a bluish-grey and, after a period, consulted her GP. He looked at it and concluded that she had banged it and that the bruise would eventually disappear. It did not. She consulted him again some weeks later, and the same GP advised, 'If you're upset about it, put some nail varnish on it,' or words to that effect. At some point after this ludicrous advice, Frances happened to bump into a dermatologist she knew from her nursing days, and she mentioned the finger. He took one look at it and, in a manner of speaking, ejaculated, 'Shit! You need to get that seen to at once: it looks horribly like a melanoma…'

Back to the GP. And then a lengthy wrangle among oncologists as to whether the finger should be amputated at once or sentinel nodes in the lymphatic system should be tested first for malignant cells. The debate was sufficiently important to be referred to in a high-level medical case conference. Frances was referred to a dermatologist whose first instinct was to go for amputation, but he was ultimately stalled and, despite the long delay caused by the GP, the sentinel nodes were tested and found to be free of malignancy. Had they not been, I should have had to be prevented from strangling Frances's GP: sadly, I have retained these unQuakerly personality traits. A date for surgery to amputate her finger was eventually set, and I flew over to provide moral support. In fact, and this is so characteristic of Frances, she seemed perfectly sanguine about both the surgery and the prognosis, the latter especially being a worry to her family. It was as if she had '*la belle indifference*' which we used to see in patients with hysterical conditions. It may also have been the case that she was receiving a high level of concern and overt affection from her two sons and their families.

And so she had the surgery, and quickly thereafter managed do everything with the remaining digits. And all went well for the next two years or so, until a lesion appeared on her leg. This turned out to be malignant, and further surgery left her with a bullet-hole in her shin. After a second surgery, of course, the prognosis was more pessimistic than after the first. Nevertheless, she emerged as well from the second bout as she had from the first.

We arranged for her to come to Crete with us in September 2007. We hired a villa deep in the countryside, to the west of Chania, the capital. The weather was brilliant, and we all had a relaxed, happy holiday. The villa had its own swimming pool and Frances, a keen swimmer, made full use of this. Despite already possessing a deep tan, she sunbathed at every opportunity – a fact which surprised me, given the nature of her disease. It was now four years since her initial diagnosis.

As a family, we endeavoured to see as much of Frances as practicable, given that we live on opposite sides of the Atlantic. In October 2008, Frances had a routine examination from one of her oncologists. Since she had been involved with the cancer services for five years, she had got to know some of the personnel well, and, on the occasion of the October assessment, had laughed and joked with the examining physician who, among other tests, was supposed to palpate her armpits and groin for lymphatic growths. But did he? She had a faint subsequent recollection that he had missed the armpits. She flew, as planned, to the UK that December for a Christmas holiday with us, but mentioned to us that, when showering prior to her departure, she had felt a swelling in her left armpit. Quite a large swelling. Resolving to enjoy her holiday with us anyway, she proceeded with her plans, having asked her GP to arrange a scan for her return. When she telephoned her GP immediately before returning to Ottawa, her GP confessed that he had not arranged a scan. My fury with the man, whom I already considered woefully negligent, was without bounds. He hastily arranged an emergency scan, and Frances was found to have a melanoma the size of a tennis ball. Surgery was scheduled for February, 2009, and I flew over for the occasion.

The tumour was duly removed, and I managed to steel myself to empty the drain emanating from the wound thereafter. As usual, Frances recovered briskly and positively from the operation and its aftermath. However, following this, her third round with 'acral lentiginous' melanoma – the most aggressive form of an already highly aggressive form of cancer, apparently – she was advised that her cancer had reached the final point of stage three,

230

meaning, evidently, that, should she advance to stage four, she was looking into the prognostic abyss. At this point, she was advised that she might have as little as six months to live. Needless to say, we were horrified by this news. And yet Frances conveyed it quite dispassionately.

When we had holidayed in Crete the year before, we had arranged for Frances to go on a day trip to Santorini, a picture of which she had had for years on her sitting room wall. I think that her friend, Pat, had been there many years before and had fallen in love with the island. Frances did likewise – by proxy. On the day of the sailing, however, a squall blew up, preventing the catamaran from crossing the choppy strait. We were mightily disappointed that Frances was unable to realise her dream.

Given the Damacletian gloom surrounding Frances's future, Marion and I resolved to take her to Santorini somehow, some day.

Frances has, for about 20 years, suffered from depression. She has had several in-patient admissions, attended day hospital and had follow-up out-patient treatment by the psychiatric services. A number of antidepressants were tried with little or no effect until, finally, she was prescribed a monoamine oxidase inhibitor (MAOI) as a last resort. I suspect that this drug has had no therapeutic effect, as Frances's depression is not a chemical but an existential one, a problem with what she perceives to be the point of life – or life for *her*, now that her children are grown and she has no partner. She had six years of what purported to be psychoanalysis, attending the analyst's office for four days a week. Mercifully, this was financed by health insurance – merciful not only because she could not possibly have afforded it, but because I could detect no benefit to Frances, and nor could she when asked to indicate any. When the analysis finally ended, Frances remained 'depressed' and occasionally in despair.

231

Gill wondered whether Frances might benefit from 'schema' therapy, a relatively recent variation of cognitive behavioural therapy, which acknowledges the influence of early life and attempts to challenge self-defeating patterns of thought. Frances's health insurance did not cover this kind of therapy, so we located the sole practitioner of schema therapy in Ottawa and 'treatment' began, financed enthusiastically by Gill, Marion and me. We were all convinced that at the root of Frances's problems were her endless and repetitive, negative and frequently 'catastrophising' loops or circuits of thinking. Things began to look up, but the new therapy coincided with Frances's finally, after years of urging, signing up to a dating agency and meeting potential partners. Apprehensive about meeting new people, she nevertheless manifestly enjoyed her dates with quite a range of men, several of whom – except the chap with the high performance motorcycle and a deep love of country music – shared her interests and met her 'person specifications'. She eventually seemed to 'click' with a retired, very senior civil servant whose range of interests was wide, but who did not share Frances's passion for classical music. They dated for well over a year.

But things started to go wrong with the schema therapy – or, more accurately, with the schema therapist. She began to cancel appointments, or to change them at the last minute. On one occasion, she showed up with a conspicuous black eye and explained to Frances that she had been in 'an abusive relationship'. Paradoxically, she soon took to calling Frances late at night, rambling incoherently about having to change or cancel appointments. It was clear that the therapeutic relationship was far from therapeutic, and it was not long before the clinic in which she worked informed Frances that the therapist had 'retired early'. To say that this was all deeply unfortunate was to understate the case mightily. This woman represented our last hope

232

that someone would be able to help Frances short-circuit her entrenched patterns of self-limiting thinking. It was fortunate that Frances was in reasonably buoyant form when the 'therapy' came to a close.

Given Frances's three encounters with melanoma, and the poor outlook for the future, we sisters decided to bring the Santorini dream to life. Her surgery had taken place in February of 2009, and we planned the holiday for September. Needless to say, we earnestly hoped that she would be physically well enough to undertake the journey...

But the months passed, and Frances did not die or become ill. She duly flew to Edinburgh and joined Marion. Then she and Marion travelled down to York from Waverley. They stayed overnight with us and we left early in the morning for Manchester airport. Nearly half of our travel time was, of course, spent in the airport, but, in a few hours, we were transported from a drizzly, grey Manchester to a warm sunset in Santorini. Just in time to drop off our suitcases in the 'studio' apartments, and convene in the pool bar for an evening meal and the first drinks of the holiday. My sisters had wine, and I had 'a few beers'...

We awoke to the soft, sweet sound of miaowing, and tiptoed out to the source under the hedge which curled round the villas. In a little furry hollow, we were able to discern five tiny bundles, curled up in one another like a powder puff. Cats and kittens became a major theme of our holiday. We ignored the guides' warning not to touch the creatures or, heaven forbid, admit them to our quarters, and each evening one or another feline group joined us for supper.

Santorini is often considered to be the most beautiful island on Earth, and there is no doubt as to its stunning blue, white and golden charm. Archaeologically, too, it is of immense interest, especially following the massive earthquake which, in 1956, destroyed much of the built environment. Much earlier, however, in about 1650 BC, the 'cauldron', or *caldera*, a deep crater surrounding the island, was formed by a huge volcanic eruption. Quite recently, too, archaeologists discovered and exposed the remains of the ancient city of Thira, the alternative name for Santorini. Some scholars believe that the myth of the lost city of Atlantis is located in the *caldera*.

We trod in the steps of the tourist millions through the streets of Kamari, Fira and Oia, glancing at the souvenir shops, inhaling the cool peace of the myriad churches and eating in the finest restaurants on the island. Santorini is famous for its fine wines, and we visited one of the wineries, where we learned the island has a unique technique for growing the vines: the pruning method trains the vines to grow in coils close to the ground – otherwise they would be blown away by the *meltemi* winds. For aficionados, the wine is of exceptional quality, with 'a refreshing acidity' and high alcohol content. Gill and my sisters sampled a selection of the wines: I did not, because if I drink before evening, I am lost for the remainder of the day – or, more precisely, I lose the remainder of the day...

Along with the excellent beers and wines, we enjoyed the splendid Santorini cuisine. The island is famous for its *fava* and a special genus of tomato, and the coastal fish restaurants, while prohibitively expensive, served huge platters of beautifully cooked, fresh fish in astonishing variety. The outdoor restaurants were typically inhabited by feral cats, the waiters ordinarily tolerant of the importuning creatures, to the point of casting leftover heaps of pasta and fish skins their way.

There was a retrospectively amusing finale to *my* otherwise idyllic holiday. For days, I awoke with a fresh host of insect bites whose itch was unlike any other I had experienced. We visited several pharmacies to request advice and purchase expensive medicines and unguents to no avail. There were times when I wanted to tear off my clothes and run over my whole body with a large Brillo pad. It was perhaps fortunate that I did not discover the cause of these unspeakably itchy bites until our very last day – when I observed a fat little bed bug crawling over my hand. I could never have slept in that bed again, and would have had to make a bit of a fuss with the proprietors: as it was, I merely reported the problem, temperately, to the travel representative. I have since learned that there has recently been a worldwide surge in this infestation. Ugh. Magnified images of the creatures reveal them to be utterly grotesque in appearance. My shoulders are itching terribly as I write this...

But Frances was in wonderful form, manifestly relishing the warm, Mediterranean sun, the delicious food and drink and the stunning scenery. We hoped that this would be an experience she could recall and treasure for ever. Our chief aim is to invest whatever time Frances has left with as much enjoyment and fun as we can contrive. She has had an unfortunate life, which seems to have consisted of one disappointment after another. Her early life, she now reports, was one of sustained fear – fear of Father's explosive temper and physical punishment, and of my bullying. She implies that I was bullying her frequently and, although I have scant recollection of this, I still have no doubt that it is true. I have expressed my profound sorrow for having treated her so abominably, and she has forgiven me over and over. But nothing on earth – no counsellor or psychotherapist – can deracinate the malignant tenacity of sin against another. You may be fortunate enough to believe that God has forgiven you, but that will never erase the fact of the sin.

But the Santorini idyll *did* happen. And it was not the last holiday Frances was able to enjoy. Quite soon after our return to the UK, Marion was busily planning a Grand Tour

235

– of Scotland, England and Wales – for Frances. I doubted that Frances would be well enough to undertake all the travel involved, but it came off with total success in the late spring of 2010.

I often reflect on the fact that we sisters, despite our different personalities, support one another through the Sloughs of Despond as well as the occasions of celebration. This is undoubtedly one of the outstanding features of our inheritance – along with intelligence, humour and grammatical pedantry.

EIGHTEEN

Nothing quite prepares you for the sheer tedium involved in travel to the antipodes. Long before you even catch sight of an aircraft, there is the check-in procedure and a series of security checks which occupy the better part of two hours. The final hour is spent desultorily wandering about the glittering designer shops, bars and duty-free section which seems to stock little apart from booze, cigarettes and perfume. A £4 espresso helps the Valium down, and we finally walk a mile or so to the departure lounge. The flight is called.

There is no turning back. I take as deep a breath as I can manage while simultaneously attempting to regulate my heartbeat, now syncopating. It is essential that I have a window seat, so that I can check our alignment with the horizon as we take off, cruise and land. It is best to be close to the wing, so that one may alert the crew should an engine catch fire.

The only thing worse than flying phobia is having a flying phobia and claustrophobia. From the moment the doors are closed, you are trapped in a hermetically sealed cigar tube from which there is no escape: although a member of ground crew at Heathrow years ago told me about an American passenger about to return to the US who, as the aircraft was taxiing to the main runway, had such a spectacular panic attack that the plane had to return to the terminal in order to release her. You could never live that sort of thing down, and you would have to consider applying for British citizenship if you were to avoid a repeat of the experience.

There is little respite when we achieve the cruising speed at 38,000 feet, for the possibility of clear air turbulence is ever present. When the miniature meals arrive, I claim a couple of miniature bottles of wine. It is said that the effect of alcohol is doubled at high altitude, but I have tested that on numerous occasions, and there is no truth in it.

There are four flights involved in this trip. The first leg, from Manchester to Heathrow, is a brief warmup for what is to come. The flying time from Heathrow is 22 hours, with a brief stop for a Thai beer at Singapore. As we resume our journey, I am surprised to find that the agony of boredom is beginning to eclipse the state of arousal and extreme vigilance which I normally experience on transatlantic flights of a mere seven hours. There is a limit to the distraction offered by books, newspapers, solitaire, 'general appeal' movies and several 'comfort' expeditions.

At last we arrive in Sydney. I remember the witticism of our Kiwi vet who advised that, when the immigration officers enquire whether one has a criminal record, the correct answer is 'Oh, do you still need one?' In fact the entry process is noticeably more relaxed than in North America. Although the airport is halfway round the world, the terminal is the same as any other: a McDonald's the first sight. I never thought that our first meal in Australia would consist of a soggy beefburger, but there it is.

Finally, the four-and-a-half hour flight to Perth. Nose pressed hard to the thick Perspex, I try to catch my first glimpse of the territory. During breaks in the cloud, I can see infinite acres of sandy-red soil with, here and there,

238

scrubby little trees. This must be the Outback. The vastness of the terrain is almost impossible to comprehend, used as we are to the tiny, patchwork fields and scattered urban areas of beetling traffic at home. Most of the population of Australia occupy a ribbon round principally the western, southern and eastern rim of the continent.

And, finally, we are in Perth terminal, watching my cousin Hallie and my aunt Thelma racing in through the entrance: they had been waiting in the international terminal, but we were on an internal flight.

My father was born in the picturesque North Yorkshire village of Bishop Monkton on the seventh of September, 1916. We presume that his father was then in the Royal Flying Corps, since there was an air base nearby. Somehow, a decision was reached whereby my paternal grandfather's sister Mary, the nun-who-did-not-take-her-final-vows, travelled down to Yorkshire from Aberdeen to collect my father when he was but a few weeks old. My Australian relatives have suggested that my father's grandparents on both sides had persuaded his parents to let them look after both my father's older sister, Mildred, and my father as his parents 'were always moving about'.

Mildred had, several years before, been billeted on her mother's parents in Aberdeen, and now her little baby brother was to be similarly billeted on his father's parents, also in Aberdeen. My father's grandfather was a stern Victorian Church of Scotland minister. Aunt Mary, still a devout Roman Catholic and a trained nurse, considered my father to be unwell and, observing the Church's teaching on the necessity for baptism where there is a possibility of an infant dying, took him to St Wilfrid's church in York. There, she either baptised him herself or had a priest carry out the sacrament. My baby father safely rescued from the prospect of Limbo – that place where unbaptised Catholic infants used to go, and where there is no prospect of heaven – Aunt Mary took him by train all the way to Aberdeen. It was not uncommon, in those days, for children to be brought up by relatives other than their parents. My father never subsequently thought it odd that his parents emigrated to Australia with little hope of seeing him again. He always believed that the reason he was left behind was so that he should have a good Scottish education.

Several years later, another child was born to my father's parents. This was Ron. But Ron was not sent to lodge with relatives, and, at the age of two, was taken with my grandparents to Australia. My father was perhaps nine years old when his mother and father emigrated. He never saw them again. By 1926, when my father was ten, his grandmother had died. He was thereafter cared for by his grandfather and Aunt Mary. Father's sister, Mildred, used to visit her little brother, as they both lived in Aberdeen.

A fourth child was born some years after my grandparents had arrived in Australia. This was William, and it was through one of William's children that my Australian link came alive. William's daughter, Hallie, came with her mother, Thelma, to the UK in the late 1990s and visited my parents in St Andrews. And when Gill and I had just moved to York in 2004, Hallie, Thelma and a sister of Hallie's, Brenda, stayed with us for a few days. I was quite delighted with their company, and we maintained contact thereafter.

Back in 1983, my parents enjoyed a six-week holiday in Australia, courtesy of my father's brother Ron, who had retired early from his job as a surveyor with a blue asbestos mining company in the east and generously invested part of his retirement 'lump sum' in tickets for them. My parents stayed with Ron and his wife, Rose, for a few weeks before flying to Perth to meet his sister Mildred and brother 'Bill'.

But Bill was not in evidence when my parents arrived in Perth, and it was Bill's wife, Thelma, who explained that this was because Bill was in prison for sexually abusing his children. I have no idea how my mother reacted to the rather startling news, but I am sure that she would not have allowed the slightest sign of shock to cross her countenance. Father, on the other hand, would undoubtedly have appeared impassive, and have said something like 'Well, well, dear me'. Whereas he tended to react with unbridled fury at minor peccadilloes, he usually took grave sin in his stride. Such was his strangely inverted value system. Thelma took Father to visit Bill, but none of us shall ever know what passed between them.

Hallie had told me that Bill married her mother when Thelma was only 16, he being ten years older. Their first child was stillborn, but she went on to have nine successful pregnancies: five boys and four girls. When the eldest girl was three years old, she wandered into her parents' bedroom, where they were having sexual intercourse. Thelma ordered the child to leave at once, but her husband insisted that she stay. Not long after this presumably bewildering introduction to the world of sex, the child began to be sexually abused by her father.

It would seem that, when she was just old enough to do so, this child did her best to protect her younger sisters from their father's predatory attentions, but she could hardly succeed in this. Only the youngest daughter was shielded from her father's incestuous urges by virtue of his imprisonment. Although the boys were not sexually compromised by their father as far as I know, they were subject to severe beatings from time to time for minor 'offences'.

Bill was a plumber in an enclosed little mining community in the far northwest of Western Australia, and managed to threaten his wife and children into silence about the abuse. He had total domination over Thelma, commanding her to keep her hair long and preventing her from ever going out without him. In addition to his sexual abuse of the girls and regular beatings of the boys, he played sadistic games with the children, firing gunshots close to them, for example, when they were outside.

We met all of my cousins except one, who worked too far away to arrange a visit to Perth. Another of the five brothers had attempted suicide by carbon monoxide poisoning in 1993 at the age of 31, following a series of failed relationships and a heroin addiction. Two children came upon the scene, called the emergency services, and the poor man was flown to a Perth hospital and placed in a decompression chamber. After six months in hospital in a semi-vegetative state, he choked on vomit during a coughing fit and died.

Several of the brothers have serious alcohol problems, and all have unskilled jobs, chiefly driving trucks. The eldest girl − the first to be abused − lives in a small town many miles south of Perth and runs a grocery store. She has changed her name and has nothing to do with her family except Hallie. She is a Jehovah's Witness, and was clearly uncomfortable with Gill's and my presence in her shop, having enquired of Hallie whether we were a gay partnership.

After years of alienation from her father, Hallie now has strictly limited contact with him, and then only in regard to the welfare of Mildred, his sister and Hallie's aunt. The second youngest girl, Brenda, has no contact with her father, and has a personal assistant post in the north of the state − a 'fly in, fly out' job, where she has ten days at work followed by ten days at home, and vice versa. The youngest girl, who is gay, has no contact with her father, and was in the midst of a painful relationship breakdown − involving their four-year-old twins − when we met.

All my cousins have had relationship difficulties, and none has had higher education, yet all are manifestly bright and a joy to meet. Hallie, whom I have got to know best, is clearly highly intelligent and could easily have gone to university had her family circumstances been different. She now devotes her free time to caring for her mother, Thelma, and her Aunt Mildred. Hallie is a senior government official in the transport department.

Before the Australian trip, I had long wondered whether my paternal grandfather had some form of personality problem, given the circumstantial evidence of his 'moving about a lot' – and having two very peculiar sons. The depositing of two of his children with grandparents prior to his emigration and the apparent poverty of his existence after settling in Australia suggested that he might be a bit of a will-o'-the wisp; a dilettante. I learned that, when he first arrived in Australia, he had a partnership in a poultry farm but terminated it when he learned that his business partner was having an improper relationship with someone else's wife. At some point, he enlisted in the Australian army, but was discharged on medical grounds after a relatively short period of service. He certainly had at least two school teaching posts, but was not a qualified teacher. It is thought that, at some point, he may also have had a shop. He appears to have moved house quite frequently, and never had much money. My cousins had been rather too young to note much about our grandfather, and Aunty Mil, at 95, could recite only one or two anecdotes, which she tended to repeat. I gathered, however, that my grandfather was generally considered a true gentleman; a practising Christian who knelt in prayer every evening before bed and was a thoroughly decent, kind man. It is clear despite this that he had not managed to build a career or vocation of any kind, having left Aberdeen University without completing an engineering degree. My father told me that his father had

243

left his course in the final year because he met and married my grandmother, Alice, who was reportedly pregnant with another man's child. Having seen my Aunt Mildred, I am convinced that she is a true blood relative in appearance and mannerisms: I imagine that Alice simply became pregnant unexpectedly, and that my grandparents married in some haste. My cousins believe that they eloped first and subsequently went through a conventional marriage ceremony.

One of the most memorable moments of our Australian trip was the day on which I met Uncle Bill. Hallie arranged things so that we would go to Aunty Mil's house on a day when Bill visited, and that he would drive Aunty Mil to the town of York, east of Perth. Hallie, Gill and I drove together, and joined Uncle Bill and Aunty Mil at a restaurant in York. Uncle Bill would undoubtedly have known that we knew his criminal history, so it would have been perfectly natural for him to feel uncomfortable. He actually appeared rather cold, and I did feel uneasy in his presence. What affected me most, however, was his eerie physical resemblance to Father – especially the upper part of his face. This was an encounter I am unlikely to forget.

I had been comprehensively briefed about my relatives on Father's side, but knew virtually nothing about my cousin Helen's daughters, Elaine and Evelyn, who live in Albany, on the south coast of Western Australia. My mother's older sister, Alice, had two children, Donald and Helen, and, especially while I was doing my nursing training, Helen and I were very good friends as well as first cousins. Poor Helen was precipitated into holy matrimony rather earlier than she had intended – if she had intended to marry the father at all – and asked me to become godmother to their daughter, Elaine. They were living in Cumbernauld, just outside Glasgow, at the time.

Helen emigrated with her family to Western Australia while the girls were still small, and she and I lost touch, although my mother and she corresponded fairly regularly. Helen held various senior nursing posts at several hospitals in the state, finally settling in Albany. Elaine married and had two children, neither of whom we met. But then she fell in love with her uncle Donald's son, Rory, her first cousin, and they married after Elaine's divorce. That was about the extent of my knowledge about Elaine's adult life. Evelyn never married, but had at least two long-term relationships.

Sadly, Helen contracted lung cancer – she and I smoked enthusiastically for decades – at the age of 60. Sensibly, perhaps, she rejected treatment, and died within three weeks of diagnosis in 2001. I was sorry that she had departed by the time we finally got to Australia; it would have been so good to see her again.

Hallie drove us down to Albany, where Elaine was living in her mother's flat. We arrived in mid-afternoon, and were – pleasantly, in my case – surprised to find Elaine and her sister smoking roll-ups and drinking tall glasses of Scotch. Because of Hallie's presence and declared dislike of 'drunk people', I reluctantly opted for tea when offered a drink, but looked forward to a bibulous evening with them when the others had returned to their accommodation on the other side of town. What I recall of the evening was very pleasant indeed, including a sensation of supreme contentment brought about by an excellent spliff – my first smoke in 11 years.

Clearly, both girls were heavy drinkers. Elaine confided that Evelyn was also a recovering heroin addict, and that she had introduced Elaine's husband-cousin to the drug so that he, too, was a recovering addict. Although Elaine and Rory were still legally married and remained on good terms, Rory was living in the former matrimonial home in Balga, a northern suburb of Perth. Both the girls were hugely entertaining and I was extremely sorry that we had only a couple of days to make one another's acquaintance. On the second day, Gill and I stayed at the home of Evelyn and her partner Kim, a Vietnam veteran, mercenary and erstwhile bodyguard to the Bee Gees, Roy Orbison and other stars undertaking Australian tours. He was also an 'Ocker' or traditional Australian, who detested 'Pommie bastards', blamed women for everything that was wrong with men, and declared Australian youth to be hopelessly Americanised. But the man was an entertainment in himself – a fascinating, obviously enormously talented individual. Shortly after our visit, Elaine wrote to say that Kim had ejected Eve from his house, on the ground that he was basically a loner who didn't 'do' family relations...

Our sojourn in Australia was simply fascinating from many points of view. Given my unquenchable interest in people in general – and my relatives in particular – I had an intensely interesting experience. For poor Gill, however, as one of her colleagues presciently observed, it was truly a busman's holiday. It was so good to meet most of my first cousins and dear Aunty Mil. Seeing Uncle Bill was, of course, a strange experience, but I try to consider that there is 'that of God' within him, and that he cannot therefore be the epitome of all evil. I suppose it was mildly depressing to find that my first cousins once removed were all affected by the monster of addiction, but only poor Rory seemed to have nothing resembling a satisfactory life – but then he, too, had a deeply problematic upbringing.

It seems to me that my family on both sides has been affected by deeply flawed parenting, and it is difficult for me to be too dispassionate about this. No doubt the roots of addiction are multifactorial, as the psychologists like to say. One thing is certain, however, and that is that substance misuse is no respecter of persons: intelligence and talent afford little protection from the hell of addiction, that

246

'baffling and mysterious' affliction – according to Alcoholics Anonymous – for which no one has the explanation – or answer.

NINETEEN

In January 2011, Frances had an MRI brain scan, following her complaint to that same inept GP that she was losing her memory. She did not seem to realise that she has had an even worse memory than mine for years, but reported that her family in Ottawa had mentioned it. Although I am hardly qualified to say so, I am convinced that industrial quantities of antidepressant for at least 20 years have served to blunt both her memory and some of her powers of perception. My own poor memory is undoubtedly the product of alcohol abuse for 40 years – and possibly the use of antidepressants for as long.

Back in York, we have been happily established in this beautiful city for almost eight years. Charlie returned after just over a year of testing out his desire to live independently. We found him a newly redecorated flat immediately within the city wall in Gillygate, and re-equipped it and him for a fresh start. At Gill's suggestion, he applied for and got a job as a temporary support worker at The Retreat, a job which he seemed to manage well, although there were a few late arrivals and no-shows. He continued to smoke cannabis, and most of the time looked as if he had recently been exhumed after a long rest in peace. There is no doubt about it: cannabis is death to the complexion. In due course, he acknowledged that he was unable to make it on his own, and we surrendered the flat. My cleaner, whom I engaged to tidy the once sparkling little place, baulked at the mess and refused the task. Once again, Gill lost her deposit.

In a weak moment, I suggested to Gill that Charlie might move into the loft room in our house, rather than into the back bedroom, which he had left in a dreadful state prior to moving to Bexhill. And so he moved back. We bought yet another basic set of furniture and bedding, and hoped for the best. Charlie was eventually successful in getting a permanent support worker post at The Retreat, and was evidently very highly thought of. But his home environment quickly degenerated into the kind of filthy mess that had led to lost deposits and utter frustration for Gill and me. I am happy to admit that I am very obsessional about my surroundings, and I grew ever more distressed and angry about the terrible state of the loft. One of the conditions under which we let him return was that he would not smoke in his room, but the carpet and shelving were covered in cigarette burns, and we regularly found the 'bongs' used to enhance the effects of cannabis smoking.

I could stand it no longer, and persuaded Gill that Charlie must find alternative accommodation. Relations between him and me were at their nadir, and we eventually managed to find a ground floor room for him in a congenial house two streets away. He moved in early November 2009. And, almost from that moment, things began to improve. I have made it clear to Charlie over the years that I do not look down on him at all with regard to his cannabis habit, and I have no doubt that, on the whole, it is less dangerous than alcohol. I have never made a secret of my own misuse of alcohol, and have tried to point out that it is the *effects* of his habit that are so worrying. Several attempts at preparing for higher education have come to naught because of his cannabis use, as have previous experiments at living independently. But now things are beginning to look up; he and I have almost healed our broken relationship, and he continues to be popular with his colleagues. Unexpectedly, however, he was, during an annual appraisal last year, assessed as 'unsatisfactory', which gave us a considerable jolt. He mislaid the written report, but we gathered that it referred to his turning up late for work, and being less than dynamic in performing his role. A subsequent Performance Improvement Plan was issued, although we have not seen it.

We do not worry about John, who completed his master's degree in forensic psychology at the University of the South Bank last summer and is now employed as a support worker in a medium secure forensic unit in London. He still enjoys the finer things in life such as exotic cuisine, designer fashion and foreign travel. He may not earn much, but puts his income to good use.

Nick married at 20, a lovely young nurse who bore him two charming children. But he was too young, he and his wife temperamentally very different. They soldiered on for several years, but ultimately divorced. To our enormous relief, the divorce was neither 'messy' nor 'acrimonious', and Nick sees his children every week. The grandchildren and their mother come up to see us several times a year. Nick has now been working in motor insurance for about ten years, and seems to enjoy it. He has the kind of mind which thrives on meticulous attention to detail.

Gill, hopefully just five years from retirement, continues to enjoy her work. She and I are trustees for Survive, the tiny local voluntary organisation which supports men and women who have been sexually abused.

Unquestionably, in my entire career I have never come across a more moving account of childhood sexual abuse than that of Susan, whom I met while working at the Mental Health Advocacy service. As usual, I was seeing a client instead of managing and developing the project. Susan was about 40, a trained teacher. She had been referred to us by her sister, a former colleague of mine who was a psychiatric social worker. Both girls had been abused from infancy by their parents and a circle of paedophiles which included a church warden and the local GP. The reason for the referral was that Susan had come to a standstill in her life: she was unable to work, and had found a cottage in the middle of nowhere where she could see anyone approaching from a distance. She was tall, slender and attractive, but wore shapeless, androgynous clothes to conceal her gender as far as possible.

She was an intelligent soul, able, in spite of everything, to smile or ruefully laugh when she had finally become secure enough to tell me about her childhood. She had been sadistically abused from the beginning of her life, or so it felt. The elder of the two girls, she was presented as a gift to a neighbouring farmer at the age of approximately 18 months. It was repeatedly emphasised to her that she was a very bad girl, and that bad girls must be punished if they were to be pardoned and made good again. One of a range of flashbacks consisted of her being tied to a tree trunk, face pressed against the bark, then buggered mercilessly, all the while being told: 'You are a very, very bad girl.' Once, in a field with one of the ring, she happened to see a wild flower, and stooped to pluck it. When he saw this, the perpetrator seized the little flower and crushed it under his boot.

You do not recover from that kind of evil and, on hearing about it, the listener does not recover either. Susan's experience is, as she put it, built in to every cell of her being. It is ineradicable, whatever any therapist may say. And it cannot be erased from the memory of the hearer. The best that can be said is that it motivates those who are privileged to be confided in to do what they can to support the victims of the worst evil that can befall another human being. And 'support' is the best that can be done.

My life in York has been considerably enhanced by my friendship with Jackie, whom I met just after we moved into Melrosegate in 2005. I was registering our lurcher, Digger, at the local vet's, when the receptionist showed me a photograph of her own lurcher, Josie, who had gone to heaven the month before. We quickly became great friends, and, in the first years of life in York, while I was still painfully grieving for my mother, she was instrumental in bringing laughter and joy into my life. I had a car, but she did not. I could not read maps, but she could. I did not know Yorkshire, but she did. With all that and our passion for dogs, we had wonderful times touring the beautiful county together. Jackie is a true Yorkie, born and bred. I have said before that I consider friendship to be one of life's greatest gifts. Sometimes, I think the greatest gift of all is laughter. And I have that in abundance.

It has taken me ten years to write this account. The tenth anniversary of Mother's death falls on June 1, 2012. I have, these ten years, tortured myself for inflicting upon her so much anxiety, hurt and disappointment. But I have decided to bring an end to my penance.

Of course there are encapsulated residues of fear, guilt and shame. But I have almost learned to live with them: they seem to be hard-wired in my brain. I shall always be tense from the moment of waking until the moment of sleep, and there will always be grotesque, graphic nightmares. Invariably, the themes are of annihilation, humiliation and terror. The brutal truth is that I am unable to attenuate the sense of sinfulness, fear or imperfection unless I am either three sheets to the wind or full of Yorkshire pudding, sausages and onion gravy.

In preparation for old age, Gill and I have moved into a tiny terraced house on the far side of York. We have given up our car and rely mainly on public transport. The household includes Tupac the cat and Basil the almost-Saluki. The closest thing to heaven is a Saturday morning in bed with mugs of tea, Tupac and Basil. We are close to our Quaker Meeting House, and have many dear friends. Unlike other Quakers, I am incapable of 'centring down' in meetings for worship: my closest approach to worship – whatever that is – is through encounters with others and listening to music. I do try to believe that 'there is that of God in everyone' and, as far as I am able, 'walk cheerfully about the earth' as George Fox advised.